SPLINTERS OF THE SUN:

TEACHING RUSSIAN LITERATURE TO HIGH SCHOOL STUDENTS

SPLINTERS OF THE SUN

TEACHING RUSSIAN LITERATURE TO HIGH SCHOOL STUDENTS

BY

BETTY KLETSKY STALEY

AWSNA

To my father, who fed me the sun with my daily bread.
To my colleague, John Wulsin, who shares my passion
for teaching Russian literature to adolescents.
To all my students who have been touched by the
beauty and depth of Russian literature.
To my future students who will join me on the path …
Let us all continue to be warmed by the splinters of the sun.

Printed with support from the Waldorf Curriculum Fund

Published by:
The Association of Waldorf Schools
of North America
Publications Office
65-2 Fern Hill Road
Ghent, NY 12075

Title: *Splinters of the Sun*
    Teaching Russian Literature to High School Students
Author: Betty Kletsky Staley
Editor: David Mitchell
Copy Editor and Proofreader: Ann Erwin
Cover: Hallie Wootan
© 2008 by AWSNA
ISBN # 978-1-888365-83-2

CONTENTS

The Sun Burst!
A million golden splinters
Fell upon the earth
And then night came …

Now men are beating each other
For a spark of Light.
But I have hidden in my heart
A splinter of the sun,
Therefore I am not cold.[1]
                    – Kulagin

Saint Basil's Cathedral, Moscow

Preface

My first connection with Russian literature was through my father, Israel Kletsky, a Russian Jewish immigrant from Belarus. He spoke very little about "the old country," as was the case with many immigrants at that time. All I knew was that his father had been a miller and a rabbi, who had married twice and had eighteen children, my father being the youngest. My father made very rare allusions to his time in Russia (Belarus was part of the Russian Empire) except to try to entice me to eat spinach by describing the rich black earth and how large the sunflowers and strawberries were in the old country. That was it. There were occasional comments about riding horses, about being caught between the Reds and Whites. No more. So, although I had a feeling, I had no knowledge whatsoever. Unfortunately, my father died when I was twenty-one, and I had no further opportunity to discuss anything with him. I had no idea I would one day steep myself in the culture of his homeland.

In 1974 when I, along with others, founded the Sacramento Waldorf High School, I spoke with my mentor, Christy Barnes, about looking at Russian Literature for the twelfth grade curriculum. Over the next three years, I began reading Fyodor Dostoyevsky's *The Brothers Karamazov* and some Tolstoy short stories. I had seen the film of Pasternak's *Dr. Zhivago* and read the book, and I felt very drawn to Russian culture.

When we had our first twelfth grade class, I taught a course based on *The Brothers Karamazov*. I was at first surprised by the way the students responded to the themes in the book, and I found myself researching more of the elements included in it. I had already heard of Solovyov, and I could relate his writings to Father Zossima, the elder in the book. After teaching the course for a few years, my enthusiasm grew stronger and stronger, and I continued to do research.

In 1985 I attended a course on Sovietology at Stanford University. This course focused primarily on the political and military aspects of the Soviet Union. During this course I became aware of the Research groups at Berkeley and Harvard as well as at Stanford, and I began receiving their literature on book reviews and films.

A seminar for high school literature teachers was held as part of the June 1986 Waldorf Teachers Conference at High Mowing School in Wilton, New Hampshire. The conversation turned to Russian literature, and we discovered our common experience of student enthusiasm about the subject. Jennifer Greene, who was then teaching at High Mowing, asked whether we should take students to Russia. Despite the fact that the United States and Russia were still embroiled in the Cold War, I answered, "Why not?"

I had organized travel tours previously and set to work to plan this trip. We had decided to take adults first before taking students. As preparation, I participated in a weekend workshop in San Francisco on Citizen Diplomacy between the United States and the Soviet Union. It was very helpful, and I came away from it with addresses of people to contact as well as a sense of how disorganized the

Soviets were in helping Americans organize such educational tours. Not only was I interested in bringing students to experience Russian culture as a background for understanding the literature, but I was interested in having us meet Russians and form a people-to-people relationship.

I attended a poetry reading in Berkeley by the Russian poet, Yevgeny Yevtushenko, and I was captivated by his recitation. In a conversation following his reading, he encouraged me to take students to the Soviet Union.

The first trip, which occurred in June 1987, was for four weeks and included quite a few Russian cities, as well as Tbilisi, Georgia, and three cities in Central Asia—Tashkent, Bukhara, and Samarkand. As the plane descended into St. Petersburg, my first impression was of families camping. Having been raised in a conflicting atmosphere of the Cold War—Don't trust the Russians!—and my father's socialistic leanings, I did not know what to expect. The thought came: "These are just families camping." They were not the evil empire of which President Ronald Reagan had spoken. They were ordinary people trying to enjoy a family vacation. This thought would weave in and out of bureaucratically staged experiences which were set up to impress us of Soviet power and strength.

St. Petersburg is a city that brings to mind palaces, churches, canals, peasants forced to stand in the swampland and dig trenches with their hands, and the terrible German blockade of Leningrad. We visited the Fortress of Peter and Paul, where Dostoyevsky had been imprisoned, and the Hermitage with its amazing art collection. We strolled the streets at midnight during the White Nights and made contact with some of the people who had been recommended at the Citizen Diplomacy workshop. We were invited into their homes, and we began to understand how important it was for Americans to make contacts with people who were trying to make changes within the Soviet Union. Computers were not yet available; letters were still being censored. So personal contact with anyone in the West was a lifeline. The people we came to know were struggling financially as well as in other ways. They appreciated the gifts and even the money we had brought, but they especially asked for certain books that were not available in their country. We learned about the pollution of the Baltic Sea and of the land by the dumping of pesticides on farmers' fields. Most of all, we were impressed by the energy and determination of Soviet citizens to reach out to other lands and people and to end the isolation of their country.

Taking the train south, we stopped at Novgorod for a tour of this ancient city—the only one that had not been destroyed by the Mongol Invasion. In our conversations, we were worried about saying too much in front of our guide, and we were paranoid that he would learn the addresses of our contacts in the various cities. A boat trip on Lake Ilmen took us to a village where homes and churches from all over Russia had been reconstructed so that we could learn about them and be able to imagine the homes in the villages as described in the nineteenth century novels.

Continuing south, we arrived in Moscow and were settled in the enormous Kosmos Hotel on the outskirts of the city. We visited the usual tourist spots and made contact with people on our list. We spent evenings in homes in deep conversation, listening and learning. However, the most impressive experience was the one in which four of us had an early dinner with the poet Andrei Voznesensky. This had been arranged through my colleague John Wulsin from the Green Meadow Waldorf School, who taught Russian literature there and who had a direct contact. Voznesensky invited us to the Dom Literatura (the House of Literature) and spoke about changes happening in the country. He was at that time working to establish a museum in Vitebsk for Marc Chagall's work. It was due to his efforts that *Dr. Zhivago* would soon be published in the U.S.S.R. I had read Voznesensky's poems in the book *Arrow in the Wall*, and I quoted these lines from his poem "Mother":

> "Don't go to America, son.
> You won't go, will you?" she asks, frightened by TV.
> "Don't go, they'll kill you."

"Did your mother really think the Americans would kill you?" I asked.

"No," he said. "You have to learn to read Russian poetry between the lines. The 'they' refers to the KGB." Aha! That was a clue I would use from then on.

I wanted very much to visit the house of Boris Pasternak, but because it was outside the perimeter of where foreigners were allowed, I was told it was impossible.

Our trip continued to the city of Kursk, the site where the Russians turned around the German tank invasion during World War II. In this city we had conversations with local people and participated in a home-hosted dinner. As about five of us sat around the table, heaped with delicious food, I asked one of the people, "Why do the Russians hate the Americans?"

"Don't you know," she said. "You invaded us." She was referring to the American support of the White Army during the Revolution. At that time I wasn't aware that we had sent troops. She also said, "You didn't help us during the Second World War until the end. We have done nothing to you."

My response was, "What about the Cuban Missile Crisis?"

She said, "What Cuban Missile Crisis?" That was when I learned that the Soviet people knew nothing about how close we had come to having World War III.

Wherever we met children, we would get the same answer to our question: "What do you like best about your country?" "It is very beautiful, and it is the most advanced and peaceful country in the world."

We visited daycare centers with their photographs of Uncle Lenin on the walls. We looked up at enormous murals on buildings that proclaimed "Glory to the Soviet People." We visited a hospital which felt as if it were from the 1930s, and the guides touted the oxygen drinks (now we have them all around in the U.S.). Our minds were continually tossed between being impressed by the people and being confused by the primitive conditions.

Our days in Tbilisi, Georgia, were very exciting. Here we felt we were in a crossroads between Athens, Istanbul, and San Francisco, socializing in the outdoor cafes, enjoying small cups of very strong coffee and chewing on delicious round bread. The people were very handsome with both European and Asian features. Georgia is an ancient land, having been Christianized in the fourth century. It is a hotbed of the arts—dance, poetry, pottery, puppetry and painting. We visited a synagogue where the prayer books lay in shreds on shelves beneath magnificent stained glass windows. Tbilisi has been a multicultural society with its population of Christians, Jews, and Muslims for centuries. We met with a psychologist who was calling for a new kind of education based on head, hands, and heart. Our awareness of the Russian Empire and the Soviet sphere of influence was heightened as Georgians spoke of their hatred of Soviet power and influence.

Central Asia awakened us to the Silk Road, the marches of Tamerlane, caravans moving between China and the West. Tea houses, brightly colored dresses, markets filled with herbs and spices, ruins of formerly tiled mosques.

Back in Sacramento, my teaching of Russian literature deepened as I internalized these experiences and began taking Russian language lessons. Meanwhile, we began to work on assembling the group of high school students who would accompany us on our second trip in the summer of 1988. Life in the area we were to visit had become more difficult because of a large earthquake in Armenia, which sent thousands of refugees into Georgia and Russia, and affected the reservations we had made. On the other hand, Gorbachev's reforms of *glasnost* and *perestroika* were changing Soviet society, making it more open to the West. The emphasis on this trip was to bring together high school students from the U.S. and the U.S.S.R. and have them share experiences as a continuation of Citizen Diplomacy. Their youthful energy made this trip more stimulating as they seemed to always find where their counterparts were hanging out. One of the most significant experiences of this trip was my visit to Boris Pasternak's *dacha* in Peredelkino. I have described this at the end of the Pasternak chapter.

This second trip continued to provide me with experiences that would deepen my understanding of Russian literature and the culture in general. More importantly was the experience of a society awakening from isolation and darkness. Despite political propaganda that would classify Americans and Russians as enemies, we found Russians had a great curiosity and interest in Americans. As one Russian said, "If the government says Americans are the enemy, that's enough to tell us we should become interested in you."

Several subsequent trips and a three-week teaching experience at Herzen University in St. Petersburg have added to my experience of Russian culture. The political changes that have occurred since the late 1980s have opened up much of what had previously been hidden by censorship and isolation. The events of 1991 and the withdrawal of a number of republics from the Soviet Union (both nonviolently and violently) have left a country caught between centuries, unsure of itself, and unstable in its understanding and commitment to democracy.

Russia is struggling to come to terms with its past. Now that much of the censorship has been removed (not all, because the government continues to clamp down on the press and television), the opportunities for authors to publish work that had been finished and hidden away and for authors to publish newly-written work are producing a flood of new literature. It will take time and the involvement of those interested in Russian literature to become familiar with the newest works and to share sources and enthusiasm with those of us who do not have ready access.

One of my regrets is that I have not become proficient in the Russian language. I have to rely on English translations for my studies. Knowing that the translation can never live up to the original, I have done the best I could do in the circumstances. Any mistakes I have made through misinterpretation are my responsibility.

I have now been teaching Russian literature to twelfth graders for about thirty-five years. My approach as a Waldorf teacher has been to use the subject as a vehicle to stimulate their interest and appreciation of the culture and to awaken self-knowledge. I am not a scholarly historian, yet understanding the history behind the literature has always seemed very important to my teaching. Therefore, I am a voracious reader and student of Russian history.

I am passionate about Russian literature, and yet I am not a specialist. My professional life has been focused on teaching a wide variety of courses from Child and Adolescent Development to American Transcendentalism and John Steinbeck; from World Mythology to *Parzival*; from Art History to the Evolution of Consciousness. Yet Russian Literature has been the class that continues to be new, no matter how many times I teach it. Each new book provides another perspective; each new first-hand experience opens up a range of sensory experiences — smells, tastes, sounds, and sights.

Through over a decade of visits to Latvia and Russia, my personal experiences have grown and deepened. When I read a story about a peasant's hut, I remember sitting in a darkened kitchen, eating freshly made mushroom soup; making my first dark rye bread in a large trough and shoving it into the brick oven fire on a wooden paddle; and warming my cold hands on the large tile wood stove. As I read about the Soviet government's destroying the barns of private farmers and forcing them into collectives (*kolhozes*), I remember walking on the stone foundations of such a barn, delivering food scraps to the pigs. When Russian life changed radically in the unstable 1990s, I had to purchase yarn with U.S. dollars as the clerk would not accept rubles. And there are many, many more stories to tell.

With all my experiences and studies, one would think I would have a solid grasp of Russian culture and character. But I am just as puzzled by the enigma of Russia today as I was forty years ago. However, one thing I am sure of. Russia holds a question that is calling to us. It is something out of the future. When I read Russian poetry, even in translation, I can feel the question, but I do not yet have the words. And so I go on teaching and learning and listening.

I hope that other teachers will be inspired to step into the wonderful, confusing, exciting, challenging and colorful world that is Russian literature and share this exploration with their students.

Betty Staley
Fair Oaks, California, 2008

Endnotes
1. I have had a copy of this poem for forty years. Despite my searching, I have not been able to locate the first name of the poet, nor any other information about him.
2. Andrei Voznesensky, "Mother," from *An Arrow in the Wall, Selected Poetry and Prose*, eds. William Jay Smith and F.D. Reeve (New York: Henry Holt & Co., 1987).

Introduction

Why Teach Russian Literature?

It must be understood that the structure of the Russian soul is all its own and completely different from that of Westerners. The more penetrating minds of the West realize this well enough and are attracted by the puzzle it presents.[1]

— Nicholas Berdyaev

Whether one is teaching in a Waldorf school or another school, the high school years are a time in which students develop their thinking further. As they learn about different cultures through history, geography, and literature, they broaden their perspectives and come to more fully understand themselves and their place in the world. All that has been learned in the lower school years is transformed through the awakening intellect of the fourteen- to eighteen-year-old phase. This puts a special responsibility on the high school teacher as he or she guides the students through these four years.

In the ninth and tenth grades, the teenagers are still trying to figure out who they are, which group they belong to, what their classmates and friends think about them, what capacities are their strengths, and what their challenges and special interests are. In the eleventh and twelfth grades, the process becomes more internalized, as youngsters pass through the sixteen- to seventeen-year change and come face to face with issues of identity and begin to wonder about and plan for their future.

Each grade possesses a question that forms a theme that connects the different subjects of study. By being conscious of the theme, the teacher can shape their subjects so that a thread runs through them, and instead of each subject sitting in a separate compartment, the subjects begin to be integrated.

The ninth grade is focused very much on the present. It is a year of grounding. What is happening now? Can I develop my observation skills so I can clearly see what is there? What is the earth on which I stand? At the same time, it is important to find areas of the curriculum to feed the students' awakening idealism.

The tenth grade looks back. How did societies develop? How does one thing relate to another? How did language develop? How does the past relate to the present? How do I find my way into the world?

The eleventh grade experience is like venturing into a new land which needs a helpful map. Questions have more to do with why things are the way they are. It is the year of questing, of going on a journey to find out how "I" connect with the world. What do I have to do in my own development to become a vessel for the "world good"?

The twelfth grade is the capstone of the Waldorf curriculum. Themes that meet and nurture the twelfth grader's consciousness are the big philosophical ones. Who am I? What is good and evil? What is the nature of freedom? What is the role of responsibility? How are the needs of the individual and the community different? What is my relationship to my country? What is my relationship to humanity? What is the role of spiritual life? Each subject that is taught offers students opportunities to awaken perspective, stimulate their feeling life, broaden their thinking, and motivate them to "right" action.

Literature exists in the realm of story. Starting with "Once upon a time," we enter the stream of time and space. We can be anyone or anywhere or in any time period. We can fly away in our imagination, and we can learn about how people live and think every day. Literature nurtures the head, the heart, and the limbs. It can motivate us to think new thoughts by disciplining our cognitive powers; it can warm our feelings toward empathy and compassion; it can inspire us to take action in the world. Like mother's milk, literature continues to feed us in our connection with the divine world and with the love of guiding spirits, mortal and immortal.

Each culture's literature is a window into the soul of the people. When students immerse themselves in a country's literature, they step into the wide ocean of language with its undersea currents and surface waves. Some themes emerge, disappear and reemerge in another poem or novel. The landscape of the literature is varied, from a nine-hundred-page novel to a six-line verse, from symbolism and imagery to description. In literature, students meet the genius of the language and the representatives of the folk in the writers and poets.

The study of Russian literature introduces students to many great writers and poets of the nineteenth and twentieth centuries. Through their words, students are carried into the big questions of the culture. Does Russia have a unique destiny? Does it matter if God exists or not? What is the true nature of brotherhood? How do we relate to each other humanely? What is the spiritual responsibility of the writer or poet? Do writers have a special responsibility to tell the truth? Through exploring these works, students not only learn about another culture and its artistic expression, but they learn about themselves.

Individual works of Russian literature can be taught at any grade level. For example, Russian fairy tales can entertain a first grader. Sixth graders can appreciate Pushkin's poems on nature. Tolstoy's "What Men Live By" can be studied to great advantage by eighth or ninth graders. In addition to individual works being studied, I believe the impact of immersing students in Russian literature as a cultural experience in the twelfth grade can have tremendous benefit. Not only are students engaged in meeting a rich and complex heritage, they can learn more about their own country through the contrast. In addition to studying the individual work, learning it in the context of history, geography, and religion connects the literary work to its roots.

Designing a Russian Literature Block

Deciding what to teach is a problem of having too much richness. The teacher has to be selective and figure out what is too much and what is too little to include. So, the first challenge is content. Then the question is, how will I teach it? What modalities will I use—oral, written, artistic, performing? Then come the tricky questions: What is my educational goal in teaching the block, and how will I evaluate it? Of course, the questions may come in a different order. But always behind the course of study lie the essential pedagogical questions: Why am I teaching this subject? What does it have to do with the students of a particular age? Does it make a difference that the student is engaged in this subject matter? One could say, "Well, I have to teach it. It is required for standards, for college entrance exams, for the curriculum of a particular school." If it just stays at that level, the teacher's approach can easily become mechanical.

The challenge for the teacher is to make an intimate connection with the material, an engagement, a dialogue. This is an artistic process by which the teacher awakens something new in himself or herself. Then it is not only creative, but also fun. If the teacher can reach this level of connection with the subject, then he or she will surely find a way to connect the subject with the students in the class. The class discussions that ensue enliven the learning process and reiterate the teacher's calling to this special vocation.

Over the years of working with Russian literature, I have developed different ways of teaching the block (usually three or four weeks of daily classes of one and a half to two hours.) Much depends on the students, their interests, and their capacity. In general, I have a framework that is flexible enough to meet the specific situation. I have taught the class to a packed classroom of thirty-six students and in a seminar format of fourteen.

Certain elements are always part of the course. I begin in the previous spring when I send a letter to the eleventh graders, telling them that their summer reading will be *The Brothers Karamazov*. (This was approved by the English faculty.) I have audiotapes which I lend out to students who have learning issues. Now that these have become more available, some families listen to them as they drive on their summer vacations. In the last years, a colleague in the English department has offered summer evenings for any students who wished, to gather with him to read and talk about the book. This was a great help and very much appreciated by the students and me. Other students plunged into the book and either struggled or loved it. Over the years the students have told me that reading the book was a rite of passage.

The block is usually placed in the late autumn or early winter. I have taught it as a three-week block and also as a four-week block, the latter being much preferable as it gives time for the students to live into the subject more deeply. Four weeks, in general, is a healthier rhythm as it allows better breathing and not so much of a feeling of rushing.

I have always started the block by having the students tell me what they know of Russia or what they identify with the word. I fill the board with their words. With some classes, I have needed two boards, in others we did not fill even one board. Usually students give words such as: "cold," "vodka," "Communist," "KGB," and "furry hats," and *Peter and the Wolf* often came first. It is always interesting to compare the first day's words with the list at the end of the block when we repeat the exercise and now need several boards.

Depending on whether I was teaching this course during the Cold War or since the end of the Soviet Union, different stereotypes appeared. The course gives students an opportunity to explore their prejudices. "They're the enemy," "They're all aggressive," "I see them in the coffee shop and they're all in the Mafia" — these expressions usually come out on the first day. By the end of the block, students are able to fill the board with phrases such as "passionate," "melancholic," "profound," "deeply spiritual," "deeply affected by the Mongol invasion," "sympathetic," "beautiful land," and "lovers of poetry."

Geography is a very important foundation for any subject as it anchors the students in a physical place. Even though the themes of the literature are universal, they also reflect the place and time in which they were written. It is important to have a good topographical map of Eurasia that shows the landscape. We would spend ten to fifteen minutes each morning locating mountains, rivers, seas, and cities on the map and placing them on individual outline maps. This was always an active time as one student would be at the front map, pairs of students shared laminated maps at their seats, and then they had their individual ones in front of them as well. We played different kinds of games in which students had to find the geographical features and places. Usually after two weeks we also made a large body map with different students becoming mountains, rivers, and so forth. This was lively and gave the students a kinesthetic experience as well.

History connects students with the stream of time. I give them a brief historical picture, especially focusing on a few themes as described in the history chapter of this book. Often the response is, "I never knew anything about this before." In some classes there have been students who were partly Russian, some Russian-Jewish, others Russian-Orthodox or Baptist. They have always been grateful to learn something about their background. Some start talking to their parents about it. Others invite their parents to speak to the class or visit a class. Another interesting group was the Germans in Russia, descendants of Germans who moved to the Ukraine in the 1800s to farm and who were caught up in the revolutionary activities. Many emigrated to the Canadian prairie and still meet annually.

I have included a sample daily lesson plan in the Appendix. I change it from year to year. It has always been important to leave room for changes to the plan as we would go further into the course. Some classes have really wanted to explore "The Grand Inquisitor" scene or the "Teachings of Father Zossima" in *The Brothers Karamazov*. Others were less interested in those. The block includes numerous biographies of writers and poets. At times I have had the students tell the biographies, but as the years passed, it became clear that they did not always have the experience to choose the significant aspects of the biography. Also, as use of the internet has become more common, the biographies have tended to become chronologies taken off the web instead of experiences developed from reading books. Rather than having student presentations of the biographies, I have more recently told them myself and involve the students more in the discussions about the biographies. Each student does give an oral report—whether about a theme or scene in *The Brothers Karamazov* or another reading, such as Solzhenitsyn's *One Day in the Life of Ivan Denisovich* or his "Harvard Address."

We would begin the morning with the usual high school opening verse and then the speaking of a poem as choral recitation. Usually I use "Russia My Country" by Andrei Biely, sometimes I use the title poem "The Sun Burst" from which the image of "splinters of the sun" is taken. This is followed by recitation of several poems from a poetry resource reader I have put together. Sometimes we do group recitation, other times the poem is divided by verses, lines, or words, or by gender, or as an individual recitation.

Each student has to memorize a poem which is presented to class, also each one would choose a poem and write a description of the poem, including figures of speech, imagery, rhyme scheme, and personal impressions.

Important to the class is the daily review. Here we go back over the previous day's material and then discuss it in relation to themes we have just been covering. The review is extremely important for the learning process. It not only helps the student who has been absent, but emphasis can be placed on certain important issues, and new themes can emerge depending on student contributions in discussion. Sometimes we would do spontaneous poetry writing or drawing, based on the course.

Another important ingredient of the course in addition to oral presentations and writing assignments is the artistic element—a drawing, painting, sculpture, music, dance, drama, or cooking. The days these have been presented have always been a festival as we enjoy the talents of the students. Some that stand out are: an original musical interpretation of two different poems, a folk dance, a cello piece, a filmed enactment of a scene from *The Brothers Karamazov*, a Chekhov drama scene, a song sung in Russian, a costume, a metal sculpture, a large acrylic painting, and, of course, wonderful examples of cooking—either a full meal in the student's home to which I was invited or a full class banquet with a dozen dishes made by various students.

In designing the block, each teacher will choose his or her special readings and activities. So it should be. Planning out the block offers an exciting creative opportunity.

Throughout these chapters, I have included examples of student writing as they reflect our study together. I have not edited their work (except for making very minor corrections in spelling and grammar appropriate for publication) and place it in this book as it was placed in their books. I believe the students' words speak for themselves as to the importance and relevance of Russian literature in the twelfth grade curriculum.

Student writing:

Over the course of the past four weeks my love for history and foreign cultures has been rekindled again and again. This course on Russian literature not only opened my eyes to a subject I have rarely taken interest in — poetry — but deepened my understanding of the Russian people and their country's rich and turbulent history. For me, this course wiped away every image and stereotype I had of Russians. For me, this course was like the fall of the Berlin Wall. It was a course that I can honestly say changed the way I view the world.

From reading Fyodor Dostoyevsky's masterpiece, *The Brothers Karamazov*, to studying poetry and its powerful relationship to the Russian people and learning about the hardships *and* suppression that sculpted a country into what it is today, these past four weeks have proven to be a rich and fascinating whirlwind of culture and history.

For me, the most interesting aspect of learning about Russia's history was its people. For centuries upon centuries they have been terrorized, tortured, and killed by not only outside forces, but the very powers that govern their country. It is no exaggeration when I say that every generation in Russian history, to this very day, has experienced hardship on a scale that most westerners cannot comprehend, and that the majority of this hardship is the direct result of the country's very own government. And what amazes me most is that, through all this, the Russian people are a proud people. Proud of their country. Proud of their poems. Proud of their culture.

When I first walked into class four weeks ago, I knew nothing about Russian literature (except, of course, *The Brothers Karamazov*) or Russian poetry — especially poetry. The fact is I had never cared much about poetry. It didn't speak to me — at least the poetry I had read before taking this course. This all changed after I started reading some of Pushkin's poetry, especially "Message to Siberia" and "The Prophet" and Balmont's "Voicelessness," Their work captured every emotion I felt when I thought of Russia and its people. Their work captured the passion of the Russian people and the persistent suffering that emanates from their lives. As the weeks went by and I read the works of other Russian poets such as Anna Akhmatova and Boris Pasternak, my appreciation for poetry, at least Russian poetry, only increased, and by the end of the course, while reading the works of Joseph Brodsky, I found myself wanting to read every Russian poem I could lay my hand on. I even spent time to look up more Russian poems on line. – *M.M.*

This block has opened my eyes. It gave me an opportunity to look at some of the major philosophical themes of recent history, while exploring the history, geography, and peoples of a distinctly unique nation. The discussions I particularly enjoyed were those on free will and responsibility, suffering, the culture of Russia, and the power of ideas. . . .

One of the arguments against God's existence that we discussed was the existence of evil and suffering in the world, which was Ivan's problem with God in *The Brothers Karamazov*. It made me think about free will and its value in the world. Obviously, this is and has been the major criticism of God for centuries. Religion is something that interests me enormously, and free will and moral responsibility are at the heart of its belief system. Before these discussions and thoughts, it was very hard for me to see the value in something that was not logical or rational, but I have begun to realize that some things can be accepted through faith alone, and I have learned the power of this irrational, inexplicable belief that so many people hold in the core of their soul.

One theme I found particularly poignant was the idea and role of suffering in the culture of Russia. When we discussed the biographies of the great Russian writers, what I found was that each one had his or her problems, whether it was a flirtatious wife, censorship, or undeserved years in a labor camp. All of the writers had major issues that they dealt with, and they discussed these issues in their writing. Tolstoy talked of his problems and beliefs in *Confessions*, Dostoyevsky played out his questions of faith in *The Brothers Karamazov*, Solzhenitsyn portrayed life in a *gulag* (where he spent fifteen years) in *One Day in the Life of Ivan Denisovich*, and Anna Akhmatova's "Requiem" tells of her grief after her son was sent to a labor camp for her dissidence. Writing the commentary about suffering made me consider the paradox of suffering: We all try to avoid it, but we have a great respect for those who survive it. Suffering is feared and respected in our society, and many people would say that most great art is the expression or reaction to human suffering. Suffering gives us a different perspective on life, or perhaps allows us to see outside of ourselves. The Russian people have had to withstand huge amounts of suffering in their history as a nation. From subjugation by a ruling class, to oppression by an iron-fisted government, they have seen the worst of the worst in the plight of the human being in this world. What is truly great about the Russian writers is that they have been the prophets, or the voices, of the people. They expressed this suffering to us in the most powerful ways. Pasternak told us about the horrors of the revolution, Solzhenitsyn told us about the Siberian labor camps, Akhmatova described the oppression of the Russian government. They made us understand and feel for the common Russian, and brought home the injustices that were occurring daily in the U.S.S.R. These writers were truly the voice for the suffering of their people.

Finally, this block gave me the history of a country and people that I did not know much about before. Russia had always been referred to as this looming power that was huge in size and influence in the world. In this block, that stereotype was not necessarily destroyed, but put in a historical and sociological context. I saw the other parts of the Russian people. I got a sense of the culture of the Russians and of some of the things that they value. I learned of the natural hardiness that the harsh climate has cultivated in the Russian people, of their love and respect for poetry and poets, and of the deep influence that the church holds in Russia. When you study a people, you start to truly empathize with them, and I feel that in some ways I can understand some parts of the Russian mentality. I have learned that once you get past the stereotypes and outer trappings of the identity of a people, you begin to find your own qualities reflected in that identity. In learning about Russia's history, I have gained a perspective on where its peoples have come from and perhaps where they will be going in the future.

Also what this block impressed upon me was the power of ideas, and their timelessness. Learning about the rise of communism and the oppression by the Russian government during the Soviet era impressed upon me the power of idealism in the world. To think that the writings of Karl Marx in the nineteenth century caused the birth of a government that killed or enslaved millions of people is staggering. There are many ideas in our society that hold sway over our future. If a certain carpenter two thousand years ago had not claimed he was the Son of God and had not tried to spread his ideas, what would our society look like today? If humanism had not arisen in Europe in the Renaissance, would democracy or capitalism exist? Our society is truly shaped and defined by the rise and fall of ideas.

I enjoyed this block, and it has made me think and question my ideas and conceptions more than most other main lessons. I can see why it was placed in senior year. Another part of the globe has become clear in my mind, and I have begun to understand a completely different kind of lifestyle and thinking." – L.S.

A Comparison of Russian and American Cultures

Another key element of teaching Russian literature is that it awakens a contrast with American literature and culture. America was founded on the idea of freedom of thought, religion, and expression. Coming out of the Enlightenment, the ideas of equality and the sanctity of the individual come to expression in the American spirit. Americans as a people are centered in the will, people who *do*. It is a matter of individual striving, working hard, overcoming obstacles, being a rugged individual. People who are willing to work to overcome odds come to America, and most everyone (except the Native people) has come here either by choice for opportunity or by being enslaved and brought here in chains. An individual has to learn to make it here; very little reaches out to embrace one.

Economic life dominates American culture. Yet there is also tremendous generosity and willingness to help others who encounter tragedy or natural disaster. There is good will. What is less evident in the American soul is the heart force connected with community. In order to find our individual identity and destiny, we often leave the community behind. We then have to search for the concept of community in our own individuality.

Before Russia developed a national identity, small villages based on democratic councils functioned independently. The cultural identity was unified by the adoption of Eastern Orthodox Christianity which connected individual life with the life of Christ. Central to that was the concept of *sobernost*, community, the individual embedded within the community. Community included the earth as a living suffering being, the spiritual world, and the people living within this interrelationship of earth and heaven. What is strongest in the Russian identity is the Soul. The struggle in Russian history has always been to find a place for individual freedom of thought and expression. Russian history is layer upon layer of authority, either cruel or benign, but authority nonetheless. The uniqueness of the Russian has been the belief in the peasant, the person of the earth, who may sin dramatically, but is redeemed because of his or her faith in God and Christ.

Russian and American cultures have similarities as well as differences. Both have had governments which at times have focused on power and expansion. America came of age in the nineteenth century, and in the twentieth century spread its wings, developed a strong army and navy, was victorious through courage and bravery in World Wars I and II, and still today struggles with *hubris*, excessive pride. America tends to isolation so we can go our own way, taking what we want and imposing what we think the world needs or how we think the world ought to be. Often this means we want them to be like us and share our values of individualism and democracy. Russian power has come through its empire, spreading out and taking in more and more land, and especially seeking accessible seaports when it is already the largest country in the world. Russian power has also been exercised internally, limiting freedom, and demanding complete obedience of its people.

Russians and Americans have been pioneers, settling the Far East and the Far West respectively, both wild places where individuals could go to seek their fortune in spices and jewels or gold and other minerals. One difference is that in America, criminals, no-gooders and other undesirables went west to get away from the eye of government; in Russia, political reformers or others of whom the government did not approve were sent to Siberia in chains or in rail cars, with terrible suffering as a result.

Both countries have much of which to be proud. America is a haven for people from all over the world seeking freedom and opportunity. Russia has great cultural achievements in literature and music and deep religious yearnings. Both countries bear guilt for the treatment of their people — America's treatment of the Native people and the African-Americans, Russia's treatment of her free thinkers and individuals who showed initiative or thoughts of freedom. The Russian concept of community and the American concept of individuality and independence create a balance in human activity.

[I]f the single man plant himself indomitably on his instincts, and there abide, the huge world will come round to him. . . . We will walk on our own feet; we will work with our own hands; we will speak our own minds.[2]

– Ralph Waldo Emerson

Through deep suffering, people in our country have now achieved a spiritual development of such intensity that the Western system in its present state of spiritual exhaustion does not look attractive. . . . The complex and deadly crush of life has produced stronger, deeper and more interesting personalities than those generated by standardized Western well-being.[3]

– Alexander Solzhenitsyn

The people and character of the West were more competently inclined towards a capable engagement with the material, practical matters of life and world than the Russians would ever be. The Russian people were much more inclined towards a deep, soulful inner life. They would never quite "get it right" with the practical, material life; whether they live in a time of *perestroika* and *glasnost*, or not.[4]

– Valentin Rasputin

Yes, the Russian's destiny is incontestably all-European and world-wide. To become a real Russian, to become fully a Russian, perhaps, means only to become brother of all men, a completely universal man, if you want.[5]

– Fyodor Dostoyevsky

Discussing the concepts in these quotations in the context of Russian literature study can broaden a student's perspectives and provoke questions which can quicken the mind and stir the heart. In this context of similarities and differences, American high school students, especially twelfth graders, can benefit tremendously by being exposed to the literature and culture of Russia.

Endnotes

1. Nicholas Berdyaev, as quoted in *Towards the Spiritual Convergence of America and Russia* by Stephen L. Lapeyrouse (Santa Cruz, CA: Lapeyrouse, 1990), p. 352.
2. Ralph Waldo Emerson, "The American Scholar," from *The Portable Emerson*, ed. Carl Bode (New York: Viking Penguin, 1981), p. 71.
3. "A World Split Apart" Solzhenitsyn's 1978 Harvard Address, from *Solzhenitsyn at Harvard, The Address, Twelve Early Responses, and Six Later Reflections*, ed. Ronald Berman (Washington, DC: Ethics and Public Policy Center, 1980), pp. 12–13.
4. Valentin Rasputin, as quoted in Lapeyrouse, *Spiritual Convergence*, p. 47.
5. Fyodor Dostoyevsky, from his 1880 "Pushkin Speech" in Moscow, as quoted in *Dostoyevsky, His Life and Work* by Konstantin Mochulsky (Princeton, NJ: Princeton University Press, 1967), p. 641.

SECTION I
EXPLORING THE BACKGROUND OF RUSSIAN LITERATURE

CHAPTER 1

GEOGRAPHY OF RUSSIA AND THE SPECIAL RELATIONSHIP OF RUSSIA'S PEOPLE TO THE LAND

What these poets loved was the beauty of the landscape of birches and pines, high mountains, endless steppes, the beauty of the Russian tongue, with its complexity and richness that enables the language to convey an incredible range of subtle nuances of emotion and thought. They shared a love for art and poetry that could not be equaled in any other country, for it was a country where hungry people gathered in cold rooms to read poetry to each other and performed experimental music based on traditions of the Russian past. And they shared a love for the people who had suffered so much and yet had endured, a love for a people who asked questions about the meaning of life and death that others had often been afraid to ask. In the process, these poets came up with answers that have influenced more major Western thinkers throughout the twentieth century.[1]
                                                – Roberta Reeder speaking about Anna Akhmatova

About one and three-fourths the size of the United States, Russia is the largest country in the world in area (one-eighth of the world's land), and it has many challenging aspects. Much of the country lacks good soil and climate—it is either too cold or too hot—for agriculture. The land can readily be compared with northern Canada with its forests and frozen land. Russia has the longest coastline, but most of the coastline is in the Arctic and unusable, with only one port, Murmansk, that can be used because it is warmed by the Gulf Stream. The most important ports are on the Baltic and the Black Seas.

A part of the continents of Asia and Europe, Russia borders fourteen countries as neighbors. Disregarding the two-mile distance across the Bering Strait to Alaska, then the United States can be considered the fifteenth neighbor. Russia has the deepest fresh water lake in the world (Lake Baikal), the highest mountain in Europe (Mount Elbrus), and the longest river in Europe (the Volga). The land is divided into five zones.

Furthest north is the Tundra. Here in this expanse of cold, marshy land where only mosses, lichens and dwarf willows grow, it is either light all night in summer or in total darkness in winter. Less than one percent of the population lives here. The soil is frozen all the time, with permafrost penetrating several meters deep. The Arctic winds blow south, making the Siberian winters very cold and the summers hot and dry.

South of the tundra is the Taiga, the world's largest forest region, an area about the size of the United States. About thirty-three percent of the population lives in this area, the coldest inhabited area in the world. Most of the taiga is in European Russia.

South of the taiga is the Steppe, what can be considered the typical Russian landscape. Similar to the American grasslands, the steppe is the treeless grassy plains between the Ukraine and Kazakhstan. Of all the Russian topography, it is most suited for agriculture and for human settlement with its moderate temperature and a good balance of sun and moisture (although there are occasional droughts). The black earth of the steppe is some of the richest soil in the world.

South of the steppe is the Arid region, a desert-like zone. Most of this belt is in the Asian part of Russia. Furthest south is the Mountainous area, particularly the Caucasus Mountains. The Caucasus shelters the land from the North winds, so the cities on the Black Sea have a relatively mild climate.

Russia is a country with a great deal of surface water, including many lakes, the Caspian and Black Seas, and 150,000 rivers. However, many of the rivers are not navigable nor do they flow out into outer bodies of water such as the Mediterranean Sea.

With more than half of its land north of the sixty-degrees north latitude, Russia is considered the coldest country in the world. For six months snow covers the permafrost. Then comes a very brief spring, a longer summer, a brief autumn, and winter again. Because of the cold, the people have adapted their housing, their crops, their transportation, their use of energy, and their clothing. About seventy-five percent of the people live in the cities and towns of European Russia, and twenty-five percent in rural areas. The total population is about 149 million people.

Russia has much to admire. There is a wealth of natural resources such as oil, natural gas, minerals, and timber. The rich farmland yields wheat, barley, oats, potatoes, and sunflowers. But since only eight percent of the land is arable, it is impossible to produce enough food for the population. The large ocean fishing fleet provides a variety of fish for food.

Although the climate is harsh and the land does not yield enough good soil for farming, Russia is a beautiful country which is loved and honored by its people. Writers and travelers have extolled the beauty of the heartland of Russia (the steppe) with its birch trees, streams, and meadows and majesty of snow-covered terrain.

Winter had begun long ago. The frost was severe. Disjoined sounds and forms without any visible connection materialized in the frozen haze. They stopped, moved, and disappeared. A crimson sphere was hanging over the forest; not the sun to which we on earth are accustomed, but some other kind, a substitute. As in a dream or a fairy tale, amber-yellow rays, thick as honey, were flowing from it, stiffening in the air and freezing on the trees.[2]

– Pasternak

The day came, white, clear and cold—the kind on which you exhale steam and on which hoar frost lies on the trees, houses, fences. In the village, grey smoke rose straight up from the chimneys. Beyond the windows was an abandoned garden. The little village stood there, pressed down to the ground by the snow. Further on stretched white fields, a ravine, and the forest. The sky was white, the air was white, and the sun did not come out from behind the white clouds.[3]

– Pilnyak

Gigantic trunks of oaks, lindens, birches, and aspens lie scattered about the forest. First they dry up, then their roots rot out, and finally they are battered down by a storm. As they fall they bend and break young neighboring trees which, despite their disfigurement, continue to grow and to blossom, picturesquely twisting to the side, stretching toward the ground, or bent into an arch. The corpses of the forest giants, while decaying internally, preserve their external appearance for a long time. Moss and grass grow around the bark. . . . This is a special kind of world and folk fantasy has peopled it with supernatural beings: goblins and wood-sprites.[4]

– Aksakov

To understand the poetry of a birch one must go to Russia. This pliant and hardy tree illuminates the depths of the Russian forests with its white moss-marbled trunk. Whether standing alone or commingled with other species, it always enlivens the wood, imparting a bit of its elegant insouciance. Russians love the birch, the *berioza*, and I understand their affection. The languid grace of this silvery tree sets it apart from all the others. In summer, when its supple branches arch over its base, or in winter, when its undulating twigs are etched against the white horizon, it is saluted like a friend: "Berioza, berioza." [5]

– Legras

There are few mushrooms here; you have to go into the birch grove for mushrooms, and I am ready to start out. For I have never loved anything more in my life than the forest with its mushrooms and wild berries, with its bugs and little birds, hedgehogs and squirrels, with the dank smell of rotten leaves which I love so much. And even now, as I write this, I can smell the birch grove of our village, such impressions last for one's entire life.[6]

– Dostoyevsky

Early in the morning, the coolness woke him in his carriage and he glanced indifferently to the right. The morning was absolutely clear. Suddenly, twenty paces away, as it seemed to him at first, he saw clean white masses with their soft outlines and the fantastical, distinct, yet ethereal line where their peaks met the distant sky. And when he realized all the distance between himself, the mountains and sky, the immensity of the mountains, and when he became aware of the endlessness of this beauty, he feared that it was all a mirage, a dream. He shook himself to wake up. The mountains remained the same. . . . At first the mountains only amazed Olenin, later, he rejoiced in them; but then, staring more and more at the sight, not from other black mountains but straight at the chain of snowy mountains which were running away and growing right out of the steppe, Olenin began, little by little, to enter into that beauty, to *feel* the mountains. From that time on everything that he saw, everything that he thought, everything that he felt, became tinged with the new strongly majestic character of the mountains.[7]

– Tolstoy

Summer arrived in the space of a week. The last migratory bird appeared and built its nestlet. Red and white poppies burst into bloom. Baby-blue flowers of silken flax poured like a sea over the field. White buckwheat peppered the whole endless path like powdery snow. . . . The linden gleamed like a solid gold arrow while the silvery oats and pale-amber wheat spread hither and yon. They covered the forests and ravines; infinitely stretching to the deep blue sky, and they were lost in the humming and abundance of preharvest insatiability.[8]

– Remizov

Student writing:

How can you imagine that the geography of Russia might influence the character of the Russians?

The geography of Russia has influenced its people for as long as they have existed. Not only is the terrain unforgiving, but the country itself is enormous. Some parts of Russia were not even habitable by its early people. To survive the harsh winter and untamable wilderness requires a determined resilience. As a result, the people of Russia have developed a unique temperament. The snow is beautiful to behold in its majestic purity, the enveloping blanket of white, the fragile snowflakes, like the tears of an angel. And yet, the snow is absolutely merciless, like a rose with its thorns, the snow's beauty is lethal, threatening to embrace you with its cold fingers and draw you into its icy depths. The people of Russia are a people of the snow, their passion and love for beauty is strong, but at the same time their hearts are steeled with a layer of frost. A snowflake on its own will easily melt away to nothing, but with many snowflakes you get a snow bank that will last long after the last snowflakes have fallen on it and the sun has returned to warm the land. The people of Russia are not unlike its permafrost; in that way, they are united.

Russia's cold and unforgiving geography is one of the reasons Russia was not able to flourish quickly like the countries around it. And yet, the very aspects that prevented Russia from developing also saved it time and time again. Eleven time zones and a half. The harsh and unforgiving winter was enough to stop any army in its tracks. Not even the great Mongol hordes could conquer the northern reaches of Russia. The land had two faces. In one way it was a harsh mistress with an icy temper that forced the Russian people to lead simple lives, always aware lest they be swallowed by the elements. At the same time, Russia's massive size and its harsh terrain protected its people like the embrace of a caring mother. In many ways Russia is like a mother to its people. She is stern perhaps, but always looking out for her children when they need her protection. – J.B.

The most unique qualities of Russia's geography is that it is extremely large, it is very cold, and it is partly in Europe and partly in Asia. These three characteristics alone will have created very interesting characteristics in the people of Russia.

Russia is the largest nation on earth and spans eleven time zones. Given this size, and the low population density of most of Russia, I imagine the peoples of Russia differ greatly in culture and traditions, and perhaps have trouble identifying themselves as one unified nation.

Most of Russia is tundra or permafrost, and this makes it very difficult to live there. This difficulty of living could create an intense will to survive, no matter what the situation. This will to survive comes along with a lot of value placed on heartiness and strength in men and women. I imagine that until recently, intelligence, altruism, and sensitivity were signs of weakness, but communities working together would be very important to survival. This level of difficulty of living would create a people very receptive to religion (particularly Christianity), as a source of comfort that this life is not it, that there is something else to look forward to.

Finally, Russia is in both Asia and Europe, which means that its people are connected to both continents, but perhaps identify with neither. Russia is unique in the world in its geography, and its people are also unique. It is a very interesting study of how the land affects its inhabitants. – *L.S.*

The Special Relationship of the Russians to Nature and to the Earth

One of the special qualities about Russian literature is the way the writers express their intimate connection with the earth. In some aspects they are similar to the Native Americans' feelings of the earth as a living being, the Great Mother. And yet there is more. In addition, Russians feel that the earth has witnessed human actions throughout history, and it has suffered because of those actions. The individual's life is an echo of the Mother Earth Soul and its suffering. By feeling the earth's pain, the Russian is united with the spiritual world. The earth was blessed because Christ walked upon it, and she shared the pain of Christ's sacrifice. The earth and all of nature is a mirror of heaven.

> The Russian soul kneels upon the earth and turns its gaze upwards to the heavenly world, which bends down to her in love. In the heavenly etheric sphere the soul's longing gaze seeks Him—the Sun of Truth; Christ, who draws near to it in angelic form.... It perceives in nature, in the humble nature of its home land, the reflection of His heavenly kingdom.[9]
>
> – Gabriele Efimowa

> And through thee, dear earth,
> blessing thee in the guise of poverty,
> Christ the Lord of Heavens, has wandered.[10]
> – Tjietschavv

While the Russian feels the earth to be a beating, suffering heart, the American experiences it as a heavy, material body providing resources for survival. The Russian soul did not need an ecology movement to awaken to the earth as a living organism. However, in the last fifty years, many modern Russians have misused the earth as much as any other people, and pollution was a serious problem during the years of the Soviet Union.

I was in the monastery in Zagorsk in 1987 when a pilgrim entered who could have been straight out of Tolstoy's world. Sporting a long white beard, wearing an ankle-length woolen coat and a worn leather backpack, he pressed himself on the ground and kissed the earth. In Medieval Russia this was a common sight. Russian pilgrims travel the earth, seeking the kingdom of God within it. From a song:

"Forgive, forgive, O Mother Earth,
Three heavy sins lie sore in me!"
The earth replies,
"I will remit the first two sins.
When you committed them you were still young.
Yet the third sin of fratricide I cannot
Forgive in all eternity." [11]

These lines are particularly poignant in view of the millions who were killed in the Stalinist purges. One can ask how the earth can recover from the blood that has seeped into her weeping heart. The following medieval song includes a dialogue between Mother Earth and Christ.

The Earth Complains to the Lord Christ:
No longer can I carry upon my breast sinful men
who commit so great crimes.
Theft and fratricide, lying and slander —
O lord, bid my depths open and swallow lawless humanity!

The Lord Christ Answers Mother Earth:
O Mother, moist Mother Earth,
Of all creatures, thou art most in pain.
By the sins of humanity thou art stained.
Have patience yet a little while until I come again.
Then Thou, O Earth, shalt rejoice and skip;
Thou shalt shine forth whiter than snow.
I shall change thee into a marvelous garden
Where beautiful flowers of Paradise shall bloom for thee!
O ye, my chosen souls, rejoice.[12]

In the Western world, it is the saints who experienced the stigmata. However, it is described that the Russian people as a whole carry the stigmata. This intimate connection of the Russian with the crucifixion awakens a dream and hope of resurrection. They seek the Holy Spirit in their devotion to the Christ.

The reflected light of heaven shines upon the Russian soul, for which everything is holy, is consecrated — the bread, the simple spoon, the grain, the water of the well. Every meal is a communion. The same is true for the plant life, as Russians have a much stronger love for wild flowers than for cultivated ones.

Rudolf Steiner described two streams of activity through which Russian people experience their identity.[13] The light of the cosmos touches the earth and its reflection is then received in the head. The other stream emanates from the rhythmic system and heart. They meet, unite, and form a channel through which the folk soul/spirit (national identity) enters to sustain the individual with its inspiration. The Russian people experience their folk soul/spirit through the flowers and grasses, in the harmonies of the spheres which flow from heaven to the flowers and rise again from earth to the heavens.

In the words of Dostoyevsky's Father Zossima in *The Brothers Karamazov*: "God took seeds from different worlds and sowed them on his earth, and his garden grew up, and everything came up that would come up. But what grows and lives is alive only through the feeling of its contact with other mysterious worlds. If that feeling grows weak or is destroyed in you, the heavenly growth will die away in you. Then you will be indifferent to life and even grow to hate it. That's what I think."[14] Dostoyevsky may have been forewarning what would happen if Russian culture were to become materialistic and isolated from its spiritual foundation. The cruelty that came under Stalin and his successors reflected both an indifference to life and a hatred of it.

Endnotes

1. Roberta Reeder, *Anna Akhmatova, Poet and Prophet* (New York: St. Martin's Press, 1994), xiv.
2. B.L. Pasternak, *Doctor Zhivago*, 1957, as quoted in *Classic Russian Idylls* by Proctor Jones (San Francisco: Proctor Jones Pub. Co., 1985), p. 32.
3. B.A. Pilnyak, *Snows*, 1920, as quoted in *Classic Russian Idylls*, p. 38.
4. S.T. Aksakov, *Notes of a Rifle Hunter from Orenburg Province*, 1851, as quoted in *Classic Russian Idylls*, p. 44.
5. J. Legras, *Au Pays Russe*, ca. 1895, as quoted in *Classic Russian Idylls*, p. 50.
6. F.M. Dostoyevsky, *Diary of a Writer*, 1876, as quoted in *Classic Russian Idylls*, p. 70.
7. L. Tolstoy, *The Cossacks*, 1863, as quoted in *Classic Russian Idylls*, p. 90.
8. A.M. Remizov, *The Black Rooster*, 1907, as quoted in *Classic Russian Idylls*, p. 98.
9. Gabriele Efimowa, "Mother Earth," *Russia, Past, Present and Future*, compiled by John Fletcher (London: New Knowledge Books, 1968), p. 9.
10. Quoted in Efimowa, "Mother Earth," p. 8.
11. Ibid., p. 4. This is from a spiritual song in which a man confesses his sin of killing his brother to Mother Earth.
12. Ibid.
13. Rudolf Steiner, *Russia: Past, Present, and Future*, compiled by John Fletcher (London: New Knowledge Books, 1969), pp. 13–14.
14. This quotation is from the "Conversations and Exhortations of Father Zossima, Book VI, The Russian Monk" in *The Brothers Karamazov* by Fyodor Dostoyevsky, trans. by Constance Garnett (New York: Signet Classic, Penguin Books, 1980), p. 311.

Spring on the Russia Plateau

CHAPTER 2

HISTORY OF RUSSIA

It is very difficult to understand Russian literature without some background in the country's complex and fascinating history. Unlike literary works of various other cultures, many works of Russian poetry and novels are intertwined with historical events. In Russian literature, poets and novelists carry out a dialogue between themselves and their times. It is therefore helpful to give the students a timeline as a framework for the historical and literary events. The timeline can also help the students place in perspective what they are learning in other history classes.

In this chapter, I have provided much more information than can usually be included in a literature main lesson block. However, it will serve the teacher to have enough background to emphasize some of the remarkable events and changes that have shaped Russian society and thus Russian literature. Generally, I take two to three class sessions to present the main information. In the first session I cover the time period from 988 to the 1880s, focusing mainly on the Christianizing of Russia, the Mongol Invasions, and Peter the Great. I weave in additional aspects as part of the biographies of Pushkin, Dostoyevsky, and Tolstoy. Before introducing twentieth century writers, I find it helpful to speak about the industrialization of Russia, the class differences in 1900, and the inner conflict felt by writers and poets who enthusiastically supported the ideas of the Revolution but were made victims by the brutal totalitarian actions of the Bolsheviks. I use the biographies of Pasternak, Akhmatova, and Solzhenitsyn to add historical details, especially for the post-Revolutionary period. If the students have already studied Karl Marx's work, this is very helpful background for speaking about the Russian Revolution and the post-Revolutionary period.

Pre-Tenth Century: The Slavic Tribes and the Rise of Kievan Rus
Russia Gains an Identity as a Nation

Who Were the Slavs?

The Slavs were a part of an ancient Indo-European culture which included German, Baltic (Latvian-Lithuanian), Romance, Greek, Celtic, Iranian, Indian (Aryan) and other people spread over a large area of land between the Atlantic and Indian Oceans west to east, and from the Arctic Ocean to the Mediterranean Sea north to south. The Slavic tribes lived mainly east of the Alps and toward the Carpathian Mountains. They were cattle-raising people who struggled for pastures and herds; they traded with copper and bronze. By 1500 BCE, the entire zone of the European deciduous forests and partly wooded steppe was occupied by these Indo-European tribes, the ancestors of the Balts, the Germans, and the Slavs.

They began to develop a settled way of life based on farming, in three major centers. In each of these centers an Indo-European language developed: in the western part of the zone, the Germanic language developed, in the middle, the Slavonic language which became Russian, and in the northeast Lettish-Lithuania (Latvian-Lithuanian). The people lived in small villages basing their economy on land cultivation, livestock breeding, fishing and hunting. Their tools — axes, knives, and sickles — were still made of stone; bronze was used mainly for decoration. Their burial rites reflected the ideas of reincarnation; the bodies were folded in an embryonic position as if prepared for rebirth.

By 1000 BCE, with the development of the plow, the Slavic farmers increased yields of grain and became the breadbasket for Ancient Greece. With the discovery of iron in the swamps and lakes, the Slavic tribes grew rich by developing a thirty-five pound plow. Some of their earliest literature portrays the Slavs defeating an evil serpent (raiding tribes). In these tales, the blacksmith is the chief hero because he taught the people to plow the land. The blacksmith did not kill the serpent with his sword but caught him in his pincers, harnessed him to the magical plow and made enormous furrows known as Serpent ramparts.

The Slav tribes along the Dnieper River built forts and defended their land against the raiding tribes who were livestock breeders. Their myths were passed down in Russian, Byelorussian, and Ukrainian folk tales that describe three kingdoms; one was the Golden Kingdom ruled by the Sun Tsar. The Scythians roamed the area in carts and competed for the available land to graze their cattle. They competed with the grain growers who every spring celebrated the holiday of the sacred plow given to them by the God of the Sky.

In the third century BCE, the Scythian state was overtaken by the Sarmatians, who became the new masters of the steppe. Aggressive, they took over trade routes, plundered Greek towns, attacked the Slavs, and pushed the grainlands northwards. The "wife-ruled" Sarmatians also left their traces in the stories about the Serpent Woman, the Serpent's wives and sisters, and Baba Yaga, the witch who lived on chicken legs in an underground house near the sea, where Russian heads were displayed on poles. During this time the Slavs moved northward from the partly wooded steppe to the forests. Here in the dense forests, near swamps, the Slav tribes reformed, building new forts and finding protection from the Sarmatians.

During the time of the Roman Empire, Rome extended its influence on the Germanic tribes and part of the West-Slav tribes along the Rhine, Elbe, and Oder Rivers.Their legions seized the Greek ports on the Black Sea. With the expansion of Roman authority to Eastern Europe (and the forced language of Latin as in Romania),Slavic trade thrived, and from the second to fourth centuries AD, a wealthy nobility developed. The Slav nobility imported luxury items and developed Kiev as a major trade center. Products traded included amber, furs, honey, slaves, wax, weapons, silk, and silver. During this time the potters' wheel gave rise to crafts.

In the third century AD, trade was interrupted by the Sarmatian invasion, and again at the end of the fourth century by the invasion of the Turkish-speaking Huns. The name *Rus* or *Ros* has been traced to sources in the mid-sixth century. It referred to the Eastern Slavs living between the Baltic and the Black Sea. Other times it referred to those living in Kiev.

When we research how the Kievan Rus state came to exist, we find two different versions. One version is that the Kievan state was a powerful and successful trading alliance with relations all the way to Baghdad in the south and in the east to Bulgaria. At some point, the Swedish Varangians (Vikings) made their way into Rus and joined the Russian traders and entered the service of a Kiev prince. Thus the Slavs in this region came to be referred to as the Rus. The other version is that in 862 AD, Slavic tribes invited the Swedish chieftain Rurik and his two brothers to rule them. Some Russian historians consider this revisionist history, claiming that the Varangians were Viking raiders who took over various communities, exacting tribute and offering protection from other Varangians. Whether the Rus were invited in or they pushed their way in, the result was an identity of a land of Slavs centered in the territory of Kiev in the Ukraine.

From the ninth to the twelfth centuries the Kievan Rus was an enormous feudal state stretching from the Baltic to the Black Sea. Its princes formed relationships with the kings of European countries and with the Byzantine Emperor. There was a great deal of infighting between cities although in their pagan religion, the Slavs did not have a god of war.

The Christianizing of Russia

One source describes that the first act that Prince Vladimir did was drive the Varangians out of Kiev. Then he established a heathen religion based on six gods headed by Perun, the god of thunder and war. Vladimir was successful and extended Rus as a state of all the Eastern Slavs. He appointed his sons to head the major cities which were joined to Kiev by highways.

Vladimir's grandmother Olga had become Christian, and she had hoped that, at her time of dying, her grandson would also adopt Christianity. The ancient Primary Chronicle relates that in 987 Prince Vladimir of Kiev conferred with emissaries from various lands about their religion. The Bulgars wanted him to convert to Islam because Muslims believe in God and Mohammed promised that, if they were faithful, they would be able to fulfill their carnal desires after death. Vladimir was impressed by that since he had been married four times and had several hundred concubines. However, Vladimir also recognized the central pleasure of drink, and knowing alcohol was not allowed in Islam, refused the offer to convert.

German emissaries had been sent by the Pope to persuade Vladimir to choose Roman Catholicism. They spoke of their light-filled faith, the worship of God as creator, and the similarities between their two countries. However, the emissary insulted Vladimir's pagan religion and its gods of wood. So Vladimir also turned down the Germans.

The Jewish Khazars explained that they believed in one God, the God of Abraham, Isaac, and Jacob. But Vladimir understood that the Jews were condemned to wander the world, and he rejected Judaism.

When his emissaries reported on their experience in Constantinople, they spoke of the Cathedral of Hagia Sophia with its magnificent interior of gold mosaics, incense, candles, and music. They said, "We knew not whether we were in heaven or earth and we are at a loss to describe it. We only know that God dwells there among men, and their service is fairer than the ceremonies of other nations. For we cannot forget that beauty."[1]

Vladimir was impressed by the description of the beauty of the Greek Orthodox service and the cathedral, and soon after 988, he agreed to convert. He was baptized and issued a decree that the land of Kiev would adopt Eastern Christianity and use the Greek alphabet and Slavonic language for church services. He began a program of beautification, incorporating Russian folk art and music, Slavic traditions of community and brotherly love. The people had a strong heart-felt attitude toward this new religion. They focused on the spiritual ideals of compassion, nonresistance, gentleness, and humility. They identified their own suffering with the suffering Christ experienced on the cross.

Over the next fifty years (988–1038) Kiev, with over four hundred churches, became one of the most beautiful cities in the world. The dedication to beauty was evidenced in the architecture of the church, with heaven being represented by the central dome. The dome represented the head or forehead, the drum was the neck, and the rounded gable the shoulder, the bosom. The number of domes carried significance: one equaled God; three equaled the Trinity; five were for Christ and the four evangelists; nine for nine choirs of angels; twelve smaller domes surrounding the main one represented Christ and the twelve Apostles. All domes carried a cross with a slanting beam across the bottom arm and often another near the top. In places a sign was hung above Christ's head and at his feet. Later a crescent moon was placed at the foot of the cross to depict the victory over the Muslim Tatars. Russian Christians view themselves not as Christian soldiers, but as children inheriting their father's house.

The beauty of worship connected mankind with the beauty of the spiritual world. Inside the cathedral was the image of Patokrator, the Divine Creator of heaven and earth. God was not only a God of truth but of beauty, who revealed Himself to His people through the beauty of art. Statues were considered graven images and were not allowed. So artists filled the churches with icons to remind the congregation of the invisible and comforting presence at the liturgy of whole companies of heaven.

Vladimir was called "the Bright Sun" who practiced mercy and reformed the Byzantine legal codes which were savage and brutal by instituting due process of law and forbidding the death penalty, mutilation, and torture. The social services he put in place were way ahead of his times. When he gave feasts of brotherly love, he sent wagons loaded with bread, meat, fish, vegetables, and mead for the poor and sick. In this way he practiced *sobornost* (community). Craftsmen from Europe were brought in to build magnificent buildings, libraries and hospitals, as well as churches.

Vladimir died in 1015, leaving twelve sons. His son Svyastopolk seized the territories of two of his younger brothers, Boris and Gleb, who refused to fight evil with evil and were murdered by him. They became saints because they had accepted suffering and death in imitation of Christ. A third son of Vladimir, Yaroslavl the Wise, ruled from 1019–1054. The greatest of the Kievan princes and a scholar of five languages, Yaroslavl founded hospitals, libraries, public baths, and schools. He established humane laws; he abolished hereditary castes or classes; peasants were free and could move about. Literacy was common, town assemblies were established which any free man could attend. Lord and peasant worshipped together. Yaroslavl sponsored artists and craftsmen from all over Europe.

For two hundred years (eleventh through thirteenth centuries), Kiev was a cosmopolitan and artistic city, often referred to as the New Jerusalem. Centered between the Baltic, Black, and Caspian Seas, Russia became a large trading empire with Novgorod and Kiev the centers. Russia was poised to develop close relations with Europe in the High Middle Ages. But that was not to happen. Tragedy befell Russia, the results of which would cause tremendous suffering and shape the Russian personality. Over time the princes continued to feud and became disunited and then—

> The black earth under the hooves
> was strewn with bones,
> was covered with blood.
> Grief overwhelmed the Russian land.[2]

The Mongol Invasions

From the East came the Mongols led by Genghis Khan. In 1211, a hundred thousand horsemen came galloping across the Gobi Desert in three streams— across the Russian steppes, through the Caucasus Mountains, and across Persia (Iran). They captured the princes, built a platform over them, and held a feast on the platform, crushing them to death.

After fourteen years the Mongols disappeared, only to return in 1227, when Genghis Khan's son Ugedey and his son Batu invaded with an army of two hundred thousand men, each with eighteen spare horses. They crossed the Urals and rode down along the Dnieper River, burning and sacking Russian towns. The Mongols could stay on horseback for days. If they had no food, they drew blood from the horses' veins and drank that. They could shoot bows backward and forward. They showed fierce and total obedience to their leaders.

By 1240 the Mongols arrived at Kiev. Their battering rams broke through the walls of the city, destroying the people and the city. The Kievan Russians lived on as Mongol vassals.

Only Novgorod escaped; the melting ice of the spring thaw made the land impassable for horsemen. The Mongols went on to conquer Hungary and Poland, Czechoslovakia, Austria, and Western Europe. However, Batu had to return to Mongolia to elect a new Khan, for the Great Khan had been poisoned, possibly by a jealous woman. Thus Europe was spared from Mongol domination.

Batu established a Saray called the Golden Horde (camp) on the lower Volga River. From there he collected tribute from the city-states of Russia. However, as the Mongols were outnumbered by the Turks in the region, the Turkish language remained and Islam became the prevailing religion in the south. This helps explain why most of the Central Asian republics are Muslim today.

In the thirteenth century, the Swedes took advantage of Russia's weakened situation, and under papal authority, in union with the Teutonic Knights of Germany, invaded Russia. They destroyed the pagan religion still being practiced in parts of the Baltic area and in parts of Russia, drowning the priests and making Russia a Roman Catholic country.

The Russian princes put up a resistance. One of the best known, Aleksandr Nevski, son of the Grand Duke of Novgorod, defeated the Swedes on the Neva River. But at the same time the Mongols were pressing in. They respected Nevski because of his courage and his victories. When they sent men to collect the tribute in 1242, Nevski refused and was able to make alliances with the Mongols, destroying an army of Teutonic Knights on the frozen surface of Lake Peipus. At the time Nevski died, holding off the Mongols, Novgorod remained the only great free city in Russia. It joined the Hanseatic League, thus connecting the city with wealthy German traders. Because of the resistance, Catholicism failed to become the dominant religion of Russia.

In 1380 the newly emerged principality of Muscovy (Moscow) defeated a Mongol army, and though conquered again shortly afterwards and reduced again to vassalage, it continued its resistance. Even after the Mongol domination was gradually broken, their successors, the Tatars (or Tartars) continued to ravage Russia from encampments in the south.

By the fifteenth century, a hundred thousand people lived in Moscow with the Kremlin (the Mongol word *kreml* means fort) as its heart. From time to time, there would be raids by the Tatars, who appeared as if out of nowhere. In 1571 the Crimean Tatars reached Moscow, killed two hundred thousand people, and carried off one hundred thirty thousand as slaves, sold in Asia, Africa, and Europe. Mongol domination was gradually broken. After that slaughter, Moscow finally broke free and became the new center of Russian culture.

The Russians Who Survived

Large numbers of Russians hid in the forests, clearing land and developing village life. They built log cabins and churches, using the forests for their needs. The icon and axe were hung on the walls of the cabins, reminding them of the power of the church and the life in the forest. They hunted game and bear, used wax for candles, gathered honey, berries, and mushrooms. They used bark for shoes and for writing, fur for clothing, moss for floors, pine boughs for beds. In these villages, peasant hospitality developed around the large earthenware stoves which served for heating the homes and for cooking. Often the oldest family member (and the cat) was given the shelf of the stove for sleeping. Russians became skilled with fire, developing techniques of smelting and making bells and cannons. People paid tribute to Mongol rulers by bowing to the ground and being completely subservient.

The only force still active was the Russian Orthodox Church. Like shepherds, monks and holy men roamed the land to comfort and help. Over the years, as the Mongols were tolerant of all religions, hundreds of new churches and monasteries sprang up. The church kept alive a Russian identity and was viewed from that time on as the comforter and caretaker of the people.

Results of the Mongol Invasions

For two hundred years all contact with the West was severed in the great silence. The Great Russians in the North became vassals of the Mongols; the Little Russians, the Ukrainians, were taken over by the Poles and Lithuanians. From then on there was fear of the East and resentment of the West because no help came during these terrible times.

After two hundred years the Russians had taken on some of the characteristics of their conquerors, especially despotic rule, and physiological features such as blue slanted eyes. As a result of the Mongol Invasions, two thirds of the population perished. Only one force survived, the Russian Orthodox Church.

Summary
- introduction of military, administrative strength, and despotic rule
- a visionary, mystical quality
- Islam
- eastward expansion
- physical changes: blue-eyed Slavs, slanted eyes
- destruction of artistic and intellectual accomplishments
- introduction of new foods such as cabbage and yogurt
- the Russian Orthodox Church viewed as the caretaker of the people
- fear of the East and distrust and resentment of the West

Russia had been separated from Europe during the time in which Europe was undergoing the High Middle Ages. In Europe, western culture developed a continuity of learning from Greece and Rome through the Middle Ages to the Renaissance, and a growing emphasis on the individual. However, under Mongols rule for two hundred years, the Russians knew only despotic authority, and there was little allowance for the evolution of free and individual development.

Tsarist Russia

The Growth of Moscow

During the time of the Mongol invasions, Moscow was a small trading post in the wilderness. The Mongols allowed the princes to rule Moscow as long as they paid tribute and bowed down to them. The Russians had to beat their heads on the ground five times before the Khan and pay large tributes. The fighting monks under Sergius urged the princes to defy the Mongols.

In 1326, the Russian Orthodox Church moved to Moscow, and Moscow became a holy city. Fortified monasteries were established in a ring around the city, and as the church and state were united, Moscow became a symbol of national consciousness.

In 1480, Ivan III threw off the Mongol yoke. He quadrupled the territory of Russia, including taking over Novgorod. He protected the monasteries and weakened the power of the nobles. In return the monks supported him as ruler.

Ivan III continued to expand Russian territory with Moscow as its center. During the sixteenth and seventeenth centuries, Moscow became a beautiful and powerful city, looking toward the East rather than the West. The contrast between Kiev at its height and after the devastation wrought by the Mongols is important as it sets the stage for the ambivalence Russians have felt toward the West and East. The role of the Russian Orthodox Church continued to strengthen its caretaker relationship to the Russian people.

Ivan IV the Terrible, 1533–1584

Ivan IV reigned for fifty-one years, the longest in Russian history. His life was complex, filled with tragedy and glory. When he was four, his father Ivan III died; at eight his mother died. He and his deaf-mute brother were tormented by the *boyars* (nobles) whose outrageous barbarity set a tone for Ivan's rule and that of later tsars. At age thirteen he asserted himself as ruler and had his regent seized and killed.

At age sixteen, Ivan announced he would be crowned not only as Grand Prince, but also as the first Tsar and Autocrat of Russia, based on the Mongolian model of rule. This decision set the tone for future tsars as well as most of the twentieth century Soviet Communist leaders. Ivan was crowned in 1547 and soon after married Anastasia Romanov, of a *boyar* family. She was a gentle and beautiful young woman, and she had a beneficial influence on her husband. This was a marriage of love and trust for thirteen years, referred to as the "good period" in which they had six children, two of whom died in strange accidents. Anastasia died of illness, and Ivan was sure that she had been poisoned. Her death left him heartbroken, and he changed radically. He became a drunkard, dissipated, suspicious, obsessive, and paranoid of everyone around him. Although he married seven more times, Anastasia remained his only love.

Ivan developed an intellectual and artistic life in Russia. He had a strong intellectual bent and was well educated. He read voraciously—church history, Roman history, Russian and Byzantine chronicles, and the Old Testament. These works inspired his leadership and he further expanded the boundaries of Russia and brought his land to greatness. His achievements included introduction of the first printing press, translation of Russian manuscripts, an encyclopedic compilation of world history, of which six volumes were devoted to Russian history. His love of music, including singing and writing hymns, inspired the Golden Age of Russian Music. He was devoted to arts, establishing large collections of painting, sculpture and jewelry. He built the Armory Palace, a network of workshops for icon painters, gold- and silversmiths, and architects. One of his greatest accomplishments was the building of the great church, the Cathedral of the Virgin of the Intersession, which came to be known as Saint Basil's. It stands in Red Square and is well known today for its brilliantly colored onion domes and colored tiles which were added later.

Ivan is credited with the building of Moscow into a great city between the East and West. He invited representatives and traders from various countries to settle in Moscow. Although they spoke of Russia as a primitive culture, Ivan respected and admired them. He corresponded with Queen Elizabeth and even proposed marriage to her.

Ivan loved to show off, hosting extravagant dinners for thousands of guests. Some of the most lavish events in history, they went on for five or six hours with displays of elegant food and drink, as well as magnificent serving vessels. Meanwhile, Ivan became convinced he alone could rid the world of evil, and he saw evil everywhere. His treatment of enemies was extremely harsh, and the more familiar meaning of the word "terrible" could be used to describe the bloodbaths, secret police actions, and heartless murders against innocent victims. His uncontrolled temper led even to his killing his beloved son, and this act drove him mad until he died in 1584.

The Romanov Dynasty

There is not enough time in a Russian literature course to describe the many tsars, but I present some of the most important. The Romanov Dynasty was established by Mikhail Romanov, who became its first tsar in 1613, and his family ruled Moscow until 1918. The early rulers of this dynasty struggled to end internal disorder, foreign invasion and financial collapse. Peter the Great is particularly significant because of his attempt to westernize and modernize Russia. His biography connects the students to contemporary changes going on in Europe and helps them to place Russia in a time period in Europe with which they are more familiar.

Peter the Great (1689–1725)

When Peter was born, his father Tsar Alexis (son of Mikhail) was excited that he had a healthy child. Of thirteen children born to his first wife, all but two had died in infancy and the surviving two were handicapped. In his enthusiasm, Tsar Alexis had a two-hundred-pound gingerbread, baked and stamped with the Double Eagle. It was the largest gingerbread ever recorded in Russia. Peter grew to be a curious, inventive boy, brimming with physical energy and will.

When Peter was four years old, his father died unexpectedly. Bitter feuds broke out, and rival families wanted the throne. Six years later his brother Fyodor died, and Peter and his retarded half-brother Ivan became joint tsars. With bloody intrigues and murders going on all around, Peter grew to hate the Kremlin with all of its terrors and secret plots. When he was ten, the palace guards murdered the supporters of his mother, and his uncle was dragged from hiding and massacred. Peter, his mother, and two small sisters withdrew to their country house outside Moscow in order to live a somewhat normal and protected life away from the Kremlin intrigues. From age twelve to fifteen, Peter was brought back to the Kremlin only on special occasions to sit on a specially built double throne side by side with his feeble brother Ivan, flanked by twelve giant guards with battle-axes.

In the countryside Peter roamed the grounds and the village. He constructed a wooden fortress on the grounds, complete with towers, bastions, and earthworks. Using the village boys as an army of soldiers and himself as leader, he played war games. He learned how to shoot a cannon and how to hunt. Some of the sons of nobles heard how much fun was going on and came out to the village to join the games. Peter was a natural leader. He felt strongly that one had to earn higher ranking, so he, himself, started as a private in his own regiment.

When he was fifteen, a remarkable experience occurred which was to affect his later achievements. He saw an English sailboat in a storeroom. The boat was unusual, and with it he learned to sail against the wind. He drew on his passion for boats and the sea, his curiosity and his mechanical talent, when he later established the Russian navy.

Peter grew to be 6' 7" tall. A formidable figure, both from his height and also from his strong personality, he drank heavily and had a ferocious temper like his father. Although he sobered quickly and forgot his anger, much damage could be done.

When Peter was twenty-four, his half-brother Ivan died, and Peter became the tsar without challenge. In the knowledge that Russia had lost most of her earlier achievements during the two hundred years of Mongol invasion, he wanted to catch her up with Europe. He had often wandered in the foreigners' quarters in Moscow and observed Western culture, but he wanted to go to Europe to see for himself. He arranged to visit Europe, the first Russian ruler to do so. Of course, he did not travel alone, but with two hundred seventy people — nobles wearing fancy jewelry, clad in long fur coats and hats, accompanied by trumpeters, drummers, interpreters, merchants, and jesters—traveling by sleigh. This must have been quite an exotic sight to behold. At one time along the journey, Peter went incognito as a sailor and demanded to see everything and understand it. In Holland he went to work in a shipyard where he learned to build ships. In England he visited Parliament and learned to make paper engravings, cut whale blubber, and do surgery. Everything interested him. He hired eight hundred people of various skills to return with him to Russia to teach his countrymen.

Upon his return, Peter shaved his beard and personally shaved off his nobles' beards. The beard had long been a sign of a true believer, but Peter did not have much enthusiasm for religious life. Later, he let men keep their beards but taxed them. He cut off the long sleeves of the *kaftan* (the long dress) from everyone except clergy and peasants, and he ordered Western style clothing. Western habits like dancing, new ideas, and innovations were brought in. Women cast off veils. They were allowed to take part in social affairs. Fathers had to swear they would not force their children into marriage. All the noble class had to speak French. Peter created a modern army and navy, founded schools of navigation and astronomy, engineering, and art. He introduced the potato, breeding of Russian horses, the first newspaper, writing paper, lace and tapestry making, mines, calendar changes, and alphabet reform, and he forbade Russians to kiss the ground. Because he changed centuries-old traditions, he was seen by some as the Anti-Christ.

His army experience served him well and he defeated Sweden in battle, earning him the name Peter the Great. The army and navy were of a very high standard for the time. Through his efforts, he established Russia as a great European power and was proclaimed Russia's first emperor.

In his personal life, he divorced the wife who had been chosen for him, and, when he was thirty, married a Livonian orphan girl, Martha Skaronskaya, from the Baltic region. She took the name Catherine, and they had twelve children, six of whom were sons. All died in childhood but two daughters, Anna and Elizabeth.

The Building of St. Petersburg

As Ivan IV had built Moscow to be a thriving center of Russian culture, art and music, gold and jewels, so Peter the Great built St. Petersburg. Whereas Moscow had more of an Asiatic flavor, St. Petersburg was influenced by European culture.

On a misty spring morning in 1703 a dozen Russian horsemen rode across the bleak and barren marshlands where the Neva River runs into the Baltic Sea. They were looking for a site to build a fort against the Swedes, then at war with Russia and the owners of these long-abandoned swamps. But the vision of the wise and bending river flowing to the sea was full of hope and promise to the Tsar of land-locked Russia, riding at the head of his scouting troops. As they approached the coast he dismounted from his horse. With his bayonet he cut two strips of peat and arranged them in a cross on the marshy ground. Then Peter said, "Here shall be a town." [3]

> On a shore by the desolate waves
> He stood, with lofty thoughts,
> And gazed into the distance.[4]
> – Pushkin

He named the town after his patron saint in Dutch, Saint Peterburkh. The spot he chose was swampy, with a terrible climate and a frozen river. He drafted 150,000 peasants, prisoners, and soldiers a year to drain the swamps by hand as they had few tools. They built wooden piles sunk into the shifting ground. They slept in the open air, drank foul water, and at least half of the workforce died. It is said that St. Petersburg is a city built on bones. Even though the work was done by hand, it took only seven years to construct this amazing city, built to look like Amsterdam with its canals, bridges, and grand palaces. Like Amsterdam, St. Petersburg was a city of ideas. Peter brought in foreign engineers to design and build. He established libraries, academies with teachers from the West, magnificent gardens, fountains, and palaces. He abolished the church structure, and became head of the church himself. He was an absolute monarch.

As he grew older, he became ill often, yet that did not stop him from being constantly on the go. Exhausted, he died at age fifty-two, ending a twenty-nine year rule. Peter had radically changed Russia, and although many did not understand what he had been trying to do, he is still considered the greatest tsar of Russia. One of the results of his actions was that the clergy and peasants were allowed to keep their Russian way of life while the small middle and upper classes were strongly influenced by his westernizing reforms. What was considered worthy was European, what was Russian was considered unworthy and lower. Before Peter's rule, rich and poor had considered themselves all children of one God, but during Peter's rule, a gulf between the classes was set in motion and would fester for the next hundred years.

Elizabeth Romanov United Court and Village

After Peter a series of women became rulers. His daughter Elizabeth (born out of wedlock before he and Catherine married), a lover of everything Russian, reestablished Russian culture as the style of the times. A very happy, charming pleasure-loving woman, Elizabeth had been constantly passed over by others to be tsar until, goaded by her guards, she claimed the power as Empress. She spoke French fluently, along with some German and Italian. She kept a balance in her advisors between Russian and European. In these ways, she reminds one of Elizabeth Tudor of England who skillfully kept a balance between rival factions. Elizabeth Romanov had a lifelong love with a peasant musician with a magnificent voice. She combined the lavishness and opulence of a French court with the everyday simplicity of a Russian village.

Elizabeth's enthusiasm for the performing arts made her reign a time of excitement, giving birth to Russian opera, ballet, theater, the collecting of Russian folk songs and the performance of folk dances. Music thrived in her court, and she herself was given to bursting out in song. Through Elizabeth's patronage, European artists were attracted to her court where their talents would find expression and appreciation. It was a time of parties and extravagant entertainment, lavish clothing and jewelry, of colorful architecture. Elizabeth died at fifty-two, having become very fat from her love of food and high living, and leaving behind a fairy-tale city.

Catherine the Great (1725–1796)

Elizabeth had chosen as her successor her fifteen-year-old nephew Peter, and the grandson of Peter the Great. He had been brought up in Germany and hated everything Russian. Elizabeth had further chosen for his wife a fourteen-year-old second cousin of Peter and a daughter of a German aristocratic family. Sophia, who changed her name to Catherine, took a great interest in everything Russian, although she never lost her German accent. Peter was a miserable, angry, orphaned boy who was even more disabled by a terrible case of smallpox. He withdrew into alcohol and his German-ness.

Catherine was quite a contrast to Elizabeth. She detested all the lavishness and opulence and preferred to read or go hunting or fishing by herself. Her outlet was the risk involved in gambling and, later, playing the game of diplomacy. She cultivated her intellect and shrewdness. After Peter died in mysterious circumstances, Catherine became Empress and used her intellect to write laws and participate in philosophical arguments.

However, as soon as she became Empress, she turned against everything Russian, tearing down palaces and closing monasteries. She went on a tirade of building European style architecture, changing the face of St. Petersburg. She did away with the bright colors of Elizabeth, choosing muted tones, milky white glass, marble, and huge chandeliers. She was called Catherine the Great because she expanded the Russian empire to include one-fourth of the area of Europe as she won Poland, the Crimea, and parts of Turkey through war. Her partner and sometimes lover was Grigory Potemkin, a brilliant soldier who was her closest friend, adviser, passionate lover of poetry, and wielder of power.

She spent money extravagantly, often using it to buy the favors of her favorites. Under her guidance, French language and culture became the style of the court, creating a huge divide between the nobility and the common people. Catherine attached millions of peasants to the land as property that could be sold, fixing serfdom for the first time in Russia. This was a radical change in Russian society and influenced Russian history over the next century. The noble class kept hundreds of serfs on their estates—tailors, shoemakers, carpenters, grooms, butlers—and even musicians, actors, poets, painters, and architects. Catherine's interest in French philosophy familiarized her with ideas of the Enlightenment, especially the idea of freedom. However, these were only ideas. She would not consider freeing the serfs although some of the nobles began to speak of it. As she aged, she became more and more conservative. She died at sixty-seven.

Tsar Alexander I (1801–1825)

Catherine had prepared her grandson Alexander for the day he would rule. He had been educated by excellent teachers along the philosophical lines and inspired by ideas of justice but never given any practical or logical training. He was taught to be brave rather than coddled. When Alexander became tsar, his good looks and charming personality made him an impressive young man. At first it seemed he was moving to liberalize Russia. He abolished censorship and allowed landowners to free their serfs. He encouraged publication of books, and establishment of schools and universities. Interestingly, he corresponded with Thomas Jefferson on the Constitution of the United States. He was seen as a golden prince, often called "the Blessed."

Alexander I wanted to make St. Petersburg the grandest, most elegant capital of Europe. He employed architects and engineers to design palaces and cathedrals in the classical style and bridges over canals.

His personality was confusing. More at home with Germans than Russians, he was fastidious and exacting in his demeanor, often regarding Russians as lazy and undisciplined. During his twenty-four-year reign, he expanded Russia by annexing Finland, Bessarabia (Moldova), and Georgia, and he colonized Siberia. He also initiated wars in the Caucasus region.

At first, he allied himself with Napoleon, but in June 1812, Napoleon invaded Russia with an army of 600,000 men. Europeans had an impression that Russians were peasants, undisciplined and suppressed. They were surprised that peasants fought side by side with officers to protect their land. Peasants burned their fields so there would be no source of food for the French army. The Russians retreated, burning their fields and the city of Moscow as they evacuated it. Although the French occupied Moscow, they found little compensation. It was an empty victory as the city was in ruins, and the French had no choice but to retreat. As they did, they were caught in the bitter Russian winter. Unable to warm or feed themselves, 125,000 Frenchmen died in battle; 132,000 died of fatigue, hunger and cold; and 193,000 were captured.[5] Only 40,000 limped back to Paris.

After this event, considered the greatest military catastrophe in history, Alexander I went through a change in his personality: He became very religious and considered that the Russian victory was a spiritual mission. The Russian army liberated Paris in 1814. (It is this scene of Alexander I riding down the Champs Elysees that the adolescent Alexander Pushkin would mock in a cartoon.) While in Paris, some of the Russian officers came in contact with the ideas of liberty, equality, and fraternity and brought them back to Russia, instilling new ideas of democracy and freedom in the minds of young Russian intellectuals. In 1815, Russia joined Prussia and Austria in the Holy Alliance and divided Napoleon's empire through a series of compromises.

After his return to Russia, Alexander I became more and more conservative. In 1823 he started arresting anyone who discussed bringing about political changes and the first deportations of revolutionary suspects were sent walking to Siberia, chains on their feet. This was to be the first of hundreds of such deportations, and when the word "Siberia" sent fear into the hearts of Russians.

The Struggle with the Western Idea of Liberalism

Alexander I died in 1825, and in the aftermath, the first revolutionary uprising occurred. The Decembrists were a group of Russian noblemen who had either been with the army in Paris or had traveled to Europe. Inspired by the French Revolution, they resolved that Russia should have a constitution. Nicholas I, the younger brother of Alexander, had been in France during the Napoleonic War and was not going to allow these ideas to threaten his rule. The liberals considered serfdom an evil, but Nicholas, often referred to as the Iron Tsar, crushed the Decembrists cruelly. His harsh treatment of the Decembrists inspired later reformers to consider the Decembrists martyrs for the cause.

During the reign of Nicholas I, art and music flourished. In the later years of Alexander I and Nicholas I, the Golden Age of Russian Poetry with Pushkin and Lermontov thrived. This was followed in 1840–1872 as the Golden Age of Russian Prose with the works of Lermontov, Gogol, Goncharov, Turgenev, Dostoyevsky and Tolstoy.

Between 1853 and 1856, the Russians fought and lost the Crimean War. This resulted in their giving up European territory, and turning toward Asia for land and trade. When Nicholas I died, his son, Alexander II (1855–1881) became tsar. A reformer, he emancipated the serfs in 1861, allowed local self-government and local taxation; he supported the building of schools, roads, and hospitals. During his reign a middle class emerged which wanted a constitution. A proletarian class also emerged. Although he tried to be liberal, Alexander II was strongly autocratic and crushed rebellions cruelly. He did not grant a constitution. During this time the *Communist Manifesto* and *Das Kapital,* which had been translated into Russian, were circulated in Russia. Many revolutionary groups emerged as young people formed secret societies. There were many attempts on Alexander II's life, and he died in 1881 as a result of a successful bomb.

Tsar Alexander III (1881–1894)

Having witnessed the violent death of Alexander II, Tsar Alexander III restored the authority of Nicholas I, reestablished censorship, and persecuted Jews and liberals. Revolutionary currents began to surge, and in the 1890s a semi-constitutional government was established, but it had little power. During this time, there was a greater impetus to industrialization and in production of iron and steel than in any other European country.

Tsar Nicholas II

In 1896, when Nicholas II was twenty-six, he became the thirty-fifth tsar, but he was not prepared for the role. He was a reserved man, unsuited to rule over one-sixth of the earth. His German-born wife was co-ruler, but she was never beloved by the Russian people. The major concern during his reign was the issue of a constitution. He refused to consider it, considering peasants as the true Russians, and concerns of a constitution to be by those who were un-Russian. There is a great deal written about Nicholas II and his family in their last years, which the students can pursue on their own outside of class. The important consideration for our class time is the overall situation in Russia in 1900.

Twentieth Century Russia: Revolution and War

Russia in 1900

The total population was 116 million: 97 million peasants, 3 million Cossacks, 13 million shopkeepers, and 3 million of the elite. Life expectancy was thirty years. Famine, starvation, mass illiteracy, and disease were common, although at the same time the upper class experienced the greatest luxury the world had ever seen.

Russia was the only country in Europe at that time in which a central figure had total authority. There were no elections, no courts, no parliament, and a censored press. The only way for people to express their despair was by terrorist activities. Between 1900 and 1905, industrialization was continuing at a high rate, as was agricultural production. Peasants became farmers, and there was a high rise in prosperity. State land was given over to peasant ownership as they were allowed to buy it. Siberia was opened up for land-hungry peasants. Advances were being made in education.

A similar pattern was evolving in the United States, as the West was opened for land grants and farming. Immigrants found opportunity as land was plentiful and agriculture thrived. Schools were included as part of the expansion beyond the Eastern states. As changes were happening between 1900 and 1905, there was reason to expect life to continue getting better. However, a series of events soon changed the course of Russian history.

Russo-Japanese War

The mention of the Russo-Japanese War is important because it was such a humiliating defeat for the Russians. At the turn of the twentieth century, Japan was also in the rapid pace of modernization and explosive growth and needed more space and land. It also wanted to gain a foot on the mainland. In 1894, Japan had defeated China, and now demanded the secession from Russia of the Liaotung Peninsula with Port Arthur, Manchuria's natural harbor. Tsar Nicholas resisted, and Germany and France joined with Russia to stop Japan. Japan took Formosa and the Pescadores. Russia became the protector of China against Japan, establishing a strong military presence in Manchuria, including continuing the building of a transcontinental railway. Russia and Japan continued fighting to divide the Far East, and in January 1904, the Japanese attacked Port Arthur. Port Arthur fell on December 21, 1904, Russia's sea power was destroyed, and Russian pride was humiliated.

1905 Revolution

During 1905 a series of workers strikes, student and peasant revolts, and army and navy mutinies met with violent response from the Tsar's troops. On "Bloody Sunday" fifteen hundred peaceful demonstrators were slaughtered by the Tsar's troops. Under pressure, the Tsar granted a constitution for the establishment of a parliament (*duma*). However, when *pogroms* (anti-Jewish rioting) and uprisings broke out across the country, the Tsar took back total authority in order to restore order, and the Revolution of 1905 was defeated. However, as a result, four groups rallied—the organized workers under Russian Social Democratic Labor Party leadership, rebellious peasants, discontented ethnic minorities, and the Soviets (councils).

The Marxists split into Bolsheviks (majority) and Mensheviks (minority). Lenin became the leader of the Bolsheviks, seeking power through revolution, conspiracy, and iron discipline. The Mensheviks, with Alexander Kerensky (1881–1970) at the head, sought power through parliamentary methods. The differences between these two groups played out in a disastrous way.

World War I (1914–1918)

When World War I broke out, Russia joined England and France in the Triple Entente alliance. Revolutionaries and radicals, including members of the *Duma* were sent to Siberia as all revolutionary organizations were crushed. During the war, Lenin was in Switzerland, and the Bolsheviks were smashed. At first the war went well, but then there were shortages of men, supplies, and food.

The Revolution of 1917

In 1917 the population again took to the streets of St. Petersburg, rioting and demanding changes. The Tsar dismissed the *Duma* which was the only other instrument of authority. A Provisional Committee of all the parties except the Right was formed to restore order. In March 1917 Tsar Nicholas agreed to a constitutional monarchy, but he was too late. He finally abdicated in favor of his brother, but at this point, the Bolsheviks demanded total power. Tsar Nicholas II and his family were taken prisoner and then murdered. With that violent act, tsarist rule came to an end. The political prisoners who had been exiled to Siberia were freed and returned to support the provisional government and the war effort.

However, just as the Bolsheviks were prepared to accept democracy, Lenin returned to Russia in a sealed car with German money to finance the revolution (and sign a peace treaty, taking Russia out of the war). Lenin seized the leadership and took complete control calling for violent revolution. At the Front, mutinies and desertions occurred, and the officers could not maintain discipline. Chaos reigned.

In July, Kerensky, the leader of the Mensheviks, became Prime Minister, but his provisional government was paralyzed as it could not satisfy both the peasants and the landowners, the military and the workers. Kerensky ordered a general offensive to defend Russia, but a popular insurrection against the war broke out.

The Revolutionary Committee arrested the parliamentary leaders. After only three months of democracy, the window of opportunity was closed. Lenin issued a call which was supported by revolutionary groups—for immediate peace, for a three month armistice with Germany, and for all private property rights to be abolished.

By November 1917 the Bolsheviks seized control and set up a Communist dictatorship. With the treaty of Brest-Litovsk signed with Germany, Lenin took Russia out of the war. Russia had lost Finland, Estonia, Latvia, Lithuania, Poland, and the Ukraine. However, Germany penetrated the Front and annexed Poland and Lithuania, with White Russia (Belarus), Ukraine, and Finland becoming independent. With this dishonorable peace, Russia lost one-tenth of her population. The intelligentsia, which had enthusiastically supported the change from a monarchy to a constitutional republic, were now victims of the government. The brutal dictatorship of Lenin, and then of Stalin, allowed for arrests, deportations, and executions.

This is the background for our study of twentieth century Russian writers. The events from 1917 to the present are readily covered in history books, and I list them here in the form of a timeline.

Russian Civil War: 1917–1919
- Reds (Communists and allies) versus Whites (monarchists, anti-Communists). Whites receive support—including an Allied army intervening in Russia—from England, France, the United States, Japan, Poland, Czechoslovakia
- Peasant revolts

1920–1921
- Famine caused by Communist agricultural policies; five million die
- Bolshevik Party renamed Communist Party (CPSU). Capital moved from St. Petersburg to Moscow (Kremlin)
- Lenin suffers stroke, November 21
- Joseph Stalin appointed head of CPSU Central Committee, shares power with Lev B. Kamenev and Grigory Y. Zinoviev

1921–1929: The Era of Controversy
- "New Economic Policy": planned economy; nationalization of mines, factories, banks, railroads; push to industrialize
- System of prison labor organized

1922 – Union of Soviet Socialist Republics (U.S.S.R.) established (the union of four republics: Russia, the Ukraine, Belarus, and the Trans-Caucasian Federation)

1923 – Deportations begin

1924 – Death of Lenin, January 21

1924–1929 – Stalin engages in struggle with rivals for control of CPSU, emerging in complete control in 1929.

1929–1954: Stalinist dictatorship
- Forced collectivization
- Deportations based on class (Kulaks), ethnicity
- Labor camps
- Police terror

1932 – Union of Soviet Writers formed, giving CPSU control of literature

1934–1939
- Purges of CPSU members
- Show trials, executions, disappearances
- Stalin-Hitler partnership enables Nazi Germany to rearm, despite Treaty of Versailles.

1939: "Molotov-Ribbentrop Nonaggression Treaty"
- Stalin and Hitler publicly agree to not invade each other. This frees each one to attack his neighbors.
- Secretly, they agree to divide up territory separating them, giving them a common border. Affected: Poland, Finland, Baltic States, Bessarabia (Moldova). Hitler invades Poland. Stalin "protects" eastern Poland with Red Army.

1941
- Germany invades Russia. Hitler-Stalin partnership dissolved. Russia joins anti-Nazi alliance with the United Kingdom, the United States and others.
- Germans besiege Leningrad, Moscow, Stalingrad.

1943 – Russians drive Nazis from Stalingrad. Turning point on Eastern Front

1945
- Yalta Conference: Churchill, Stalin and Roosevelt plan for post-war Europe.
- Russia promises free and democratic elections in territories occupied by Red Army.
- Russia promises to declare war on Japan.
- Russia agrees to formation of United Nations.
- With end of wartime alliance, Russia becomes extremely isolated from non-Communist world.
- With end of wartime need for national unity; anti-semitism reemerges
- Russians forbidden to have contact with foreigners
- Punishments again are extremely heavy, deepening role of fear.
- Atomic bombing of Hiroshima and Nagasaki by U.S. triggers Japanese surrender.

1945–1948

- Growing tension between U.S.S.R. and Western allies
- Communist takeover of Central and Eastern European countries
- Occupation of Germany
- Berlin Blockade

1949 – Collapse of Kuomintang (non-Communist) regime in China

1950 – Chinese Communists establish control of Mainland China.

1953

- Death of Stalin. Beria removed, executed
- U.S.S.R. ruled by *troika* under Georgii Malenlov

1955 – Nikita Krushchev emerges as CPSU leader and head of government.

1956

- Stalin's crimes disclosed by Krushchev to CPSU and soviet people
- Thousands of prisoners amnestied, released from Siberian camp
- Relaxation of censorship, other controls
- Warsaw Pact formed by U.S.S.R. and satellites, in response to NATO (North Atlantic Treaty Organization)
- Hungary revolts, tries to withdraw from Warsaw Pact
- Red Army puts down revolt, installs leadership loyal to Kremlin

1958 – Boris Pasternak, author of *Dr. Zhivago*, wins Nobel Prize for Literature. *Dr. Zhivago* banned in U.S.S.R. and Pasternak is forbidden to accept his prize.

1961: "The Thaw"

- "Peaceful coexistence": a period of relaxed oppression inside the U.S.S.R. and softening of anti-Western propaganda
- Berlin Wall
- Cuban Missile Crisis

1962 – Publication of *One Day in the Life of Ivan Denisovitch* by Alexander Solzhenitsyn

1963 – End of "Thaw": Krushchev struggling to keep control; return of strict censorship, tightening of other controls

1964 – Krushchev deposed, replaced by Aleksei Kosygin

1966 – Kosygin replaced by Leonid Brezhnev

1968

- Revolt in Czechoslovakia, suppressed by Red Army. New Czech government installed
- Publication (in the West) of *Cancer Ward* and *The First Circle* by Solzhenitsyn, winning for him the Nobel Prize for Literature

1979 – Afghans overthrow pro-Moscow regime. Russia invades, is drawn into catastrophic guerrilla war with Afghans secretly supplied by the U.S. (Red Army withdraws in 1988)

1985 – Mikhail Gorbachev elected general secretary (chief) of CPSU; assumes control of Kremlin

1987 – Gorbachev announces programs of *perestroika* and *glasnost* (economic restructuring and open discussion of political and social issues), to include greater personal freedom and democratization

1988 – First-ever multi-candidate elections since Bolshevik takeover. All candidates are CPSU members but they compete for votes in local elections

1991

- August 19 – Anti-*perestroika* forces attempt to overthrow Gorbachev's reforms. Popular demonstrations protested the coup. Boris Yeltsin, head of the Russian Federation (largest part of the U.S.S.R.), defies coup leaders, supports succession by non-Russian republics, and calls for a general strike.
- August 21 – Coup fails; Gorbachev returns to Moscow; Yeltsin seen as hero
- August 24 – Gorbachev resigns as CPSU chief (but remains head of state until the U.S.S.R. was dissolved in December). Several republics, including Russian Federation, declare independence.
- August 29 – Supreme Soviet shuts down CPSU, ending the domination of the Communist Party exercised over all aspects of Russian life since 1917.
- December 26 – U.S.S.R. dissolved. Red Flag of the U.S.S.R. taken down and replaced by the tricolor of the Russian Federation

1993

- September 21 – President Yeltsin dissolves Parliament and calls for new elections. His rivals in the parliament respond by declaring him deposed from office and barricading themselves inside the parliamentary headquarters ("the White House").
- October 3 – Yeltsin orders the army to take control of the parliamentary building. In the ensuing battle, about 140 persons are killed and more than 150 arrested.
- December 12 – Russia adopts a first post-Soviet constitution, creating a very strong presidential position.

1999 – December 31 – Yeltsin resigns, naming former KGB spy Vladimir Putin as interim president.

2000
- January 1 – Putin becomes acting president and candidate for the March 26 presidential election.
- March 26 – Putin elected; first democratic leadership in Russian history.

Student writing:

How would you contrast the effects of the Christianizing of Russia with the Mongol invasions?

The effects of Christianity and the Mongols on Russia are polar opposites. Christianity built civilization in Russia, and the Mongols tore it back down. The only similarity that can be drawn is that both caused sweeping change in Russia.

The Christianizing of Russia under Vladimir and Yaroslavl caused a flourishing in the civilization and culture. In Kiev, hundreds of churches were built along with schools, hospitals, and other important pieces of infrastructure. The acceptance of the Eastern Orthodox Church meant that the death penalty was outlawed and, most importantly, that all classes prayed together, or that everyone was equal in the eyes of God. Christianity effectively modernized Kiev and Russia centuries beyond their counterparts of the time.

When the Mongols invaded in the thirteenth century, Kiev had started to fracture in the aftermath of Yaroslavl's death. This made it easy for the warlike Mongols to conquer it and almost every other city in Russia. They swept in on their horses, caught the locals by surprise, and pillaged and looted whatever they could. They were notorious for their relentlessness, and would stop at nothing to avenge a fallen friend or an insult suffered. They destroyed everything that Christianity had built up, and every city in Russia except Novgorod was conquered by the Mongols.

Eventually the Mongols settled down, and Russia was able to rebuild itself, but this early build up and tear down has still left its mark on the modern country. – *L.S.*

By studying the literature of a people, we get a glimpse into their history through the eyes of individual participants and observers. Through personal perspectives we can begin to understand the values of the culture and how the people as a whole think. Learning only about the political history of a country does not allow us to see into the soul of its people and leads us to misunderstanding the culture. It is equally important to learn about the events that shape a country and to know how the people of that country respond to and meet those events. By reading works by Dostoyevsky, Pushkin, Pasternak, Akhmatova and many others, I have gained a picture of the passions, struggles, longings, and motivations of the Russian people.

The history of Russia lays the backdrop for understanding why her people have evolved to be the resilient, passionate and persevering Russians portrayed today. Russia's past is filled with tragedy, from the Mongol invasions in the twelfth century to Stalin's Reign of Terror in the 1930s and 1940s. The oppression experienced by the Russian people under the rule of the tsars from the seventeenth century until 1917 was nothing compared to Stalin's strict regime. Many "Westernizers" longed for the adoption of democratic measures in Russia, however the promise of the Revolution for change was dashed as the Communist Party gained power. First Lenin and then Stalin systematically centralized and homogenized Russia.

Stalin tried to gain absolute power by enforcing his decrees with the KGB prison camps and firing squads. He attempted to eliminate all people with differing views or ideas, killing off large portions of the artists and intellectuals of Russia. With the threat of death or hard labor to any nonconformist, one would think that Russian art and culture would have suffered greatly and deteriorated or even disappeared. However, the tighter the government clamped down, the more persistent the people became to preserve their culture. Ordinary people risked their lives for the sake of freedom of expression and thought. During the Communist rule, the Russian people proved their dedication to their art and culture and their inexhaustible passion for freedom.

Holding firm to their ideals, the Russian people turned to poetry. It became the vehicle for the expression of their passions. Using metaphors and allusions, free thinkers spoke their political convictions through poetry. Poetry became the binding tissue of the Russian people. Poets such as Pasternak circulated their work underground, not only to a select group of "radicals" but throughout Russia.

The Russian people have proved their strength, determination, and will power by keeping their faith in Mother Russia through unimaginable hardships. I picture the Russian people like Dmitri Karamazov, after his awakening to spirituality and his sense of purpose and duty in the world. The Russians, like Dmitri, have fiery hearts and enduring souls. They are proud, loyal, loving, compulsive, erratic, dedicated, and steadfastly striving for the good.

Of course my impressions are broad generalizations and fail to represent the spectrum of personalities found in any culture. However, from reading a sampling of Russian poetry and writing, I was left with a strong feeling of the Russian nature. This nature seems to live at the heart of what the poets describe as "true Russians." Along with the images of the faithful and ever hope-filled Russian is the idea of the true Russian transcending national borders and ethnic barriers. In a speech honoring Pushkin, Dostoyevsky said, "To become a real Russian, to become fully a Russian, perhaps, means only to become brother of all men, a completely universal man, if you want." Living at the core of the Russian soul is a longing for liberty, equality and brotherhood. Perhaps these live in the heart of the universal man as well. – *R.H.*

Endnotes

1. Suzanne Massie, *Land of the Firebird, The Beauty of Old Russia* (New York: Simon and Schuster, 1980), p. 22.
2. From *The Lay of Igor* as printed in Massie, p. 35.
3. Orlando Figes, *Natasha's Dance, A Cultural History of Russia* (New York: Metropolitan Books, Henry Holt & Co., 2002), p. 4.
4. From Alexander Pushkin, "The Bronze Horseman" (1833), as printed in Figes, p. 5.
5. J.G. Lockhart, *The History of Napolean Buonaparte*, http://www.gutenberg.org/ebooks/17579.

Bibliography

Billington, James H. *The Icon and the Axe, An Interpretive History of Russian Culture*, New York: Vintage Books, Random House, 1970.

Figes, Orlando. *Natasha's Dance, A Cultural History of Russia*, New York: Metropolitan Books, Henry Holt & Co., 2002.

Kaiser, Robert J. *Russia, The People and the Power*, New York: Washington Square Press, Pocket Books, Simon and Schuster, 1976.

Kohn, Hans. *The Mind of Modern Russia, History and Political Thought of Russia's Great Age*, New Jersey: Rutgers University Press, 1955.

Massie, Suzanne. *Land of the Firebird, The Beauty of Old Russia*, New York: Simon and Schuster, 1980.

Rybakov, Boris. *Kievan Rus*, tr. Sergei Sossinky, Moscow: Progress Publishers, 1989.

Saint Petersburg Patriotic War Order II Degree

CHAPTER 3

Russia's Mission of Universal Brotherhood and Relationship to Christ and the Grail

The mission of universal brotherhood is a fundamental part of Russian culture. For centuries, Russians expressed this unconscious impulse as part of their religious nature which connects them with the suffering Christ. At first it is difficult to see this impulse because atheism and philosophical materialism inherent in communist teachings quashed any practice of religion and was intolerant of any reference to spiritual life. However, on further examination, we can see that the true underlying character of communism, the ideal, would appeal to this impulse of brotherhood in Russia. All would be equal. No one would have more than any one else. It also appealed to those progressives who wished to correct the vast economic and social differences between the peasant and middle classes. However, communism was imposed upon the Russian people through force, through a power that did not tolerate differences of opinion or freedom of thought or expression. Because it was forced, it took on the nature of the double (or shadow) of what could have become a significant development in human consciousness.

Rudolf Steiner referred to this Russian impulse toward community and brotherhood as an expression of people of the Grail and of Christ.[1] This impulse touched on something that will occur in the future when brotherhood is a goal of humanity, just as freedom is the goal in our times. We can look to Russian writers and poets (as well as scientists such as Sakharov) as precursors who are preparing the soil on which the new impulse will reach fruition.

The following excerpt from a poem by Andrei Biely characterizes Russia in her special spiritual nature. For many years I have spoken it with my class at the beginning of each school day.

From Christ Is Risen: 23[2]

> Russia,
> My country,
> You
> Are the woman clothed with the sun,
> To whom
> All eyes
> Are lifted …
> I see clearly:
> Russia,
> My Russia,
> Is a God-bearer
>   Slaying the serpent …

The peoples
Inhabiting her
Have stretched out their arms
Through the smoke
To her spaces,
That are filled with song,
    That are filled
    With the fire of a swooping seraph.
    And I, beholding,
Feel my throat
    Lock with emotion.

The Grail Path

The path to the Grail is the path of awakening to the suffering of others and asking, "What ails thee?" As in the medieval legend of Parzival, this question is the turning point toward a true community life. Parzival began his journey as a young fool, and, as he continued on his way, he caused pain to others out of his näivite and immaturity. He had to learn to resist temptations as he purified himself and began to take responsibility for his actions. His true awakening occurred when he met his spiritual teacher, Trevrizent. Here he learned of his destiny and his connection to the spiritual world. Parzival, the fool, with the aid of Trevrizent, the hermit, underwent spiritual awakening and transformation. He was then able to integrate parts of himself and reach out in compassion to ask the question of the suffering Fisher-King Anfortas, "What ails thee?" And thus Parzival became King of the Grail. The Grail story is a universal story describing the path of transformation through suffering and love that needs to occur all over the world. The task in the future is for all of humanity to ask, "What ails thee?"

The path of transformation for the Russian is through suffering. As the fool suffers, he experiences his isolation, his separation. Through his suffering he is put through a forge of inner transformation. Out of this, his true Self arises and he is able to relate to all human beings out of love and compassion.

Images of the fool are found in many Russian fairy tales and novels. The fool is innocent with a pure heart. He is often taken advantage of by his older, more worldly brothers, but the innocence of the fool wins the day. Purity and innocence are celebrated in many of the fairy and folk tales. Ivan the Fool is a typical example. This is also true in the stories about peasants who seem foolish but actually have a kind of cleverness. This stage of being the fool is an early stage of development. The fool does not yet have compassion for others, but he is showing a kind of simplicity that is the foundation for developing faith. Faith is seen as stronger than rational thinking and more appropriate to the Russian soul.

In many of the stories the fool transforms into a pilgrim and, as he comes to know the world, expresses wisdom. In *The Brothers Karamazov*, Alyosha goes through such a transformation. In *Dr. Zhivago*, Yuri Zhivago embodies the innocence of the fool as a naïve poet who matures through the horrors of war. This transformation according to the Russian must take place within the community and not in isolation.

Fyodor Dostoyevsky's path of understanding the Russian mission arose as he searched for answers to understanding the human being. At first he sought them in the Western ideas of rationalism and democracy, but it was only when he spent time in a labor camp, surrounded by illiterate peasants, that he discovered an understanding of the Russian mission and its unique destiny—it has to come through faith and inner freedom, through being part of a community. This is why in *The Brothers Karamazov*, the elder Father Zossima sends the young Alyosha away from the monastery into the world. It is through the relationship between himself and his family and with the schoolboys that Aloysha will learn to develop his Self and be able to bring love to his community.

In "What Men Live By" Leo Tolstoy explores this question of faith and compassion as the peasant and his wife interact with Michael, the angel sent by God to discover the answers to the three questions of what men live by. He can find these only by living on earth and finding the answers in the hearts of common people. Tolstoy paved the way to an individual spiritual path that was uniquely Russian. He was punished for it by being excommunicated from the church, but nevertheless, he continued his search for truth right to the end of his life.

Some modern Russian writers search for the essence of Christianity independent of the Russian Orthodox Church. They are trying to find a path to compassion and brotherhood out of individual striving rather than as part of institutionalized religion. They courageously search for spiritual meaning in the midst of inhumanity.

Boris Pasternak was tormented by the Soviet government even after he was awarded the Nobel Peace Prize. Yet he kept his idealism.

> Even so, one step from my grave,
> I believe that cruelty, spite,
> The powers of darkness will in time
> Be crushed by the spirit of light.[3]

Pasternak risked his life by speaking to a Western journalist in an interview at this time. "In our age people are moving towards a new attitude toward life. Let me point out one thing. During the nineteenth century it was the bourgeoisie that ruled. Our own literature tells you about this. Mankind sought security in money, land, and things. Man's dream of security was happiness and stability. Today mankind has realized that there is no security in property. This applies not only to Russians. In this era of world wars, in this atomic age, the values have changed. We have learned that we are the guests of existence, travelers between two stations. We must discover security within ourselves. During our short span of life we must find our own insights into our relationship with the existence in which we participate so briefly. Otherwise, we cannot live! This means, as I see it, a departure from the materialistic view of the nineteenth century. It means a reawakening of the spiritual world, of our inner life—of religion. I don't mean religion as a dogma or as a church, but as a vital feeling. Do you understand what I mean?"[4]

In his poem "Babiy Yar," Yevgeny Yevtushenko identifies with Jews who have been persecuted over the centuries. Babiy Yar is a ravine outside Kiev in the Ukraine where tens of thousands of Jews were murdered by the Nazis during World War II. As the Soviet Army approached from the East, the Nazis tried to cover up the evidence of these terrible war crimes. The Soviet government did not acknowledge that the murdered were Jews, and Yevtushenko, in writing this poem, was challenging official anti-semitism. He was not able to speak this poem in public until after the fall of the Soviet Union in 1991. At that time, he stood at the site of Babiy Yar and in his deep sonorous voice spoke to the living and the dead.

Babiy Yar[5]

Over Babiy Yar
There are no memorials.
The steep hillside like a rough inscription.
I am frightened.
Today I am as old as the Jewish race.
I seem to myself a Jew at this moment.
I wandering in Egypt.
I crucified. I perishing.
Even today the mark of the nails.

I think also of Dreyfus. I am he.
The Philistine, my judge and my accuser.
Cut off by bars and cornered,
ringed round, spat at, lied about;
the screaming ladies with the Brussels lace
poke me in the face with parasols.

I am also a boy in Belostok,
the dripping blood spreads across the floor,
the public-bar heroes are rioting
in an equal stench of garlic and of drink.
I have no strength, go spinning, from a boot
Shriek useless prayers that they don't listen to;
with a cackle of "Thrash the kikes and save Russia!"
the corn-chandler is beating up my mother.

I seem to myself like Anna Frank
to be transparent as an April twig
and am in love, I have no need for words,
I need for us to look at one another.

How little we have to see or to smell
separated from foliage and the sky,
how much, how much in the dark room
gently embracing each other.
They're coming. Don't be afraid.
The booming and banging of the spring.
It's coming this way. Come to me.
Quickly, give me your lips.
They're battering in the door. Roar of the ice.

Over Babiy Yar
rustle of the wild grass.
The trees look threatening, look like judges.
And everything is one silent cry.
Taking my hat off
I feel myself slowly going grey.
And I am one silent cry
over the many thousands of the buried;
am every old man killed here.
O my Russian people, I know you.
Your nature is international.
Foul hands rattle your clean name.
I know the goodness of my country.

How horrible it is that pompous title
the anti-semites calmly call themselves,
Society of the Russian People.
No part of me can ever forget it.
When the last anti-semite on the earth
is buried forever.
let the International ring out.
No Jewish blood runs among my blood,
but I am as bitterly and hardly hated
by every anti-semite
as if I were a Jew. By this
I am a Russian.

In another of Yevtushenko's poems, "I Would Like,"[6] which is included in its entirety later in this book, he identifies with people all over the world—with "a victim of Paraguayan prison tortures, a homeless child in the slums of Hong Kong, a living skeleton in Bangladesh, a holy beggar in Tibet, a black in Cape Town…," and so forth. What does Yevtushenko want? He wants "happiness but not at the expense of the unhappy" and "freedom, but not at the expense of the unfree." Yevtushenko tells us how much he wants to be everyone in every place, but he ends his poem:

> I would like to fight on all your barricades,
>   humanity,
> dying each night
>   an exhausted moon,
> and being resurrected each morning
>   like a newborn sun,
> with an immortal soft spot
>   on my skull.
> And when I die,
>   a smart-aleck Siberian François Villon,
> do not lay me in the earth
>   of France
>   or Italy,
> but in our Russian, Siberian earth,
>   on a still green hill,
> where I first felt
>   that I was
>   everyone.

Despite the evils of Stalinism, Russian writers kept their idealism intact as they heeded the voice of Russia's spiritual mission—to develop a community of brotherhood. Alexander Solzhenitsyn gave up a plush prison sentence in the scientific institute to be sent to one of the worst labor camps so that he could bear witness and suffer the worst the Russian had to suffer. He said, "I will battle with death. I will face evil directly."

In his poem "Chagall's Cornflowers,"[7] Andrei Voznesensky identifies with the Russian-Jewish painter Marc Chagall and chastises Russia for discriminating against him so that he fled to Paris, taking his memories of the Russian village of Vitebsk with him. Voznesensky describes how tears came to Chagall's eyes when, on a visit to Peredelkino, he was presented with a bouquet of cornflowers, a reminder of his childhood in Vitebsk. One of Chagall's paintings is of the image of a fiddler on the roof, which became well known through the musical of that name. Voznesensky was severely criticized by the Soviet press for this poem. The phrase "rolled up in a tube" refers to the fact that most of Chagall's paintings in Russia were kept out of sight and not exhibited.

Chagall's Cornflowers

> Your face is all of silver like a halberd
> Your gestures light
> In your vulgar hotel room
> you keep pressed cornflowers.
>
> Dear friend, so this is what you truly love!
> Since Vitebsk, cornflowers have wounded
> and loved you—those wildflower tubes
> Of squeezed-out devilish sky-blue.

An orphaned flower of the burdock family,
its blue has no rival
The mark of Chagall, the enigma of Chagall —
A tattered ruble note at a remote Moscow station.

It grew around Saint Boris and Saint Gleb,
Around guffawing speculators with their greasy fingers,
In a field of grain, add a patch of sky.
Man lives by sky alone.

Cows and water nymphs soar in the sky
Open your umbrella as you go out on the street —
Countries are many, the sky is one.
Man lives by sky alone.

How did a cornflower seed chance to fall
on the Champs Elysees, on those fields?
What a glorious garland you wove
for the Paris Opera.

In the age of consumer goods there is no sky.
The lot of the artist is worse than a cripple's
Giving him pieces of silver is silly —
man lives by sky alone.

Your canvasses made their escape
from the fascist nightmare, from murder.
The forbidden sky rolled up in a tube.
But man lives by sky alone.

While God failed to trumpet
over the horror.
Your canvasses rolled up in a tube
Still howl like Gabriel's horn.

Who kissed your fields, Russia,
until cornflowers bloomed?
Your weeds become glorious in other countries.
You ought to export them.

How they hail you, when you leave the train,
The fields tremble.
The fields are studded with cornflowers.
You can't get away from them.

When you go out in the evening – you seem ill!
Eyes of the unjustly condemned stare from the field.
Ah, Marc Zakharovich, Marc Zakharovich.
Is it all the fault of those cornflowers?

Let not Jehovah or Jesus
but you, Marc Zakharovich, paint a testament
of invincible blue —
Man lives by sky alone.

The cost of standing up to the tyranny of communism and fascism was tremendous. Many disappeared into labor camps, into psychiatric hospitals, into depression and suicide. Some escaped and were recaptured. Some fled and became émigrés to other countries. Russian xenophobia was so strong that when a Russian soldier returned from a prisoner of war camp during World War II, he was then sentenced to time in a Soviet labor camp as a traitor because he may have been tainted with Western ideas of freedom.

Consider the terrible waste of human lives and the suffering, first in World War II when twenty-four million Russians were killed by Nazis, and then during the Stalinist purges when another estimated thirty million were killed. Still, Russians continued to fight, as we have seen during the 1980s and 1990s, as tremendous changes took place and continue to do so.

Another courageous soul was Andrei Sakharov, who changed from decorated Hero of the Soviet Union for his scientific studies leading to the H-bomb to Enemy of the People as he protested the government's mistreatment of dissidents. After his untimely death, Tatyana Ivanova described her feelings about his courageous stand against tyranny: "We were happy to be alive at the same time as Andrei Sakharov. He displayed heroism before our very eyes; he had absolutely no fear. Neither his exile, nor hunger strikes lasting for many days, nor the official licentious harassing that went on for many years, nor vile slanderous gossip on a huge scale, not lies, nor the well-organized 'contempt of all the people' from women textile workers with decorations to a well known writer, nor whistling and foot-stamping—nothing frightened him. Nothing could ever make him betray his conscience, renounce the truth or fail to defend goodness or justice. All this happened before our very eyes."[8]

The love of all people is the creative expression of the future mission of humanity. Russia is carrying the banner for this transformation through the voices of its writers. Fyodor Dostoyevsky expressed the uniqueness of Russia's mission in the inaugural address at the Pushkin Centenary, June 6, 1880: "Yes, the Russian's destiny is incontestably all-European and world-wide. To become a true Russian, to become fully a Russian, perhaps, means only to become a brother of all men, a completely universal man, if you want."[9]

Endnotes

1. Rudolf Steiner, *From Symptom to Reality in Modern History*, Lec. VIII (London: Rudolf Steiner Press, 1976), p. 189. Also printed in *Man and the World in the Light of Anthroposophy* by Stewart C. Easton (Hudson, NY: Anthroposophic Press, 1989), p. 116.

2. Joshua Kunitz, ed., *Russian Literature Since the Revolution*, New York: Boni and Geer, 1948), p. 21.

3. www.rgeib.com/heroes/pasternak/paster.html.

4. Robert Payne, *The Three Worlds of Boris Pasternak* (Bloomington: Indiana University Press, 1961), p. 202.

5. Reference a different translation in *Yevgeny Yevtushenko, The Collected Poems, 1952–1990* (New York: Henry Holt & Co, 1991), pp. 102–104.

6. Yevgeny Yevtushenko, *The Collected Poems,* pp. 342–346.

7. Andrei Voznesensky, *An Arrow in the Wall, Selected Poetry and Prose*, trans. Vera Dunham and H.W. Tjalsma, 1973 (New York: Henry Holt & Co., 1987).

8. Andrei Sakharov, *Lessons of Andrei Sakharov* (Moscow: Novosti, 1990), p. 101.

9. Konstantin Mochulsky, *Dostoyevsky, His Life and Work* (Princeton, NJ: Princeton University Press, 1967), p. 641.

Bibliography

Anatoli, A. (Kuznetsov). *Babi Yar, A Document in the Form of a Novel* (uncensored), New York: Farrar, Straus and Giroux, 1970.

Voznesensky, Andrei. *An Arrow in the Wall, Selected Poetry and Prose*, New York: Henry Holt & Co., 1987.

Yevtushenko, Yevgeny. *Collected Poems 1952–1990*, New York: Henry Holt & Co., 1991.

Nanilovsky Monastery

CHAPTER 4

THE ROLE OF RELIGION IN RUSSIAN CULTURE

Religion in pre-Christian Russia was pagan. There were gods of many things, but there was no god of war. Humility, compassion, nonresistance, gentleness, community, brotherly love, and peacefulness were valued. The main elements in Russian culture are the visionary and the earthly with the theme of beauty at its heart. (See the fairy tale "Maryushka and the Firebird.")

All of these qualities were incorporated into Eastern Christianity as it shaped a distinctly Russian culture in which religion and brotherhood play key roles. Central to its beliefs were the importance of community and identification with the suffering Christ. Meekness and acceptance of fate were in imitation of the deeds of Christ as the golden thread through Russian life and art.

The word for *cathedral* was the same as for *community* — *sobor* or *sobornost* — gatherings in which the authority of God was invoked. Each service was built around the communal experience of the sacrifice of Christ. The worshipper was not expected to approach the service intellectually, but to have an experience of drawing close to the spiritual world. The role of the church was to unite heaven and earth. With the ornaments and vestments of gold, precious stones, and incense, worshippers would experience richness of their senses of sight, hearing, and smell, and they would feel praise, awe, and being one of the community. The Russian view of the earth as the ideal of eternal womanhood, fertility, and compassion were incorporated into Christianity as the Mother of God.

In order to understand Russian culture and Russian literature, it is necessary to have some understanding of the teachings of the Russian Orthodox Church. In Dostoyevsky's *The Brothers Karamazov*, the elder Father Zossima is a central figure involved in the transformation of each of the characters. He represents the attitude of the church. Understanding the key elements of these teachings will help one understand the book in a deeper way. I will develop this theme further in the chapters on *The Brothers Karamazov*.

Summary: Beliefs of the Russian Orthodox Religion
- The human being can perceive the beauty of the spiritual world through worship. Man is most himself when he is worshipping God.
- It is possible to recognize the presence of the Holy Spirit in a man and to convey it to others through artistic means. For example, the icon painter was like a priest. The combination of the icons and music of the choir gave the feeling of being in heaven.
- The Russians were the first to stress the humble aspect of Christ's nature, which was not emphasized in the West until Saint Francis.

Both the Eastern Orthodox Church and the Roman Catholic Church claim to be the true church founded on the teachings of Jesus Christ. The Roman Catholic Church recognizes the Pope (the Bishop of Rome) as the leader of the church (with his lineage going back to Peter). The Eastern Orthodox Church does not. All Councils of Bishops are equal and they do not interfere with each other's Episcopal see. The Patriarch of Constantinople holds a position of authority if decisions cannot be reached within the Council of Bishops. The Roman Catholic Church does not recognize divorce; the Eastern Orthodox Church considers divorce a tragedy, but it allows divorced men and women to remarry under specific circumstances. Priests can be married before they enter the priesthood.

In Orthodox Christianity there is no purgatory. Everyone is in the hands of God until Judgment Day. The church's role is to heal the sin-filled person rather than to punish him. The congregation is as important as the priest. Easter is celebrated every Sunday ("Christ is risen" is the Sunday greeting). Icons are not to be worshipped as idols, but for focus, for meditation. In Orthodox Christianity the land holds all of the sins of man.

The Orthodox Christian churches include national churches such as Russian Orthodox, Serbian Orthodox, and Greek Orthodox. Throughout this book I use Russian Orthodox or Eastern Orthodox to refer to the Orthodox Church as practiced in Russia.

An important aspect of Russian Christianity is the role of the *staretz* or elder. Staretz Amvrosy began the tradition of the elder, and he was considered a very holy man. This role traces itself back to the beginning of Russian Orthodoxy which was brought by the early monks. It was founded on New Testament teachings that the Christian must pursue perfection through self-renunciation; the individual human ego is removed to the periphery, and in its place in the center of the human personality is God Himself. This shift is very difficult to attain and takes the greatest effort so that the soul will die to this world so that it may pass into the next world. The next world was created by Christ and will culminate in His Second Coming.

It is very difficult to make this transition, for many challenges confront the person because the enemy, Satan, is trying to drag the human soul into nonexistence and pull the person away from God. This is such a difficult struggle that no person can succeed by himself. The Christian needs a battle plan, a spiritual map to guide him past the traps along the way.

The monks laid the foundation for these teachings in the fourth century when Christianity was adopted in Constantinople by Emperor Constantine. Many monks did not trust this kind of Christianity because they saw that it was connected with spreading an empire rather than focusing on spiritual enlightenment. They retreated to the desert which they thought was the dwelling place of Satan (the devil). They felt that by living in the desert, they would have to confront Satan and deal with the passions and temptations such as pride and sensual lust that he inspired. Over generations the monks developed the map. When the map is followed, the world is illuminated with the light of Christ. If it is ignored or suppressed, then people will grope as if blind. They will lose their way and the devil will trap human beings.

This training centers on the role of the *staretz*, an elder who is recognized for his spiritual capacities. He has the authority to guide his fellow monks toward spiritual perfection by carrying out three steps. First the monk has to open his heart in total confidence to the elder, even revealing his most secret thoughts to him. Second, he has to give perfect obedience to the elder. Third he has to carry out the "prayer of the heart." By constantly repeating the Jesus Prayer ("Lord Jesus Christ, Son of God, have mercy on me a sinner …"),[1] Christ descends into the heart of the monk. While short prayers help the monk concentrate his mind, the Jesus Prayer is like a spiritual sword.

The elder can live and work in the desert, but he can also live in a monastery and interact with the common people in the village. He is able to see into the soul of a person, consider his family, his vocation, his place in the community, and offer him advice. The elder's viewpoint is the same as it would be from that of Christ. His aim is to help the person reveal his higher self, overcome sin, and find union with God.

In our minds, we are overwhelmed with different thoughts and emotions connected with those thoughts. This is the work of Satan who is keeping us from focusing on God. The way to fight against these thoughts is by an effort of will. However, if a person tries to focus only on his mind, he will fail because the center of man is not his mind but his heart. His "I" which is his unique essence lives in his heart, which is the center of the conscious and the unconscious, the soul and the spirit, as well as of the body.

The object of the spiritual life is to bring the mind into the heart; otherwise it remains "fallen," prone to sin. There is a difference between knowing about God and knowing God. To know God, one has to have exceedingly great love which comes from the whole person, from his heart. This is not a path that asks the person to give up his intellectual powers—reason, too, is a gift from God, which is needed as part of human life—but he is called to descend with the mind into the heart. When he is able to do this, his mind and heart are in alignment, and he experiences unity with God and the spiritual world. This is a difficult process because the human being has a strong will and does not want to give up his relationship to his earthly desires. Therefore, the rebellious human will has to be broken by obedience to an elder.

Another way in which God is able to temper our egoism is through sickness. When we become ill, we have an opportunity to focus on the big questions of life, and often people have a resurgence of faith in their struggle with illness. In this way, it is thought, illness provides an opportunity for God to lead us back to Himself and to salvation.

Historically, this mystical path set out by the monks, became stronger after the Mongol Invasions. The monasteries became the carriers of the Russian folk-soul when the survival of the people was threatened. Through the teachings, especially of Saint Sergius, the contemplative aspect of Christianity was strengthened and acted as a spiritual salve to heal the stricken people.

During his reign Peter the Great secularized the church, placing himself as the head. The rituals and traditions of the church took precedence, and the contemplative aspect was weakened. However, about one hundred years later, Paisy Velichkovsky (1722–1794) reestablished the contemplative aspect of Russian Christianity, describing the "map" further by journeying to Mount Athos, collecting ascetic writings, and translating them. He called particular attention to the Jesus Prayer in his writings. The emphasis on the mystical practice grew stronger after his death and continued in the nineteenth century as his monastic following increased.

Connection of Russian Orthodox Church with the Slavophils

Two different views regarding Russia and the West became particularly extreme during the nineteenth century as relations between Russia and the West intensified. They are expressed through the philosophies of Slavophils and Westernizers. An understanding of the ardent beliefs of the Slavophils helps to understand Dostoyevsky and other writers of the nineteenth century. Likewise, it is necessary to have some understanding of Marxism as well to understand the Russian writers of the twentieth century.

The Slavophils, along with the Russian Orthodox Church, held that Russia had a special mission in the world based on the unique "history, character, and mission of the Russian people." The hope of salvation for Russia was to be true to Russia's spiritual mission. This is most clearly in contrast to the view of the Westernizers. Europe was seen as decadent, especially due to the liberal democratic idea of freedom. This philosophical schism between Westernizers and Slavophils continues to this day, although it has softened. Dostoyevsky was a strong proponent of the Slavophils, but over time he embraced a more balanced view.

The Slavophils believed that the Russians were the people carrying a spiritual essence different from that of any other people, and that this essence was constantly in danger of being diluted or tainted by Western ideas and so must be protected. When the Slavophils looked at Europe, they saw greed and sterility, which came from the Western capitalist society. They were convinced that middle class life was based on materialism and egotism, and as a result, the people no longer were strong in their religious faith. The ideas coming from the Enlightenment, especially rationalism, served to segregate people and led to many diverse viewpoints, creating instability and disunity. Thus they feared ideas coming from the West and did everything they could to stymie ideas of freedom of speech, expression, and thought, even if it meant censorship, arrest, and imprisonment.

The Slavophils felt that Russia had been better off before Peter the Great Europeanized their culture. For example, at that prior time, the court, the church, and the common people all shared the same religious views, participated in the same rituals, celebrated the same holidays, and of course, spoke the same language. Even though Peter wanted the population to change, the common people resisted. However, the upper classes did change, and so from that time on, the common people and the upper classes went their separate ways. The masses maintained their traditional way of living and their melancholy songs and festival celebrations. The upper classes "forgot" everything Russian, even the language, the beauty of their land, the passion-filled songs, and the connection to the seasons.

For all these reasons, the Slavophils saw the West as being ill and strived to stay away from the contagion which could sicken and destroy the unique character of Russia. Although the Slavophils did see ways Russian society could be improved, they felt that the process should and would come out of Russia itself, out of her traditions and her culture.

Beginning in the 1840s, the Slavophils expressed that the West had completed what it brought to the world in the ideas of the Renaissance and Reformation. Now the new ideas to guide civilization were to be brought by Russia. The downfall of the West was evident in the questioning of spiritual life, in doubt, and in allowing various religious views as a result of the Reformation. What was unique in Russia's spiritual life was its unity with the Russian Orthodox Church and its embracing of community and brotherhood. This was evident in the common Russian people, untouched by Western civilization.

The Slavophils held that Russia was above all a Christian Empire, and revolution was anti-Christian. Russia was a land of faith, the Eastern Empire the Ark which would rise when the West went down in destruction. The Russian educated class would return to their faith, folklore, and soil. The land was sacred, especially when the peasants worked it. The social being of man was central, and the individual is an inseparable member of the community, a member of the collective. The Slavophils wanted emancipation of peasants, redistribution of lands, freedom of spiritual life, and social justice, not political rights or constititutional guarantees. With unity of faith, Russia would not need democracy. The peasant commune was immune to the extreme individualism and materialism of the West.

The Views of the Westernizers or the Reformers

The Westernizers experienced Russia as a backward country, superstitious and poor. They felt that the only way for Russia to progress was to imitate the West and learn from it. They did not look to the Orthodox Church to change Russia, but in fact, they felt the church was suppressing the Russian people with its mysticism and rituals. Russia would change through political and economic reform. The Westernizers were interested in the emancipation of the serfs as essential to the economic as well as the social health of Russia. They opposed the monarchy and everything that preserved the status quo. Many became radical, even anarchistic. Many were banished to Siberia, exiled to western Europe, imprisoned, or executed.

They supported what Peter the Great had accomplished by doing away with what they believed were archaic customs and traditions, and they wanted to wake the masses of people who continued to live in a primitive life style, in a kind of sleep. The upper classes had changed under Peter's reforms and under the impact of Western culture. The Westernizers wanted to raise the standard of living of poor Russians by shaking up the society and instituting reforms. They felt change could come only when the people would overcome their fear of the church and the tsar and begin to enjoy freedom of thought and expression. They emphasized education, the emancipation of women, and scientific achievements.

It is easy to understand that the Westernizers must have had a difficult time because they were threatening both power structures — the church and the absolute monarchy. Because the reformers could not publish their views publicly without being arrested, they had to find indirect ways. They found this in literature and literary criticism, where they could express political and social demands without attacking directly. But even there, they had to be very careful as letters were censored and spies were placed in discussion groups.

The Westernizers were successful in affecting townsfolk, artisans, petty tradesmen and manufacturers. These people interacted with foreigners and began to see new ways of thinking and doing things. They began to get educated and to shake off old habits of laziness. Much of the fear the peasants had of new ideas and new tools stemmed from the notion that they would be expected to do more work. They were suspicious of anything coming from outside. However, as groups of them began to change their ways of living, they grew increasingly interested in improving living conditions, and they formed connections with reformers. They were ready to become players in the revolutionary movements.

On the other hand, some of the middle class who were interacting regularly with foreigners grouped together to use their education to benefit themselves, not necessarily to bring about any change that would help the masses. The class most isolated from the common people was the upper class which increasingly imitated the foreign way of living — in language, clothes, manners, and interests.

One leader of the Westernizers, Vissarion Belinsky (1811–1848), became convinced that Western culture would be a help in changing Russia, especially in fighting against serfdom. He wrote a drama on this theme, for which he was banished from the university and threatened with exile to Siberia. He would have been arrested if he had not gone to the West for treatment for tuberculosis, from which he died at age thirty-seven. Belinsky's "Letter to Gogol" was what Dostoyevsky was reading when he was arrested and charged with treason.

Both the Slavophils and the Westernizers felt that Russia had a special mission. The Slavophils wanted to protect Russia's uniqueness by keeping out any Western influence. The Westernizers felt that in the short run, Russia needed to imitate the West, and in the long run, as Russian social conditions improved, then new cultural ideas would spring out of Russian soil. Thus, in time Russians would develop their own literature and no longer be dependent on or imitate Europeans.

They expressed it this way: "We don't want to be Frenchmen or Germans. We want to be Russians in the European spirit. Pushkin began it, we want to continue in this way."

Endnote

1. www.svots.edu/Faculty/Albert-Rossi/Articles/Saying-the-Jesus-Prayer.html, St. Vladimir's Orthodox Theological Seminary, Crestwood, New York.

Bibliography

Billington, James H. *The Icon and the Axe, An Interpretive History of Russia's Culture*, New York: Vintage Books, Random House, 1970.

Dunlop, John B. *The Distinctive Features of Orthodox Spirituality, from Staretz Amvrosy*, Belmont, MA: Nordland Publishing Co., 1972.

Kohn, Hans. *The Mind of Modern Russia, History and Political Thought of Russia's Great Age*, Rutgers, NJ: Rutgers University Press, 1955.

Kizhi Island- Karelia- Russia

CHAPTER 5

THE LIVES OF PEASANTS AND LANDOWNERS

A penetrating look at nineteenth century village life of the Russian heartland is most helpful in trying to understand Russia's culture. Over the last hundred years we find many different ways Russians tried to "return to the land," some in a sentimental way imagining the good old days and others, filled with guilt of their own family's misuse of the peasantry, wanting to go and live like the people and hopefully help them to improve their lives. Such varied views of the peasantry are portrayed in numerous works of Russian literature, painting, and music.

Set among the hills and meadows of central Russia, the countryside included the peasant villages, the manor houses of the landowner, churches and monasteries. Life in the village was very different from life in the manor house, and each was dependent on the other. But it was not always that way. Let us look at some historical background.

In 1840, Ivan III threw off the Mongol yoke and set up the position of tsar. Subservient to the tsarist family were several positions of status. The nobles (*dvoriane*) were the military class, charged with the duty to protect the tsar. The noble was given certain lands to support his family while he was doing his military service. Over time, these lands became hereditary, although the custom of military service for the state continued. The nobles, who had now become landowners, drew their quota for military service from the peasants who were independent workers of the land. In exchange for using the land, the peasants designated a number of their men to the noble. Such was the hierarchical arrangement that developed.

Until the sixteenth century the peasants enjoyed some freedom of movement, and they could choose where to live and whom to serve. Changes took place each year at a specified time in the week after Saint Yuri's Day, after the main harvesting was completed. The peasants looked around and tended to move to the estates of the rich landowners. This created a problem for the landowners who were not as rich, because they could not get enough peasants to fulfill their military obligations. In 1580 a decree was issued that peasants could no longer move around; thus began three hundred years of serfdom.

Over the next centuries, the nobles received more privileges from the tsars as to how they controlled their property, and they were granted ownership in perpetuity. As a result, the serfs became the property of the landowners who could do whatever they wanted to them—they could beat them, send them into the military (lifetime service), or even send them off to Siberia if they wished. With these changes, the original arrangement of serfdom—the contract that the peasant would work the land and, in exchange, provide men to serve in the military for the noble—was lost. The serf was no longer considered a person, but property.

Peasant life was primitive and harsh. They lived in small, dark thatched huts with earthen floors. Wood had to be cut and stoked in the large wood-burning stove for heat and cooking. The peasants had to walk to the village pump and carry back water in buckets. The roads were frozen in winter, deep mud in spring, and difficult to traverse most times. They could cultivate small plots for their family's use and grew mostly root vegetables. Anything extra would be sold. They worked the nobles' land with hand tools such as the sickle, while in the rest of Europe, peasants were using the scythe. Most peasant families had a horse, a cow, some sheep, some pigs, and a few chickens, geese, and ducks. Mushrooms and berries from the forest were precious commodities. The families were large, and illness and death were constant visitors. Alcoholism was common, as vodka was not only a means to forget the harshness of life, but often a means of currency for extra jobs the peasants did for the landowners. A woman's life was particularly difficult, as she not only worked from morning to night caring for the house, the children, and the animals, but wife beating was sanctioned, and in fact, expected. Not only was the landowner the master of the peasant, but the land itself required obedience. The farmer had to care for the land in each season as demanded, and there was no ignoring it.

The landowners' life was quite a contrast. Their manor houses were often more like sprawling, yet cozy family homes—what we think of as French *chateaus*. In some ways, they were like American plantation houses, set in beautiful parkland with birches, streams, and meadows. Their lands included the village and the church as well. The family was what we often refer to as landed gentry, the men "country gentlemen."

The sons served for two or three years in the Guards regiment, and then retired to their estates with their handsome military uniforms (which they donned for photographs and formal occasions) and a stipend. They often spent winters in St. Petersburg or Moscow and summers enjoying the beautiful landscape and pleasant lifestyle at the family estate. Family and friends came to visit and spent several months, reading aloud books from their large libraries, playing music, putting on dramas, and entertaining each other in a rather European upper class lifestyle.

The playwright Anton Chekhov portrays the rather boring life of the upper class in his dramas *Three Sisters*, *Uncle Vanya*, and *The Seagull*. The landowning class often suffered from boredom, wishing something interesting would happen, not feeling any real meaning in their lives. At times, they would lose themselves in gambling, sexual affairs, or dueling. It was as if time were ticking away, and they knew something was supposed to happen but it was not.

The landowners often separated the lazy peasants from the more ambitious or talented ones. The lazy ones might be settled in a separate village, the more talented ones sent for training in music, architecture, or other arts. Children of the lazy ones were sometimes taken away to learn a trade or married into other peasant families to increase the number of children.

The serfs were suspicious of any new methods of agriculture that the landowners tried to introduce. For example, when English estate managers introduced carrots, turnips, beets, potatoes, and beans, and the serfs were not familiar with these vegetables, they mostly ended up feeding them to the pigs. Ironically, although the peasants refused to harvest potatoes in particular, for religious reasons, potatoes became the main food of rural Russia. This refusal was so strong that in the 1840–1844 period, there were violent potato uprisings by the serfs.

The life of the serf was especially hard because the land itself was poor. When landowners suggested new ideas of fertilizing the soil, the serfs rejected them. Why should they work harder to make the land better for the landowner or produce more food for his family? They would get no more out of it for themselves. If they had any ambition, they were better off taking extra jobs that paid.

The emancipation of the serfs in 1861 affected both the serfs and the landowners. Freeing the serfs from the land was welcomed at first. But regulations which bound them to the landowner through harsh debts, dues, and taxes, did not leave them better off at all. The best land was reserved for the landowners as their own property, and the rest of the land was given to peasant communes to allot to their families. An outstanding book for a detailed description of the life of the peasants is *Village Life in Late Tsarist Russia*, listed in the bibliography of this chapter.

The landowners lost much of their agricultural support because the freed peasants no longer had to obey them. Further, with the rise of transatlantic shipping and the building of railroads in Europe, the landowners had to compete with new suppliers from the fertile farms in southern Russia and America. Many landowners could not afford to keep up their estates and had to mortgage them or sell off lumber and land parcels. One result of this competition was that by 1900, eighty percent of the landowning class could no longer support their families on earnings from their lands alone.

Bibliography

Chekhov, Anton. *Anton Chekhov Five Plays*, Oxford World's Classics, New York: Oxford U. Press, 1998.

Figes, Orlando. *Natasha's Dance, A Cultural History of Russia*, New York: Henry Holt, 2002.
_____. *Peasant Russia, Civil War, The Volga Countryside in Revolution, 1917–1921*, London: Phoenix Press, 1989.

Maynard, Sir John. *The Russian Peasant and Other Studies*, New York: Collier Books, 1962.

Schmemann, Serge. *Echoes of a Native Land, Two Centuries of a Russian Village*, New York: Alfred A. Knopf, 1997.

Tian-Shanskaia, Olga Semyonova. *Village Life in Late Tsarist Russia*, Bloomington: Indiana University Press, 1993.

Street Vendor

Kerchief Vendor

Lemonade Vendor

CHAPTER 6

FAIRY TALES AND MYTHS

Many students lovingly remember in their early school years when they heard Russian fairy tales about the Firebird, Vassili and Vassilika, and Baba Yaga. Myths and fairy tales describe human journeys. They tell the story of what it is to be human. The fairy tale is usually archetypal—the individual character may not even have a name—and teaches a moral value. Myths, on the other hand, are more detailed, and often involve spirit beings in their relation to earthly life.

When we try to find the earliest myths, we find the Slavic and Siberian stories which were created during pagan times. Because of the harsh climate and darkness, the Russians turned to their pagan gods for comfort and to keep up their spirits. The earliest cults were based around the sun, the god of sun, light, and fire. They not only told stories about the sun, but they built their festivals around the sun's appearance and disappearance, the light and darkness of the year. Many stories and songs celebrate the power of the sun and its loving connection with the earth and earth's people.

Another important pagan god was the earth goddess, whom they considered to be very close to them and in daily contact. When the Russians looked for refuge in the forests, they turned to her for protection. In many fairy tales, the characters live in the forest, gain their food and housing from forest resources, and interact with forest creatures—all under the loving care of the earth goddess.

Some gods could be relied on, and others were tricksters. Some lived outside in nature and some in the home. The house spirits were called *domovoi* and were either invisible or hairy old men who wandered the house and sat on the stove. They were seen as spirits of the ancestors.

A familiar forest-spirit is Baba Yaga who lives in a house with chicken feet, surrounded by a picket fence made of bones. She propels herself around the forest with a pestle, nestled in its mortar. As she goes, she sweeps behind her with her broom to hide her tracks. She can be a frightening creature and plays the role that the boogey man does in Western culture.

Another familiar character is Ivan the Fool. He is the youngest son, lazy and stupid, who sits on the stove all day while the rest of the family works. Like the primeval *domovoi*, when it comes to completing a challenge before his brothers, he is always the one to find the jewel or marry the princess. The fool becomes the hero.

Among the hundreds of Russian fairy tales, there are several that I enjoy telling. The first one, "The Firebird," has many versions. I particularly like to tell it at the beginning of the Russian literature course because of the role beauty plays in it. This segues nicely with our look at Eastern Orthodox Christianity and its emphasis on beauty.

"The Firebird"[1]

Once upon a time very long ago there was an orphan girl named Maryushka. She was a quiet, modest and gentle maiden. None could embroider as beautifully as she. She worked with colored silks and glass beads, making for one a shirt, for another a towel or a pretty sash. And she was always content with the money she received, however small.

The fame of her skill reached the ears of merchants beyond the seas. From near and far they came to see her marvelous work. They gazed and were amazed, for they had never thought to find anything so beautiful. One after another, they tried to persuade Maryushka to come away with them, promising her riches and glory. But she would only lower her eyes and reply modestly: "Riches I do not need and I shall never leave the village where I was born. But of course I will sell my work to all who find it beautiful." And with that, although they were disappointed, the merchants had to be content. They left, spreading the story of her skill to the ends of the earth, until one day it reached the ear of the wicked sorcerer Kaschei the Immortal, who raged to learn that there was such beauty in the world which he had never seen.

So he took the form of a handsome youth and flew over the deep oceans, the tall mountains and the impassable forests until he came to Maryushka's cottage. He knocked at the door and bowed low to her, as was the custom. Then he asked to see the needlework she had completed. Maryushka set out shirts, towels, handkerchiefs and veils, each more beautiful than the other. "Kind sir," said she, "whatever pleases you, you may take. If you have no money now, you may pay me later, when you have money to spare. And if my work should not find favor in your eyes, please counsel me and tell me what to do, and I shall try my best."

Her kind words and the sight of all that beauty made Kaschei even angrier. How could it be that a simple country girl could fashion things finer than he, the great Kaschei the Immortal, himself possessed? In his most cunning tones he said, "Come with me, Maryushka, and I will make you Queen. You will live in a palace built of precious jewels. You will eat off gold and sleep on an eiderdown. You will walk in an orchard where birds of paradise sing sweet songs, and golden apples grow."

"Do not speak so," answered Maryushka. "I need neither your riches nor your strange marvels. There is nothing sweeter than the fields and woods where one was born. Never shall I leave this village where my parents lie buried and where live those to whom my needlework brings joy. I shall never embroider for you alone."

Kaschei was furious at this answer. His face grew dark and he cried, "Because you are so loath to leave your kindred, a bird you shall be and no more a maiden fair."

And in an instant a Firebird flapped its wings where Maryushka had stood. Kaschei became a great black falcon and soared into the skies to swoop down on the Firebird. Grasping her tight in his cruel talons, he carried her high above the clouds.

As soon as Maryushka felt the power in those steel claws and realized she was being taken away, she resolved to leave a lasting memory of herself. She shed her brilliant plumage, and feather after feather floated down on meadow and forest. The mischievous wind covered the feathers with grass and leaves, but nothing could rob them of their glowing rainbow colors.

As the feathers fell, Maryushka's strength ebbed. And although the Firebird died in the black falcon's talons, her feathers continued to live, down on the ground. They were not ordinary feathers, but magic ones that only those who loved beauty and who sought to make beauty for others could see and admire.

* * * * *

Here is a fairy tale, very similar to some of the tales from many other lands, to teach children that good behavior is rewarded and naughty behavior is punished.

"Frost"[2]

The children in their little sheepskin coats and high felt boots and fur hats, trudged along the forest path in the snow. Vanya went first, then Maroosia, and then old Peter. The ground was white and the snow was hard and crisp, and all over the forest could be heard the crackling of the frost. And as they walked, old Peter told them the story of the old woman who wanted Frost to marry her daughters.

Once upon a time there were an old man and an old woman. Now the old woman was the old man's second wife. His first wife had died and had left him with a little daughter, Martha she was called. Then he married again, and God gave him a cross wife, and with her two more daughters, and they were very different from the first.

The old woman loved her own daughters, and gave them red kisel jelly every day, and honey too, as much as they could put into their greedy little mouths. But poor little Martha, the eldest, she got only what the others left. When they were cross they threw away what they left, and then she got nothing at all.

The children grew older, and the stepmother made Martha do all the work of the house. She had to fetch the wood for the stove, and light it and keep it burning. She had to draw the water for her sisters to wash their hands in. She had to make the clothes, and wash them and mend them. She had to cook the dinner and clean the dishes after the others had done before having a bite for herself.

For all that, the stepmother was never satisfied and was forever shouting at her, "Look, the kettle is in the wrong place." "There is dust on the floor." "There is a spot on the tablecloth." Or, "The spoons are not clean, you stupid, ugly, idle hussy." But Martha was not idle. She worked all day long. She got up before the sun, while her sisters never stirred from their beds till it was time for dinner. And she was not stupid. She always had a song on her lips, except when her stepmother had beaten her. And as for being ugly, she was the prettiest little girl in the village.

Her father saw all this, but could do nothing, for the old woman was mistress at home, and he was terribly afraid of her. And as for the daughters, they saw how their mother treated Martha, and they did the same. They were always complaining and getting her into trouble. It was a pleasure to them to see the tears on her pretty cheeks.

Well, time went on, and the little girl grew up, and the daughters of the stepmother were as ugly as could be. Their eyes were always crossed, and their mouths were always complaining. Their mother saw that no one would want to marry either of them while there was Martha about the house, with her bright eyes and her songs and her kindness to everybody. So she thought of a way to get rid of her stepdaughter, and a cruel way it was.

"See here, old man," said she. "It is high time Martha was married, and I have a bridegroom in mind for her. Tomorrow morning you must harness the old mare to the sledge, and put a bit of food together and be ready to start early, as I'd like to see you back before night."

To Martha she said, "Tomorrow you must pack your things in a box, and put on your best dress to show yourself to your betrothed."

"Who is he?" asked Martha with red cheeks.

"You will know when you see him," said the stepmother.

All that night Martha hardly slept. She could hardly believe that she was really going to escape from the old woman at last, and have a hut of her own, where there would be no one to scold her. She wondered who the young man was. She hoped he was Fedor Ivanovitch, who has such kind eyes, and such nimble fingers on the balalaika, and such a merry way of flinging out his heels when he danced the Russian dance. But although he always smiled at her when they met, she felt she hardly dared to hope that it was he. Early in the morning she got up and said her prayers to God, put the whole hut in order, and packed her things into a little box. That was easy, because she had such few things. It was the other daughters who had new dresses. Any old thing was good enough for Martha. But she put on her best blue dress, and there she was, a pretty little maid as ever walked under the birch trees in spring.

The old man harnessed the mare to the sledge and brought it to the door. The snow was very deep and frozen hard, and the wind peeled the skin from his ears before he covered them with the flaps of his fur hat.

"Sit down at the table and have a bite before you go," said the old woman.

The old man sat down, and his daughter with him, and drank a glass of tea and ate some black bread. And the old woman put some cabbage soup, left from the day before, in a saucer, and said to Martha, "Eat this, my little pigeon, and get ready for the road. But when she said, "my little pigeon," she did not smile with her eyes, but only with her cruel mouth, and Martha was afraid.

The old woman whispered to the old man. "I have a word for you, old fellow. You will take Martha to her betrothed, and I'll tell you the way. You go straight along, and then take the road to the right into the forest … you know … straight to the big fir tree that stands on a hillock, and there you will give Martha to her betrothed and leave her. He will be waiting for her, and his name is Frost."

The old man stared, opened his mouth, and stopped eating. The little maid had heard the last words and began to cry.

"Now, what are you whimpering about?" screamed the old woman. "Frost is a rich bridegroom and a handsome one. See how much he owns. All the pines and firs are his, and the birch trees. Anyone would envy his possessions, and he himself is a strong noble hero, a man of strength and power."

The old man trembled, but said nothing in reply. And Martha went on crying quietly, though she tried to stop her tears. The old man packed up what was left of the black bread, told Martha to put on her sheepskin coat, set her in the sledge and climbed in, and drove off along the white frozen road.

The road was long and the country open, and the wind grew colder and colder, while the frozen snow blew up from under the hoofs of the mare and spattered the sledge with white patches. The tale is soon told, but it takes time to happen, and the sledge was white all over long before they turned off into the forest.

They came in the end deep into the forest, and left the road, over the deep snow through the trees to the great fir. There the old man stopped, told his daughter to get out of the sledge, set her little box under the fir, and said, "Wait here for your bridegroom, and when he comes, be sure to receive him with kind words." Then he turned the mare round and drove home, with the tears running from his eyes and freezing on his cheeks before they had time to reach his beard.

The little maid sat and trembled. Her sheepskin coat was worn through, and in her blue bridal dress she sat, while fits of shivering shook her whole body. She wanted to run away, but she had not strength to move, or even to keep her little white teeth from chattering between her frozen lips.

Suddenly, not far away, she heard Frost crackling among the fir trees, just as he is crackling now. He was leaping from tree to tree, crackling as he came.

He leapt at last into the great fir tree, under which the little maid was sitting. He crackled in the top of the tree, and then called down out of the topmost branches, "Are you warm, little maid?"

"Warm, warm, little Father Frost."

Frost laughed, and came a little lower in the tree and crackled and crackled louder than before. Then he asked, "Are you still warm, little maid? Are you warm, little red cheeks?"

The little maid could barely speak. She was nearly dead, but she answered, "Warm, dear Frost; warm, little father."

Frost climbed lower in the tree, and crackled louder than ever, and asked, "Are you still warm, little maid? Are you warm, little red cheeks? Are you warm, little paws?"

The little maid was benumbed all over, but she whispered so that Frost could just hear her, "Warm, little pigeon; warm, dear Frost."

And Frost was sorry for her, leapt down with a tremendous crackle and a scattering of frozen snow, wrapped the little maid up in rich furs, and covered her with warm blankets.

In the morning the old woman said to her husband, "Drive off now to the forest and wake the young couple."

The old man wept when he thought of his little daughter, for he was sure that he would find her dead. He harnessed the mare and drove off through the snow. He came to the tree and heard his little daughter singing merrily, while Frost crackled and laughed. There she was, alive and warm, with a good fur cloak about her shoulders, a rich veil and costly blankets round her, and a box full of splendid presents.

The old man did not say a world. He was too surprised. He just sat in the sledge staring, while the little maid lifted her little box and the box of presents, set them in the sledge, climbed in, and sat down beside him.

They came home, and the little maid, Martha, fell at the feet of her stepmother. The old woman nearly went off her head with rage when she saw Martha alive, with her fur cloak and rich veil, and the box of splendid presents fit for the daughter of a prince.

"Ah, you slut," she cried, "you won't get round me like that." And she would not say another word to the little maid, but went about all day long biting her nails and thinking what to do.

At night she said to the old man, "You must take my daughters, too, to that bridegroom in the forest. He will give them better gifts than these."

Things take time to happen, but the tale is quickly told. Early next morning the old woman woke her daughters, fed them with good food, dressed them like brides, hustled the old man, made him put clean hay in the sledge and warm blankets, and sent them off to the forest.

The old man did as he was bid—drove to the big fir tree, set the boxes under the tree, lifted out the stepdaughters and set them on the boxes side by side, and drove back home.

They were warmly dressed, these two, and well fed, and, at first, as they sat there, they did not think about the cold. "I can't think what put it into Mother's head to marry us both at once," said the first, "and to send us here to be married. As if there were not enough young men in the village. Who can tell what sort of fellows we shall meet here?" Then they began to quarrel.

"Well," said one of them, "I'm beginning to get the cold shivers. If our fated ones do not come soon, we shall perish of cold."

"It's a flat lie to say that bridegrooms get ready early. It's already dinnertime."

"What if only one comes?"

"You'll have to come another time."

"You think he'll look at you?"

"Well, he won't take you, anyhow."

"Of course he'll take me."

"Take you first! It's enough to make anyone laugh!"

They began to fight and scratch each other, so that their cloaks fell open and the cold entered their bosoms.

Frost, crackling among the trees, laughing to himself, froze the hands of the two quarrelling girls. They hid their hands in the sleeves of their fur coats and shivered and went on scolding and jeering at each other.

"Oh, you ugly mug, dirty nose! What sort of housekeeper will you make?"

"And what about you, boasting one? You know nothing but how to gad about and lick your own face. We'll soon see which one of us he'll take."

And the two girls went on wrangling and wrangling till they began to freeze in good earnest. Suddenly they cried out together, "Devil take these bridegrooms for being so long in coming! You have turned blue all over." And together they replied, shivering, "No bluer than yourself, tooth-chatterer."

And Frost, not so far away, crackled and laughed, and leapt from fir tree to fir tree, crackling as he came.

The girls heard that someone was coming through the forest. "Listen! There's someone coming. Yes, and with bells on his sledge."

"Shut up, you slut! I can't hear, and the frost is taking the skin off me." They began blowing on their fingers.

And Frost came nearer and nearer, crackling, laughing, talking to himself, just as he is doing today. Nearer and nearer he came, leaping from treetop to treetop, till at last he leapt into the great fir under which the two girls were sitting and quarreling. He leaned down, looking through the branches, and asked, "Are you warm, maidens? Are you warm, little red cheeks? Are you warm, little pigeons?"

"Ugh, Frost, the cold is hurting us. We are frozen. We are waiting for our bridegrooms, but the cursed fellows have not turned up."

Frost came a little lower in the tree, and crackled louder and swifter. "Are you warm, maidens? Are you warm, my little red cheeks?"

"Go to the devil!" they cried out. "Are you blind? Our hands and feet are frozen."

Frost came still lower in the branches, and cracked and crackled louder than ever. "Are you warm, maidens?" he asked.

"Into the pit with you, with all the fiends," the girls screamed at him. "You ugly, wretched fellow!" And as they were cursing at him, their bad words died on their lips, for the two girls, the cross children of the cruel stepmother, were frozen stiff where they sat.

Frost hung from the lower branches of the tree, swaying and crackling while he looked at the anger frozen on their faces. Then he climbed swiftly up again, and crackling and cracking, chuckling to himself, he went off, leaping from fir tree to fir tree, this way and that through the white, frozen forest.

In the morning the old woman said to her husband, "Now then, old man, harness the mare to the sledge, and put new hay in the sledge to be warm for my little ones, and lay fresh rushes on the hay to be soft for them, and take warm rugs with you, for maybe they will be cold, even in their furs. And look sharp about it, and don't keep them waiting. The frost is hard this morning, and it was harder in the night."

The old man had not time to eat even a mouthful of black bread before she had driven him out into the snow. He put hay and rushes and soft blankets in the sledge, harnessed the mare, and went off to the forest. He came to the great fir and found the two girls sitting under it dead, with their anger still to be seen on their frozen, ugly faces.

He picked them up, first one and then the other, and put them in the rushes and the warm hay, covered them with the blankets, and drove home.

The old woman saw him coming, far away, over the shining snow. She ran to meet him and shouted out, "Where are the little ones?"

"In the sledge."

She snatched off the blankets, pulled aside the rushes, and found the bodies of her two cross daughters. Instantly she flew at the old man in a storm of rage. "What have you done to my children, my little red cherries, my little pigeons? I will kill you with the oven fork! I will break your head with the poker!"

The old man listened till she was out of breath and could not say another word. That, my dears, is the only wise thing to do when a woman is in a scolding rage. And as soon as she had no breath left with which to answer him, he said, "My little daughter got riches for soft words, but yours were always rough of the tongue. And it's not my fault, anyhow, for you yourself sent them into the forest."

Well, at last the old woman got her breath back again and scolded away till she was tired out. But in the end she made her peace with the old man, and they lived together as quietly as could be expected.

As for Martha, Fedor Ivanovitch sought her in marriage, as he had meant to do all along—yes, and married her; and pretty she looked in the furs that Frost had given her. I was at the feast, and drank beer and mead with the rest. And she had the prettiest children that ever were seen—yes, and the best behaved. For if ever they thought of being naughty, the old grandfather told them the story of crackling Frost, and how kind words won kindness and cross words cold treatment. And now, listen to Frost. Hear how he crackles away! And mind, if ever he asks you if you are warm, be as polite to him as you can. And to do that, the best way is to be good always, like little Martha. Then it comes easy.

The children listened, and laughed quietly, because they knew they were good. Away in the forest they heard Frost, and thought of him crackling and leaping from one tree to another. And just then they came home. It was dusk, for dusk comes early in winter, and a little way through the trees before them they saw the lamp of their hut glittering on the snow. The big dog barked and ran forward, and the children with him. The soup was warm on the stove, and in a few minutes they were sitting at the table, Vanya, Maroosia and old Peter, blowing at their steaming spoons.

Endnotes

1. Suzanne Massie, *The Firebird* (New York: Simon and Schuster, 1980), pp. 17–19.
2. Arthur Ransome, *Old Peter's Russian Tales* (London: Puffin Books, 1916).

Bibliography

Massie, Suzanne. *The Firebird*, Simon and Schuster, New York, 1980.
Ransome, Arthur. *Old Peter's Russian Tales*, Puffin Books, London, 1916.

Estate House in Rural Russia

Alexander Pushkin

Leo Tolstoy

Fydor Dostoyevsky

Boris Pasternak

Anna Akhmatova

Alexander Solzhenitsyn

Andrei Sakharov

Osip Mandelstam

Marina Tsvetayeva

Joseph Brodsky

Irina Ratushinskaya

Andrei Voznesensky

Yevgeny Yevtushenko

CHAPTER 7

Alexander Sergeivich Pushkin (1799–1837)

Pushkin is at the beginning of the journey we make of the Russian writers. If the students have studied the English Romantic poets, his character will be somewhat familiar. In some ways, he is like Byron, and in other ways, he is like Shelley. He is exciting, rebellious, witty, and he is in love with love. He seeks adventure, defies boundaries, lives a sensual, rollicking life, and yet—he is Pushkin. He turns his genius to the concerns of the poor, of the downtrodden, and of those who are imprisoned. His biography familiarizes the students with the historical situation of the time and introduces them to the complex relationship between Russia and the West. The language of his poetry, even in translation, is gripping and exciting.

> Pushkin is an extraordinary occurrence, perhaps the sole manifestation of the Russian spirit; a Russian in full flower, a Russian such as might appear two hundred years hence. In him the Russian character, the Russian soul, the Russian language and temperament are seen in all the immaculate beauty of a landscape reflected on the convex surface of an optic lens.[1]
>
> – Nikolai Gogol

> Everything we have comes from Pushkin. His turning to the people so early in his career was so unheard of, so astonishing, such a new and unexpected a departure it can only have been a miracle or, failing that, the fruit of the singular grandeur of genius—one, I might add, we cannot fully appreciate even today.[2]
>
> – Fyodor Dostoyevsky (1876)

Childhood and Adolescence

Alexander Pushkin was born May 28, 1799, to an old patrician family in St. Petersburg. His father was an authoritarian gentleman, well educated, and a member of the Guards regiment. His mother was a rather spoiled young woman whose great-grandfather was Abyssinian prince Ibrahim Hannibal who was taken as a hostage in childhood by Turks and given to Tsar Peter the Great as a gift. Peter adopted him and sent him abroad for education.

This background bothered his mother, and she disliked the child because he reminded her of her African bloodline and she said he looked like a monkey. If that were not cruel enough, she disliked his mannerisms, found ways to humiliate him, and was cold and disinterested.

Pushkin's family lived in a wing of the palace in Moscow where his parents spent most of their time in parties and the carefree life of the aristocratic class. But young Pushkin was neglected and unloved. The only people who showed him affection were his grandmother and his forty-five-year-old serf nanny Arina

Rodionovna. It was this warmhearted, mild-tempered countrywoman who told him old proverbs and tales that stimulated his imagination and connected him with Russian language and customs.

His tutors introduced him to reading *The Iliad* and *The Odyssey* when he was nine years old. He filled his mind with images out of these adventurous epics, and he also filled his mind with erotic imagery. These two elements were to inspire his behavior and his poetry during the years to come.

When he was twelve, he was invited to join the Lyceum in St. Petersburg at the Tsar's palace. He was a rascal who got himself into a fair amount of trouble. Although it was an honor to be accepted in this school, Pushkin felt he was imprisoned for the six years of his stay.

One area that was exciting for him was poetry. A group of boys developed this passion, vying with each other to write poems, often staying up at night rhyming. They were so intensely involved that they were forbidden to write any more poetry and they would share the results of their writing in secret. After a time the ban was lifted and they continued their poetry and storytelling sessions. Pushkin composed poetry constantly, on walks, in classes, in church, in any free time he had. His classmates knew when he was in the creative moment because he would screw up his face, write down his thoughts, bite his fingernails, furrow his brow, puff out his lips, and with fire in his eyes, read his latest verse.

When the Napoleonic War broke out and the French troops and their allies marched into Russia, the schoolboys followed each new report with great interest. They saluted the regiment of the guards at the entrance of their school. The situation worsened when Napoleon invaded Moscow. However, the citizens of Moscow had evacuated just before the French occupied it, leaving a burning city with no food for the exhausted troops. In typical schoolboy sarcasm, Pushkin wrote, "They complain and curse the French, speaking French all the while."

Things got more exciting and dangerous when it seemed the French would occupy St. Petersburg, and there was the possibility of evacuating the boys. However, instead the exhausted and starving French troops began the famous retreat from the Moscow winter, leaving behind thousands of corpses of horses and soldiers. Because Tsar Alexander had shown such strength in refusing to negotiate with the French, even after Moscow was burned, and in sending the Russian army to defeat the enemy, he was truly welcomed as a hero.

In July 1814 his mother, the Empress Maria Feodorovna, gave a reception at Pavlovsk to which she invited the most famous generals and statesmen of the day. She also invited boys who were studying at the Lyceum, the newly created French-speaking school for the sons of the elite. The boys were dressed in blue serge jackets with red piping and high red collars and gilt buttons, white vests and three-cornered hats. While the Tsar was being celebrated for his great victory as conqueror of Napoleon, a fourteen-year-old boy, sitting with his classmates in a box seat, was not impressed at all. In fact, he was drawing a cartoon of the rather large tsar, stuffed with a series of elegant dinners, trying to get through the Triumphal Arch in Paris, constructed for this special occasion. He was stuck in the narrow arch and his generals were trying desperately to enlarge the arch with their swords. The boy passed the cartoon around to the enjoyment of his classmates. Famous at school for his pranks and his talent, this same boy had recently published a poem in a St. Petersburg newspaper. Of course, this boy was Alexander Pushkin, destined to become the greatest and most beloved poet in Russia.

In his last school year, at eighteen he enjoyed more freedom and often spent it with the Guards, gambling and womanizing. He was also an accomplished athlete and excelled in swimming, swordsmanship, and riding. He had already written dozens of love poems.

> ...You love me. . . . Your caresses
> Are full of fire! When we're alone, you're so
> Sincere, so tender, your love's warmth, its glow
> Are in each word you utter! ... My distress is
> As foolish as my doubts. . . . You love me. . . . No,
> Allow me to insist . . . . Pray have compassion,
> Torment me not; spare me, O spare me, please!
> You do not know how great my anguish is,
> You do not know how boundless is my passion.[3]

Adulthood

Pushkin was given a minor appointment for his vocation. Jobs were given mainly as rewards for upper class lads to occupy them so they would not get into too much trouble.

Although he technically had a post, what Pushkin had most of was free time to do whatever he wanted since he was far from the tsar's sight. He journeyed to the Caucasus Mountains where the exciting life of the gypsies and the fast life in the Crimea stimulated his romantic imagination. He hung around with revolutionaries. He drank too much, romanced too much, and waited for the day he would be freed from exile.

He spoke out for freedom for the serfs and for governmental reforms, and he enjoyed freedom in his personal life which included criticizing the tsar, participating in duels, and having affairs with many women. He wrote the Romantic epic *Russlan and Liudmilla*, which won him fame especially among the younger generation. His poem "Ode to Liberty" expressed his political views and caused him to be exiled to Kishinev, Bessarabia (now Moldova) in southern Russia.

He received another post in Odessa (still part of his exile) where he continued to live the life of a free spirit. He was involved in a number of romantic entanglements and wrote out his ideas on atheism, which led him to be dismissed from government service in disgrace. A positive aspect of his time in Odessa was his familiarity with Italian opera which inspired later writings.

Pushkin was banished to the estate of his old grandfather where he was spied on by police, priests, and, it is said, even by his father. Although the estate had been neglected, his joy was that his old nanny was living there. She became the warm inspiration of his life. He voraciously read Russian history, she told him fairy tales. They shared with each other. He not only wrote poetry, but, inspired by Shakespeare, he wrote *Eugene Onegin* and *Boris Godunov*. The richness of his writing—including French style and common speech—modernized the Russian language and documented Russian customs. He was hailed as the Byron of Russia, and his work inspired Tolstoy and Dostoyevsky. Because he was in forced seclusion at the estate, he did not take part in the Decembrist Uprising of 1826, and thus he probably escaped being executed.

In 1826, when Pushkin was twenty-seven, Tsar Alexander I died. Pushkin was recalled to Moscow and looked forward to freedom again, but the new Tsar Nicholas I made him the court poet so that secret police could keep an eye on his actions.

His interest in women reached a peak when he fell in love for the hundredth time; the object of his love was sixteen-year-old Natalya Goncharova, a beautiful girl but without much intelligence. Despite his passionate attention to her and wish to marry her (after all, he was nearing thirty), his mother did not approve of Natalya and would not agree to the union. He was very upset, and, as was his style when he was upset, he went into action. He traveled to the Caucasus and joined a regiment, and along the way he collected legends of the area. In time his mother softened and approved the wedding. He was happy about that, but he also felt a sense of dread. Before the wedding, he escaped to the gypsies for a last fling. At the age of thirty-one, with Natalya eighteen, he married and settled in St. Petersburg.

The young couple had a promising start. Pushkin had a job in the foreign office, and Natalya occupied herself with the social life. Pushkin was bored with the round of dances and parties, but accompanied Natalya who loved being the center of attention. Over the next few years, when Natalya was not pregnant and having babies, she was flirting with the men and, like his own mother, neglectful of her children. Pushkin did not handle the gossip well and left to the family estate where he wrote some of his most famous works, "Bronze Horseman" and "Queen of Spades" among others. But life was not easy; he gambled, struggling to earn enough money to pay off his debts and for Natalya's party dresses. He implored the Tsar to release him from his service so he could earn more money, but the Tsar refused.

The situation deteriorated further as Pushkin wanted to concentrate on his work; but even Natalya had no interest in his writing. Her routine involved going to balls and returning home in the early morning. One of her flirtations got out of control, and an anonymous letter arrived mocking Pushkin. In response, he challenged Baron Jeorges Charles D'Anthes to a duel. A reprieve occurred because D'Anthes was about to marry Natalya's sister. But Natalya did not hold back, the flirting grew more intense, and rumors flew around St. Petersburg that Natalya and D'Anthes had been spending time alone. After a second anonymous letter, Pushkin could bear no more, and he again challenged D'Anthes. The following description by Suzanne Massie in *The Firebird* captures the dramatic event.[4]

They met on the dueling ground in the late afternoon of January 27, 1837, a bitterly, cold, snowy day. D'Anthes fired first, shattering Pushkin's thigh near the pelvis. Pushkin managed to fire, but only slightly wounded his adversary. Mortally wounded, bleeding profusely, Pushkin rushed home in a sleigh. When his wife saw him mounting the stairs, bloodstained and supported by his valet who had tears in his eyes, she screamed and fainted. As it was late and difficult to find his own doctors, he was treated first by the only one available, an obstetrician. When the Pushkin family physician, Dr. Spassky, finally arrived, Pushkin asked that a priest, the first one that could be found on the streets, be summoned. He confessed and took Communion. Spassky found his pulse weak. Pushkin said wearily, "Death is coming," and then added, "I am waiting for word from the Tsar to die in peace." Around midnight, when the surgeon, Dr. Arendt, came to examine him, Pushkin repeated the same words. After his examination, Dr. Arendt hastened to the palace and, finding that Tsar Nicholas was at the theater, left a message with his valet. The poet Vasily Zhukovsky, Pushkin's closest friend, was also at the bedside and upon hearing his words also went himself to try to find the Emperor.

Hardly had Arendt returned when a messenger arrived from the Tsar, urgently asking that the doctor provide him with all details at once, and adding, "I shall not sleep. I shall be waiting to hear from you." There was also a personal note written in pencil by the Tsar, which he asked to be delivered immediately to Pushkin and then returned. The letter said, "If we are not destined to see each other again, here is my forgiveness and my last advice to you, die like a Christian. Do not worry about your wife and children. I shall care for them." Pushkin, according to his close friend Prince Vyazemsky, who was at the scene, "was extremely moved by these words."

Meanwhile Zhukovsky had gone to the Winter Palace and found the Tsar waiting for news. He told Nicholas that Pushkin had taken Communion and that, as dueling was both against the law and considered a sin by the church, he was concerned about the fate of his second, Danzas. The Tsar, according to Zhukovsky, said, "I cannot change legal procedure, but I will do everything I can." He then congratulated Pushkin on his compliance with his Christian duty and repeated his promise to care for his wife and children. Wrote Zhukovsky, "I returned to Pushkin with his Majesty's answer. Having raised his hands heavenward impulsively, he said, 'How I am consoled. Tell his Majesty that I wish him a long reign, that I wish him luck with his son, that I wish him happiness with his Russia.' He said these words weakly, with difficulty, but distinctly.'"

Pushkin lingered for two days, suffering horribly. In moments of calm, he called his wife and comforted her. "Do not worry—you are innocent of my death. It has nothing to do with you." He sent word to D'Anthes that he pardoned him. D'Anthes, who was barely wounded, only laughed lightly and said, "Well, tell him that I forgive him, too."

To the grief-stricken friends who had kept constant vigil by his bedside, he said, "Farewell. Be happy." During the last hours before his death, he asked that Natalya spoon blackberries and syrup into his mouth, a last warm memory of the generous Russian countryside. A short time later, he sighed, "Life is over." At thirty-seven, he was dead. Collapsed over his body, Natalya screamed hysterically over and over, "Forgive me. Forgive me!"

Pushkin was the embodiment of the Golden Age of Russian poetry in 1820s to the 1830s. His themes of freedom, nature, and love inspired a hungry populace, and they poured out their love for him after his death. His funeral brought the country alive, and country people as well as city people shared their pain and suffering. They traveled by train and by foot, the intelligentsia and the illiterate, to pay homage to their treasure. It is said that for three days 32,000 people marched past his house each day, filing past his casket. The crowd was so large that a wall of his house had to be taken down. Copies of his poetry disappeared from the stores. Strangers shared their tears. The concept of what it was to be a Russian was exemplified by the name "Pushkin."

Message to Siberia[5]

Deep in the Siberian mine
Keep your patience proud
The bitter toil shall not be lost,
The rebel thought unbowed.

The sister of misfortune, Hope,
In the under-darkness dumb
Speaks joyful courage to your heart:
The day desired will come.

And love and friendship pour to you
Across the darkened doors,
Even as round your galley-beds
My free music pours.

The heavy hanging chains will fall,
The walls will crumble at a word,
And Freedom greet you in the light,
And brothers give you back the sword.

Student writing:
Thoughts on Pushkin's "Message to Siberia"

Alexander Pushkin's "Message to Siberia" is a wonderfully rebellious and very political piece of poetry written during a dark and turbulent time in Pushkin's life. He wrote the poem to the few survivors of the great "Decembrist Revolt" of 1825 in which a small force of young army officers and students (many of whom were close friends of Pushkin) staged an armed revolt in St. Petersburg, demanding a constitution for Russia. The uprising was short-lived and many of the rebels were executed or sent to work in the lifeless salt mines of cold Siberia. It was to these few survivors struggling to survive in the salt mines that Alexander Pushkin wrote the inspirational and hope-giving "Message to Siberia" — a poem written clearly and with very simple metaphor so that even the poorest soul could gather strength from its message. – M.M.

The Prophet[6]

Athirst in spirit, through the gloom
Of an unpeopled waste I blundered,
And saw a six-winged Seraph loom
Where the two pathways met and sundered.
He laid his fingers on my eyes:
His touch lay soft as slumber lies,
And like an eagle's, his crag shaken,
Did my prophetic eyes awaken.
He touched my ears, and lo! They rang
With a reverberating clang!
I heard the spheres revolving, chiming,
The angels in their soaring sweep,
The monsters moving in the deep.
The vines low in the valley climbing.
And from my mouth the Seraph wrung
Forth from its roots my sinful tongue.
The idle tongue that slyly babbled,
The vain, malicious, the unchaste.
His hand drew forth and so effaced,
And the wise serpent's sting he placed
In my numb mouth with hand blood-dabbled;
And with a sword he clove my breast,
Drew forth the heart which shook with dread,
And in my gaping bosom pressed
A glowing coal of fire instead.
Upon the wastes, a lifeless clod,
I lay and heard the voice of God:
"Arise, oh prophet, look and ponder.
Arise, charged with My will, and spurred!
As over roads and seas you wander.
Kindle men's hearts with this, My word."

Student writing:

Thoughts on Pushkin's "The Prophet"

"The Prophet" by Alexander Pushkin describes, in the first person, a story about how an ordinary man is turned into a prophet of God. The story starts with the man, who seems to be lost in life, being overtaken by a six-winged Seraph. The Seraph changes his eyes and ears so that he can hear and see the heavens. It rips his tongue and heart out of him and replaces them with "the wise serpent's sting" and "a glowing coal of fire." As he lies dead upon the wastes, God calls to him and charges him to rise and speak to the world, not with his old, mortal voice, but with the voice of God Himself.

The mental images that sprout from this poem are numerous and spectacular. "Athirst in spirit," the first image talks about how the person is lacking guidance in the world. "Through the gloom/Of an unpeopled waste I blundered" describes how he feels utterly alone, or perhaps lost to a point that there is no one nearby to steer him back on course. The next line introduces the "six-winged Seraph" as possibly a figure of inspiration or literally some sort of angel or "divine" occurrence. Then, when the Seraph "Did my prophetic eyes awaken," the character sees "angels in their soaring sweep" and several other things that all lead to the idea that for the first time in his life, the poet seems to feel as though he can actually see the world for what it is. Then the Seraph rips out the poet's "sinful tongue … that slyly babbled" and his "heart which shook with dread," showing that the old poet, who could not speak well and was perhaps even afraid to say what he wanted or needed to say, now had that fault taken from him. Instead, he is given "the wise serpent's sting," which implies that he has become cleverer in his verse and can say more than ever before. He is also given a "glowing coal of fire," which, among other things, can show an ability to say what needs to be said without fear. A glowing coal of fire may also represent never-dying inspiration. "Upon the wastes, a lifeless clod, I lay" describes how tiring pure inspiration can be because of its fleeting, intense nature.

In my opinion, the poem describes how Pushkin becomes a great poet. The message is that when he was young, his "vain, malicious … unchaste" tongue was the only thing he wrote with and therefore his poetry was but earthly mumblings. When this divine inspiration came into his life—mind you, it is very definitely divine and was in fact given by God—he ceased to write poetry of mere mortals but started writing using God's words. In this poem he very clearly states that his poetry is not only divinely inspired, but directly divine.

I absolutely love this poem. It is hard for me to say much else because, for me, the poem speaks for itself. It is immediately pompous and absolutely divine. The descriptions that Alexander Pushkin uses are engrossing to a degree that very few poems I have ever read in my life are. "The Prophet" is descriptive in the way I would suspect a short story would be descriptive. In very few lines, Pushkin was able to describe a scene that is vividly imprinted on my mind's eye. This is very definitely one of my favorite poems ever. – A.S.

Storm Cloud[7]

O storm-cloud, the tempest's survival alone
Like mad do you rush o'er the heavenly dome;
Alone do you cast as you drift on your way
A dark, brooding shade on the jubilant day.
A short while ago you lay cloaking the sky,
And great forks of lightning flared round you on high.
You thundered and roared over forest and plain
And fed thirsting earth with a bounty of rain.
Enough! Make you haste! Do not tarry … Begone!
The earth is refreshed and the rainstorm has flown,
And tame though the wind is, it stubbornly tries
To make you desert the now radiant skies.

To the Poet[8]

Hark poet! Do not prize the mob's love, I beseech you:
Too soon does loud praise die: discount it. Should a fool
Deride your verse, be calm: should the cold laughter reach you
Of many, of a crowd, stay firm, impassive, cool.

You are enthroned a tsar: so follow lofty-minded
The road of freedom, lone, by thought unfettered led:
Perfect the fruit of toil to noble genius wed
And ask for no reward: within yourself you'll find it.

You are your own most stern judge and meant so to be:
None will your work appraise with more severity.
Say, does it please you—this, your proud hen has created?
It does? Then let the mob against it crude declaim
And at your altar spit and try to douse the flame
And with a young imp's glee the tripod rock, elated.

Endnotes

1. Irina Zheleznova, ed. *Russian Nineteenth Century Verse* (U.S.S.R.: Raduga Publishers, 1983), p. 26.
2. Ibid.
3. Pushkin, 1823, in Zheleznova, p. 35.
4. Suzanne Massie, *The Firebird* (New York: Simon and Schuster, 1980), pp. 240–241.
5. Pushkin, 1827, trans. Max Eastman, accessed at www.sad34.net/~globalclassroom/ Library/ Russianmessagetosiberia.
6. Pushkin, 1826, available in Zheleznova, a slightly different translation than the one I have included in this chapter.
7. Pushkin, 1815, in Zheleznova, p. 69.
8. Pushkin, 1830, in Zheleznova, p. 61.

Bibliography

Guerney, Bernard Guilbert. *The Portable Russian Reader*, New York: Viking Press, 1964.
Massie, Suzanne. *The Firebird*, New York: Simon and Schuster, 1980.
Mirsky, D.S. *A History of Russian Literature*, New York: Random House, 1958.
Zheleznova, Irina, ed. *Russian Nineteenth Century Verse*, U.S.S.R.: Raduga Publishers, 1983.

Ice Sailing on the Volga River

CHAPTER 8

LEO TOLSTOY (1828–1910)

I have loved truth more than anything; and I do not despair of finding it, but I am still searching and searching. . . . But I'm alone, and it is hard and terrible, and it seems that I have lost my way.[1]

– From a letter to a friend when Leo Tolstoy was almost forty

Leo Tolstoy was a charismatic character, on fire with ideals and frustrated by his human flaws. He is the author of a significant body of work, including two epic novels, *War and Peace* and *Anna Karenina*, short stories, nonfiction, and folk tales. His life was long and dramatic, and his genius influenced people all over the world. His struggles to bring his ideals into action were inspiring and at the same time chaotic, and they remind us that, although we may fail along the way, we must continue to strive. His life stimulates profound spiritual questions as to the nature of truth and happiness, the role of a church in one's religious life, the role of poverty, the value of education, and the manner in which we live our lives.

His short stories such as "What Men Live By" and "Master and Man" easily lend themselves to class discussion. Some students may be inspired to read *Anna Karenina* or *War and Peace* on their own and appreciate the rich descriptive imagery and development of the characters.

Childhood

Leo Tolstoy was born on August 28, 1828, at Yasnaya Polyana [Clear Glade], a beautiful wooded estate in Tula Province, one hundred thirty miles south of Moscow. His family belonged to the Russian nobility, and his lifestyle was that of the typical aristocratic class of nineteenth century Russia. He was the fifth child, with three older brothers and followed by a younger sister. It was shortly after the birth of his sister that his mother died, leaving his father, Count Nicholas, alone to rear the children. Cousin Tatayana stepped in to care for them and did so with love and guidance. However, Tolstoy was never able to get over the loss of his mother. Even in his eighties, he spoke about walking in the garden and dreaming of her.

Yasnaya Polyana, with its extensive lands nestled within the rolling Russian countryside, its lakes and streams, wild game, and the lovely mansion house, was an ideal surrounding for the Tolstoy children to experience the joy of the seasons and the beauty of nature. Attached to the estate were about thirty house servants and hundreds of field serfs who lived in cottages on the estate. The nobility, the Russian Orthodox Church, and the tsars had made a legal arrangement by which peasants could be bought and sold. This system was commonly practiced throughout the country. House servants became close to their masters over several generations and often were considered part of the family. A serf stood behind each person at the table, cutting meat and helping with other aspects of the meal. When the master's children ran past the cottages, serf children bowed to them. This was the milieu in which Leo Tolstoy experienced his childhood. He especially loved this house as it was a link between him and his mother, who died when she was thirty and he was two.

When Leo was five years old, he experienced his older brothers huddled together whispering. When Leo came nearer, the eldest, Nicholas, announced that the secret to happiness was written on a green stick buried on the edge of the ravine during that year, 1833. How could they find it? Nicholas told them that they had to pass certain trials, the first was that they had to train themselves to stand in a corner and not think about a white bear. Leo took up the challenge and tried to accomplish this, but more important, he thought about the message on the green stick for the rest of his life.

Despite the loss of their mother, Leo and his brothers had a childhood filled with dramatic play, acting out hunting scenes and heroic battles, music, and dancing. (A full orchestra of serfs played Haydn each morning while the children ate breakfast.) Tutors lived with the family to educate the children. The children took for granted the religious pilgrims who, on their journey from monastery to monastery, stopped at Yasnaya Polyana to be fed and sheltered according to custom. Leo's greatest joy was lying in bed and listening to Stepanovich, a barefooted, blind pilgrim who was a great storyteller. Leo was already writing his own stories, and was inspired by this.

When Leo was nine years old, it was time for the whole family, including his grandmother, aunts, and thirty house servants, to move to Moscow so the children could study with able tutors and so the older boys could prepare for university entrance. Already as a boy, Leo pondered questions of life and death, happiness and pain. Sometimes he would test himself to bear pain by holding heavy dictionaries at arm's length. At other times he would decide happiness was only in the present and he would indulge himself with sweets and laze around.

His world was shattered again when he was thirteen with the sudden death of his father. Now his grandmother became the tyrannical ruler of the household. Leo was not a good student and resented the sternness of his tutor, and especially resented being locked in a dark closet as punishment. He referred to these terrifying experiences later in his life when he spoke against any type of violence.

Once more Tolstoy's inner world was challenged when one of his brothers' friends came to visit and announced that at his high school a great discovery had been made—there was no God. On that same day, their grandmother died and the boys became orphans. The one consolation was that Cousin Tatayana took the younger children back to Yasnaya Polyana and became their French tutor.

Tolstoy's moral awakening occurred when he observed a serf being dragged into a barn for a beating. When his aunt asked him, "If you were upset, why did you not stop him?" Tolstoy realized that as one of the master's children, he had the power to call a stop to the beating, but he had not done so. The feeling of shame haunted him for years.

His world was further disturbed when Aunt Alexandra died in 1841. Within four years the Tolstoy children had lost their father, grandmother, and aunt. Since Cousin Tatayana was not really a blood relative, the children were put in care of Aunt Pelagya, their father's sister, who moved the family to Kazan. The family furniture and serfs were sent by barge down the Oka River to the Volga River and on to Kazan.

Adolescence

In Kazan his brothers attended university. While his brother Dmitry was intensely interested in religion, Leo decided to stop believing in "church" religion, although he would never stop believing in God.

Leo was tormented by the feeling that he was ugly. His nose was too big, his other features too small. He was further disheartened by the fact that he failed his exams for college. After cramming all summer, he passed the exams and headed for college. However, he struggled with alternating shyness and false bravado. In the midst of this, he found his best friend, Mitya Dyakov, who would be his friend for forty-five years. With Mitya, Leo could let go of his conflicting emotions and have deep discussions. He began keeping a journal, setting himself rules to live by, but he was constantly breaking the rules and feeling guilty. He became interested in girls but was awkward in making advances to them. Leo received a letter from the college that he had failed in his classes and would not be allowed to take the final examinations. He retreated to Yasnaya Polyana, to its comforting landscapes and the warmth of Cousin Tatayana. His thoughts about serfdom began to change as he became a devoted reader of Rousseau's ideas of equality.

In his return to the university, he began to study law, and found this more satisfying. Yet his work was still not acceptable, and he was asked to leave the university. Again he returned to Yasnaya Polyana and decided to study on his own. He set himself a strict schedule to study law, medicine, French, Russian, German, English, Italian, Latin, agriculture, history, geography, and statistics.

When he reached age eighteen, the family divided their mother's property, and to his joy, Leo received Yasnaya Polyana with its 4000 acres and 339 serfs. With this new responsibility, Leo decided to set up a school for the children of the serfs and to provide better housing and sanitary conditions. He tried to interest them in iron plows to replace wooden ones, but the serfs were suspicious that he was trying to make them work harder. Why was he working in the fields alongside them? This was not becoming a master. Although at first they allowed their children to attend his school, then they kept them away. They would not move into the more comfortable houses he provided. In frustration, Leo gave up his attempts and felt failure here also.

Adulthood

For a change, Leo spent the next three years in St. Petersburg and Moscow, trying to fit into high society. He passed the law exams, but instead of practicing law, he lost himself in gambling, piling up enormous debts and having to sell off some of his lands and serfs. As things became worse, a new idea awakened in him—he would become a writer, and he began work on the novel *Childhood*.

He accompanied his older brother to the Caucasus Mountains where he joined an artillery regiment, enjoying the excitement of military life, gambling, and visiting gypsy camps. He was able to keep cool under fire. While he was in Romania, he read Goethe and Schiller, and a translation of *Uncle Tom's Cabin*, which was banned in Russia at this time. This book caused him to reexamine his thoughts about serfdom and to decide to free his serfs. His continued gambling caused him to lose part of Yasnaya Polyana with the central structure of the house being taken down board by board and sold to pay his debts.

The Crimean War broke out in 1854 when Leo was twenty-five years old. He was sent to command men in the Danubian provinces where the Russian army was retreating. He requested to be sent to Sebastopol where the Russians were heroically fighting the English and French along the Danube River in present-day Romania. While the war raged in Sevastopol, a few hundred miles away in Kishinev, the Tsar's sons were having wild parties. This contrast bothered Tolstoy, and he received permission to go as a lieutenant into the difficult battle zone; when he arrived there and experienced the intense suffering of amputees and the dying, he realized what a small experience of war he had had. He wanted to write the truth about the courage and heroism of Russian soldiers. He also realized that the Russians carried old-fashioned muskets while the Allies had rifles, and that the generals were incompetent, having been chosen because they were from well-known families rather than because of skill. Tolstoy wrote stories depicting the brutality of war, and these stories reached the Tsarina who wept when she read them. Leo's battery was ordered into battle under fire from the French, and he experienced six weeks of nightmarish fighting. When the siege of Sevastopol ended with the city in flames after eleven months of horrible fighting, half a million people had died. By May 1855, Tolstoy no longer idealized patriotism, but he wanted people to know the horrors of war as experienced by the men under fire. He decided he would not pursue a military career, but he would commit himself to writing, as this would help him pursue his search for truth. In his book *Sevastopol* Tolstoy recorded sketches of everyday horrors during the siege, and this book would become a model for Stephen Crane and Ernest Hemingway.

During his engagement in battle, he also found time to think about bigger ideas. He wrote,

> A conversation about Divinity and Faith has suggested to me a great, a stupendous idea, to the realization of which I feel capable of devoting my life. That idea is the founding of a new religion corresponding to the present state of mankind: the

religion of Christ but purged of dogmas and mysticism—a practical religion, not promising future bliss but giving bliss on earth. I understand that to accomplish this the conscious labor of generations will be needed. One generation will bequeath the idea to the next, and some day fanaticism or reason will accomplish it. Deliberately to promote the union of mankind by religion is the basic thought which I hope will dominate me.[2]

This idea became one of the guiding influences in his life. Tolstoy was taken into the circle of writers in St. Petersburg, and he continued to experience acclaim as his war stories were published. However, he tried to forget his wartime experiences through wild parties and gambling. This behavior was temporarily interrupted when his brother Mitya died of tuberculosis. Scenes of his brother's suffering appeared later in the character Nicholas in *Anna Karenina*.

Leo returned to Yasnaya Polyana, determined to free the serfs and lease them land, letting them pay rent for thirty years and then owning it. Despite his Cousin Tatayana's disapproval, he gathered his serfs and explained his plan. However, there were rumors that Tsar Alexander II would free them, and the serfs awaited a more liberal emancipation, which did not come at that time. He busied himself writing short stories and short novels. He escaped a possible marriage by taking off to western Europe, visiting France, Switzerland, Italy, and Germany, where he carefully observed social class distinctions and beautiful scenery.

Upon returning to Yasnaya Polyana, he decided to give up his writing and focus on helping the serfs. First he decided he should take up the plow and work alongside the serfs. He also decided that changes would best come about by education, so again he tried to establish a school for the children. Since the idea of emancipation was still circulating as a rumor, the serfs could now see value in their children's learning to read and write. Twenty-two children joyously participated in the lessons, loving reading and learning under his guidance.

During Leo's summer break, his brother Nicholas became seriously ill with tuberculosis. His sister Marya and her three children and Leo accompanied Nicholas to southern France where the favorable climate was said to be helpful, but Nicholas died soon after their arrival. Leo used this opportunity to travel and study educational methods. He felt the German and French schools crushed the inquisitive nature of children's minds by rote teaching and harsh discipline. In London he listened to a lecture on education by Charles Dickens and observed schools in action. While there, he saw a newspaper headline that the Russian serfs had been emancipated, but with full freedom not to take place for two years in 1863. Tolstoy returned to Yasnaya Polyana and established fourteen peasant schools in the district and a magazine in which he published his ideas of pedagogy.

Leo had been thinking for quite some time about marriage and family. While he spent time in Moscow sharing his educational ideas founded on freedom, he considered a number of eligible young women and decided on Sonya Andreyevna Behrs, one of the lovely daughters of Dr. and Mrs. Behrs. The family expected that he would ask for the hand of the older daughter, Lisa, but it was Sonya who was destined to become Countess Tolstoy. Although he felt that, at thirty-four, he was too old to marry an eighteen-year-old, he overcame his shyness and handed Sonya a letter proposing marriage. Despite the hysterics of her sister Lisa, Sonya accepted, and Leo, in his impulsiveness, insisted they be married within a week. A few days before the wedding, he asked Sonya to read his old diaries, complete with descriptions of his low life and a listing of his sins. She was shocked, but decided to marry him anyway. They were married according to Orthodox tradition and settled in Yasnaya Polyana to begin their lives together.

A city girl, Sonya at first felt bored and isolated. However, soon she began assuming the task of managing the estate. It was also the beginning of a tempestuous relationship between them, despite a love that grew and strengthened over the years. With the birth of their first child, Sergei, Tolstoy settled down to writing his first epic novel, *War and Peace*.

Sonya acted as his secretary, copying the manuscript by hand, as she would for many decades. After their third child was born, she wrote her sister, "I keep weaning or nursing or washing or boiling and apart from that there are the children, the pickling, the jam-making, the ... copying."[3] Writing the drafts of the novel was continued frustration as Leo changed phrases and rewrote paragraphs between 1865 and 1869 until its completion. Despite this, she was thrilled with the novel and proud of Leo's work.

On Leo's side, he was immersed in researching the War of 1812, but at the same time he was depressed by the deaths of more friends and relatives. He wrote, "I shall soon be forty — and I have loved truth more than anything; I do not despair of finding it, and I am still searching and searching. . . . But I'm alone, and it is hard and terrible, and it seems that I have lost my way." [4]

War and Peace tells the story of five families and their experiences during Napoleon's invasion of Russia in 1812. It covers family life and military life, the tsar's court, and the battlefield. When it was published, the response was enthusiastic; people of all ages rushed to buy it and saw themselves in one or the other characters. They felt proud to be Russian as they reexperienced the defeat of Napoleon by the Russians. People in other countries also recognized it as a great epic with universal themes.

Tolstoy's forties were filled with despair as he asked himself questions: Why do I live? Is there a God? Yet to the world, he appeared a successful and happy man. He had good health, a loving wife, a growing family of six children, international fame, solid earnings from *War and Peace*, and he was completing another novel, *Anna Karenina*, as well as readers for peasant children. Family life was filled with gaiety, visitors, music, costume balls, berry and mushroom picking, drama performances, swimming, horseback riding, chess, star-gazing, and delightful meals. Despite his obsession with death and many bouts of depression, Leo was in the middle of the fun, roughhousing, joking, and organizing military campaigns with the children, reading aloud, and celebrating festivals.

During these years, death did visit with the passing of Cousin Tatayana, his guardian Aunt Pelagya, and three of his infant children. He remembered the time when one of his brothers' friends had revealed the secret that there is no God, and he was tortured by this thought.

In his fifties, Tolstoy had an existential crisis in which he turned his back on aristocratic living. He felt that in his two great novels he had celebrated this elite life. Now he wanted nothing more to do with it. He moved into a simple room in the back of the house, dressed in peasant style, ate very frugally, withdrew into himself, worked in the fields with the peasants, and made his own shoes. For the next thirty years he lived in two different worlds. Masses of people began to hail him as a prophet and made the pilgrimage to Yasnaya Polyana. On the home front, his wife and family did not agree with his ideas, criticized him, and saw him as an eccentric who cared more about the poor than about his own family. It was a lonely life. In *Confessions*, Tolstoy described the following:

> One day, walking through an early spring forest, listening to the birds and looking at the twisted leaves of new green, from old habit he began to pray. And despairing that there was no God, he shouted into the stillness of the woods, "Lord, have mercy, save me." The distraught questioner became suddenly, gloriously aware that a compassionate Someone understood his struggling search.
>
> "He exists," Tolstoy exclaimed with joy. And the instant that he admitted God's existence, new life welled up within him.
>
> "What more do you seek?" asked a small voice. "This is He. He is that without which one cannot live. . . . Live seeking God and then you will not live without God." And the searcher was saved. And he began to live again.[5]

Tolstoy responded to this experience by trying to reconnect with the Orthodox Church which he had previously rejected. But although his heart longed for the rituals, his reason would not allow him to accept them. He turned away from the church again and began an intense study of the New Testament, resolving to not write fiction from then on. He wrote about the hypocrisy of the church, the goodness of the peasants, and the uselessness of the rituals, but especially of the truth in the teachings of Christ. The church condemned his writings and refused to allow them to be published, but they still managed to be shared illegally. His family was horrified by his writing and did not understand his deep searching for truth. New ideas were emerging in his mind and heart that would isolate him from his family for the rest of his life.

Sonya was particularly upset when Leo gave up writing fiction. She wrote to her daughter Tanya, "There is something lacking in my life, something that I loved, and that is Lyova's literary work, which had always given me such joy and inspired me with such reverence. You see, Tanya, I'm a true writer's wife, so greatly do I take his writing to heart."[6]

In his essay "What I Believe" Tolstoy listed the principles which informed his doctrine of nonviolence: "Live at peace with all men, anger is not justified;

never resist the evildoer by force. . . . If they beat you, endure it; if they take your possessions, yield them up; if they compel you to work, work…; and Love all men and be good to them."[7]

Tolstoy tried to apply his ideas after the assassination of Alexander II when he petitioned the new tsar to forgive the murderers and not execute them. Alexander II had been one of the most benevolent tsars, freeing the serfs, signing a peace treaty after the Crimean War, and, at the time of his death, working to bring representation in parliament. However, the new tsar, Alexander III, was oppressive and controlled the press and speech.

On the home front, Tolstoy had signed over to Sonya the rights to his books written before 1881. She reprinted them and earned enough money to allow her family to live in the elegant style of aristocracy. Tolstoy wanted no royalties on books written after 1881.

Later Life

By the time Tolstoy was sixty-one, Sonya had borne five more children, two of whom died in childhood. The relationship between Sonya and Leo continued to be extremely difficult. They had fierce fights and passionate reunions. However, he lost the lightheartedness of earlier years and had become a stern prophet. She still copied his manuscripts and tried to accommodate his new habits. He preached celibacy but did not follow it. He preached vegetarianism, and she tried to share it. But she could not agree with his faith or ideas. She expressed distaste for the long lines of pilgrims who came to their house to speak with Tolstoy or ask his advice. They called themselves "Tolstoyans" because they embraced the ideas of nonviolence and protection of the masses. Leo came to abhor the wealthy lifestyle of his family, believing that property was evil.

During a famine caused by draught, Tolstoy's ideas were tested. He had given up any faith in government and felt that the only action should be love. When he and two of his daughters traveled to the drought areas, he saw the terrible results of starvation and decided he had to act rather than philosophize. He wanted to help, but he had no money of his own as he had given up the rights to his later writings. He had to turn to Sonya to ask for money and to let her know he would be gone for months. Despite her anger at his leaving, she did give him money. Leo and two of his daughters, Tanya and Masha, bought firewood and set up soup kitchens. After three months, thirty soup kitchens had been opened, feeding ten thousand people daily. Tolstoy supervised the volunteer workers and wrote articles asking the government to help with the disaster. The government did not help, and it ignored the plight of the starving. Although the articles were censored in Russia, money and volunteers came from abroad. Tolstoy's actions were admired both within and outside of Russia.

Sonya's heart was touched by the description of the poor, and she wrote letters for help which appeared in the newspapers in Russia, Europe, and America. These brought donations which overjoyed Leo. But more importantly, Sonya herself came to help. She left her life of luxury behind to handle the account books, to sew coats for freezing children, to help in the kitchens, and then to appeal for more help. Other Tolstoy children joined their efforts of help. The government still would not acknowledge the famine which had been going on for over a year. Instead, it urged priests to tell the peasants to stay away from the kitchens because Tolstoy was the Antichrist. Yet it was only Tolstoy and his workers who served food to the peasants.

The next year, 1893, the drought ended and the crops were successful. The emergency was over and Tolstoy returned to Yasnaya Polyana. He wrote another story, "Hadji Murad." Distinguished visitors came from all over the world to honor him and listen to him.

Old Age

Tolstoy continued to live a simple life, working in the fields, emptying his own chamber pot, and developing his religious ideas. One group of his followers, the Dukhobers, a group of seven thousand Orthodox Christians who were against bearing arms, were being persecuted by the State. It was a great relief when Canada offered them refuge and land. Tolstoy worked unceasingly to raise the money for their transportation. He finalized the manuscript of *Resurrection* and arranged for the profits to go to their travel expenses. *Resurrection* was read by a large audience in Russia where it awakened an awareness of exploitation of the poor by the government and the church. The government became fearful that Tolstoy's writing would encourage the poor to unite and rebel against it. To punish him, the church excommunicated Tolstoy at the age of seventy-two, claiming he was a false prophet. Massive demonstrations as well as telegrams, letters, and visitors rallied in support of Tolstoy. He responded by writing a simple article of faith which was copied and circulated and reprinted in newspapers around the world. He went further and petitioned the Tsar to institute reforms such as freedom of the press and religion, care for the poor, equal rights, and so forth. But the Tsar did not respond.

Sonya often became hysterical as she complained about Leo's ideas and about his followers. Her tirades caused him to wish to run away to a calm place where he could think. Now in his seventies, Tolstoy was weak and often ill, and so he arranged for a doctor to come live at Yasnaya Polyana. Despite his illness, Tolstoy continued to champion the poor and the oppressed. Russia was humiliated by losing the war to the Japanese in 1905, and workers were striking in many Russian cities. The country was like a tinderbox ready to explode. Meanwhile Leo and Sonya continued to fight over the copyrights of his earlier books. She wanted to keep them as additional income for her family. He wanted to give the royalties to the public. She had fits in which she threatened to kill herself, creating more stress on Leo who was ailing. His stubbornness and changing ideas created stress on her. The family was divided as siblings chose sides with their father or mother.

Leo's eightieth birthday in 1908 was a time of great celebration with two thousand telegrams arriving to wish him well. However, the battle went on between the two over control of his diaries and over his will. When he could take it no more, at age eighty-two, he decided to leave secretly at night with his doctor to somewhere far away from his home. When Sonya realized he was gone, she tried to drown herself in the icy pond, to do anything to force Leo to return.

Leo became ill on the train en route and had to be taken off and cared for at the stationmaster's house. A telegram was sent to his family at Yasnaya Polyana, letting them know of his condition. Fearing the hysteria of Sonya who had arrived post haste, they put Leo in a private railway sleeping car that was not in use. The children slipped in to say goodbye to Tolstoy, but Sonya remained in the railway station shouting, crying, feeling sorry for herself, and frustrated that they would not let her in to see him.

Tolstoy's words as he weakened were, "Searching, always keep searching." And his last words were, "Truth … I love much."[8] When he slipped into unconsciousness, the children took their mother in to say her goodbye. Tolstoy died on November 7, 1910. As the train made its way back to Yasnaya Polyana, crowds gathered along the way to honor this great Russian. He was buried in the place of the "green stick," where he had first learned that there was a secret of happiness.

Comments

In describing the death of Leo's brother Dmitri, Henri Troyat, one of Tolstoy's biographers, wrote: "There seemed to be propensity in the Tolstoy blood for swinging from good to evil, humility to pride, lechery to virtue, with unusual facility: they were all more or less creatures of extremes, lost in a world of happy medium. Only in Leo reason moderated instinct, whereas Dmitri followed his impulses to the end, however absurd their consequences."[9]

However, Tolstoy was also driven by extremes and suffered constantly from the consequences. Dostoyevsky described the same propensity for extremes as part of the Karamazov personality in *The Brothers Karamazov*.

According to Sonya, Tolstoy was always changing his mind. "Furthermore, there was not one idea in his whole arsenal that he had not contradicted at some point in his career. Sonya was not sharing the destiny of one man but of ten or twenty, all sworn enemies of each other: aristocrat jealous of his prerogatives and people's friend in peasant garb; ardent Slavophil and Westernizing pacifist; denouncer of private property and lord aggrandizing his domains; hunter and protector of animals; hearty trencherman and vegetarian; peasant-style Orthodox believer and enraged demolisher of the church; artist and contemptuous scorner of art; sensualist and ascetic. . . . This multiplicity of psychological impulses made it possible for Lyovochka to put himself inside the skin of many characters and hence to be a matchless writer of fiction, but it also complicated his partner's task."[10]

Student writing:

What is the role of suffering in human life? Refer to Tolstoy and also to your own thoughts.

Suffering is in some ways a paradoxical quality in human life: we try our hardest to avoid it, and yet there is a respect that is awarded someone who has suffered a great deal, and we even feel sometimes that it is essential to fully appreciate life or to create great art. It can be something that we carry with us forever afterwards, and often defines part of a person's character.

Leo Tolstoy (1828–1910) was a novelist who had to deal with a lot of suffering, beginning in his childhood. His mother died shortly after his birth, and his father died when he was thirteen. At this time, he was confronting his beliefs about God and faith, years before the average person does. In his later life, Tolstoy became extremely sympathetic towards the Russian serfs. He did everything he could to raise them up, and even sometimes lived like them. He also broke with the church, though he retained his faith, and was an outspoken critic of religion. These two issues put immense strain on his marriage. Dealing with the guilt from the serfs' plight, the concern and exile from religion, and a difficult marriage must have been extremely difficult. Tolstoy was a man who truly knew the meaning of suffering.

It is interesting that many of the great artists have been people with extremely difficult lives. It seems that although suffering is something terrible to have to experience and live with, it creates in us an opportunity to grow and learn, and the strongest people are those who take this opportunity and gain insight into life. – *L.S.*

Tolstoy's School for the Peasants

Tolstoy, who tried very hard to improve the conditions of the serfs, decided to start a school especially for their children. Before starting the school, he traveled through many European countries and studied their education. But in general, he was dissatisfied with what he saw. He wanted a school in which everybody could enter and leave freely. He did not believe that education should form the character and improve the morals of the students. He felt that these were matters of family life. His students were taught reading, writing, grammar, history, drawing, music, mathematics, natural science and religion.

The education provided was free and therefore accessible to everyone. Since his students were not forced to learn anything, but everything had to come out of their own free will, the children loved his school and often stayed longer than the regular school day. Even though his theories of education were strongly disagreed with during his own times, since then there has been a tendency to acclaim him a brilliant innovator and one of the most significant of educational reformers. – *G.M.*

Excerpt from "The Religious Philosophy of Leo Tolstoy"

Tolstoy was always possessed of a religious questioning that intensified as he grew older. As a young man, he was so terrified of death that he rejected life because it could only end in death. Life seemed a cruel trick that had been played on him. Did life, he asked, have any meaning which inevitable death did not destroy? To answer this question and to relieve his mental and spiritual anguish, Tolstoy turned to the study of religion. In Orthodox Christianity he found no answer. He called its teachings hollow and found no guidance in its words. But in the pure teachings of Christ he found answers. The purpose of life was to develop the self to its highest nature, to recognize the kinship of men's consciousness, and to do good through the power of reason.

Tolstoy developed a theory of the nature of man. Man consisted of an animal personality contained in time and space, and a reasonable consciousness, the self, which was immortal. The reasonable consciousness was the same for all men, and it was the extent to which man's animal personality was subjected to it that made men unique. The animal personality must be subject to reason. God existed both in man and outside of him. The self and God were virtually indistinguishable. The self in each man was also the Son of God. The self was in consciousness, but consciousness will pass as the self will not. This seems contradictory, but he may be emphasizing the divinity of the self. There was another infinite consciousness to which the highest self of everyone was linked. The self is also the individual character; it existed beyond the personality. The reasonable consciousness, the self, the ego, like the Logos, was at the beginning and will always exist. Life must be full of self-renunciation and love of God. A man must not live for himself, his family, or his nation, but for and through a love of all men. – M.M.

The following story is one I have used every year. It is a simple and profound story.

"What Men Live By" [11]

A shoemaker named Simon, who had neither house nor land of his own, lived with his wife and children in a peasant's hut and earned his living by his work. Work was cheap, but bread was dear, and what he earned he spent for food. The man and his wife had but one sheepskin coat between them for winter wear, and even that was torn to tatters, and this was the second year he had been wanting to buy sheepskins for a new coat. Before winter Simon saved up a little money: a three-ruble note lay hidden in his wife's box, and five rubles and twenty kopeks were owed him by customers in the village.

So one morning he prepared to go to the village to buy the sheepskins. He put on over his shirt his wife's wadded nankeen jacket, and over that he put his own cloth coat. He took the three-ruble note in his pocket, cut himself a stick to serve as a staff, and after breakfast started off. "I'll collect the five rubles that are due to me," thought he, "add the three I have got, and that will be enough to buy sheepskins for the winter coat."

He came to the village and called at a peasant's hut, but the man was not at home. The peasant's wife promised that the money should be paid next week, but she could not pay it herself. Then Simon called on another peasant, but this one swore he had no money and could pay only twenty kopeks which he owed for a pair of boots Simon had mended. Simon then tried to buy the sheepskins on credit, but the dealer would not trust him.

"Bring your money," said he. "Then you may have your pick of the skins. We know what debt-collecting is like." So all the business the shoemaker did was to get the twenty kopeks for boots he had mended and to take a pair of felt boots a peasant gave him to sole with leather.

Simon felt downhearted. He spent the twenty kopeks on vodka, and started homewards without having bought any skins. That morning he had felt the frost; but now, after drinking the vodka, he felt warm, even without a sheepskin coat. He trudged along, striking his stick on the frozen earth with one hand, swinging the felt boots with the other, and talking to himself.

"I'm quite warm," said he, "though I have no sheepskin coat. I've had a drop, and it runs through all my veins. I need no sheepskins. I go along and don't worry about anything. That's the sort of man I am! What do I care? I can live without sheepskins. I don't need them. My wife will fret, to be sure. And, true enough, it is a shame; one works all day long, and then does not get paid. Stop a bit! If you don't bring that money along, sure enough I'll skin you, blessed if I don't. How's that? He pays twenty kopeks at a time! What can I do with twenty kopeks? Drink it—that's all one can do! Hard up, he says he is! So he may be—but what about me? You have a house, and cattle, and everything; I've only what I stand up in! You have corn of your own growing; I have to buy every grain. Do what I will. I must spend three rubles every week for bread alone. I come home and find the bread all used up, and I have to fork out another ruble and a half. So just pay up what you owe, and no nonsense about it!"

By this time he had nearly reached the shrine at the bend of the road. Looking up, he saw something whitish behind the shrine. The daylight was fading, and the shoemaker peered at the thing without being able to make out what it was. "There was no white stone here before. Can it be an ox? It's not like an ox. It has a head like a man, but it's too white; and what could a man be doing there?"

He came closer, so that it was clearly visible. To his surprise it really was a man, alive or dead, sitting naked, leaning motionless against the shrine. Terror seized the shoemaker, and he thought: "Someone has killed him, stripped him, and left him there. If I meddle I shall surely get into trouble."

So the shoemaker went on. He passed in front of the shrine so that he could not see the man. When he had gone some way, he looked back, and saw that the man was no longer leaning against the shrine, but was moving as if looking towards him. The shoemaker felt more frightened than before, and thought: "Shall I go back to him, or shall I go on? If I go near him something dreadful may happen. Who knows who the fellow is? He has not come here for any good. If I go near him he may jump up and throttle me, and there will be no getting away. Or if not, he'd still be a burden on one's hands. What could I do with a naked man? I couldn't give him my last clothes. Heaven only help me to get away!"

So the shoemaker hurried on, leaving the shrine behind him—when suddenly his conscience smote him, and he stopped in the road. "What are you doing, Simon?" said he to himself. "The man may be dying of want, and you slip past afraid. Have you grown so rich as to be afraid of robbers? Ah, Simon, shame on you!" So he turned back and went up to the man.

Simon approached the stranger, looked at him, and saw that he was a young man, fit, with no bruises on his body, only evidently freezing and frightened, and he sat there leaning back without looking up at Simon, as if too faint to lift his eyes. Simon went close to him, and then the man seemed to wake up. Turning his head, he opened his eyes and looked into Simon's face. That one look was enough to make Simon fond of the man. He threw the felt boots on the ground, undid his sash, laid it on the boots, and took off his cloth coat.

"It's not a time for talking," said he. "Come, put this coat on at once!" And Simon took the man by the elbows and helped him to rise. As he stood there, Simon saw that his body was clean and in good condition, his hands and feet shapely, and his face good and kind. He threw his coat over the man's shoulders, but the man could not find the sleeves. Simon guided his arms into them, and drawing the coat well on, wrapped it closely about him, tying the sash round the man's waist.

Simon even took off his torn cap to put it on the man's head, but then his own head felt cold, and he thought: "I'm quite bald, while he has long curly hair." So he put his cap on his own head again. "It will be better to give him something for his feet," thought he; and he made the man sit down and helped him to put on the felt boots, saying, "There, friend, now move about and warm yourself. Other matters can be settled later on. Can you walk?"

The man stood up and looked kindly at Simon, but could not say a word.

"Why don't you speak?" said Simon. "It's too cold to stay here, we must be getting home. There now, take my stick, and if you're feeling weak, lean on that. Now step out!"

The man started walking, and moved easily, not lagging behind. As they went along, Simon asked him, "And where do you belong to?"

"I'm not from these parts."

"I thought as much. I know the folks hereabouts. But, how did you come to be there by the shrine?"

"I cannot tell."

"Has some one been ill-treating you?"

"No one has ill-treated me. God has punished me."

"Of course God rules all. Still, you'll have to find food and shelter somewhere. Where do you want to go to?"

"It is all the same to me."

Simon was amazed. The man did not look like a rogue, and he spoke gently, but yet he gave no account of himself. Still Simon thought: "Who knows what may have happened?" And he said to the stranger, "Well then, come home with me, and at least warm yourself awhile."

So Simon walked towards his home, and the stranger kept up with him, walking at his side. The wind had risen and Simon felt it cold under his shirt. He was getting over his tipsiness by now, and began to feel the frost. He went along sniffling and wrapping his wife's coat round him, and he thought to himself: "There now—talk about sheepskins! I went out for sheepskins and come home without even a coat to my back, and what is more, I'm bringing a naked man along with me. Matryona won't be pleased!" And when he thought of his wife he felt sad; but when he looked at the stranger and remembered how he had looked up at him at the shrine, his heart was glad.

Simon's wife had everything ready early that day. She had cut wood, brought water, fed the children, eaten her own meal, and now she sat thinking. She wondered when she ought to make bread: now or tomorrow? There was still a large piece left. "If Simon has had some dinner in town," thought she, "and does not eat much for supper, the bread will last out another day." She weighed the piece of bread in her hand again and again, and thought: "I won't make any more today. We have only enough flour left to bake one batch. We can manage to make this last out till Friday."

So Matryona put away the bread and sat down at the table to patch her husband's shirt. While she worked she thought how her husband was buying skins for a winter coat. "If only the dealer does not cheat him. My good man is much too simple; he cheats nobody, but any child can take him in. Eight rubles is a lot of money — he should get a good coat at that price. Not tanned skins, but still a proper winter coat. How difficult it was last winter to get on without a warm coat. I could neither get down to the river, nor go out anywhere. When he went out he put on all we had, and there was nothing left for me. He did not start very early today, but still it's time he was back. I only hope he has not gone on the spree!"

Hardly had Matryona thought this, when steps were heard on the threshold, and someone entered. Matryona stuck her needle into her work and went out into the passage. There she saw two men: Simon, and with him a man without a hat and wearing felt boots. Matryona noticed at once that her husband smelt of spirits. "There now, he has been drinking," thought she. And when she saw that he was coatless, had only her jacket on, brought no parcel, stood there silent, and seemed ashamed, her heart was ready to break with disappointment. "He has drunk the money," thought she, "and has been on the spree with some good-for-nothing fellow whom he has brought home with him."

Matryona let them pass into the hut, followed them in, and saw that the stranger was a young, slight man, wearing her husband's coat. There was no shirt to be seen under it, and he had no hat. Having entered, he stood, neither moving, nor raising his eyes, and Matryona thought: "He must be a bad man — he's afraid."

Matryona frowned, and stood beside the oven looking to see what they would do. Simon took off his cap and sat down on the bench as if things were all right. "Come, Matryona. If supper is ready, let us have some."

Matryona muttered something to herself and did not move, but stayed where she was by the oven. She looked first at the one and then at the other of them, and only shook her head. Simon saw that his wife was annoyed, but tried to pass it off. Pretending not to notice anything, he took the stranger by the arm. "Sit down, friend," said he, "and let us have some supper." The stranger sat down on the bench.

"Haven't you cooked anything for us?" said Simon.

Matryona's anger boiled over. "I've cooked, but not for you. It seems to me you have drunk your wits away. You went to buy a sheepskin coat, but come home without so much as the coat you had on, and bring a naked vagabond home with you. I have no supper for drunkards like you."

"That's enough, Matryona. Don't wag your tongue without reason. You had better ask what sort of man—"

"And you tell me what you've done with the money?"

Simon found the pocket of the jacket, drew out the three-ruble note, and unfolded it.

"Here is the money. Trifonof did not pay, but promises to pay soon."

Matryona got still angrier; he had bought no sheepskins, but had put his only coat on some naked fellow and had even brought him to their house. She snatched up the note from the table, took it to put away in safety, and said, "I have no supper for you. We can't feed all the naked drunkards in the world."

"There now, Matryona, hold your tongue a bit. First hear what a man has to say—"

"Much wisdom I shall hear from a drunken fool. I was right in not wanting to marry you—a drunkard. The linen my mother gave me you drank; and now you've been to buy a coat—and have drunk it, too!"

Simon tried to explain to his wife that he had spent only twenty kopeks; he tried to tell her how he had found the man—but Matryona would not let him get a word in. She talked nineteen to the dozen, and dragged in things that had happened ten years before. Matryona talked and talked, and at last she flew at Simon and seized him by the sleeve. "Give me my jacket. It is the only one I have, and you must needs take it from me and wear it yourself. Give it here, you mangy dog, and may the devil take you."

Simon began to pull off the jacket, and turned a sleeve of it inside out; Matryona seized the jacket and it burst its seams. She snatched it up, threw it over her head and went to the door. She meant to go out, but stopped undecided—she wanted to work off her anger, but she also wanted to learn what sort of a man the stranger was.

Matryona stopped and said, "If he were a good man, he would not be naked. Why, he hasn't even a shirt on him. If he were all right, you would say where you came across the fellow."

"That's just what I am trying to tell you," said Simon. "As I came to the shrine I saw him sitting all naked and frozen. It isn't quite the weather to sit about naked! God sent me to him, or he would have perished. What was I to do? How do we know what may have happened to him? So I took him, clothed him, and brought him along. Don't be so angry, Matryona. It is a sin. Remember, we all must die one day."

Angry words rose to Matryona's lips, but she looked at the stranger and was silent. He sat on the edge of the bench, motionless, his hands folded on his knees, his head drooping on his breast, his eyes closed, and his brows knit as if in pain.

Matryona was silent, and Simon said, "Matryona, have you no love of God?"

Matryona heard these words, and as she looked at the stranger, suddenly her heart softened towards him. She came back from the door, and going to the oven she got out the supper. Setting a cup on the table, she poured out some *kvas*. Then she brought out the last piece of bread and set out a knife and spoons. "Eat, if you want to," said she.

Simon drew the stranger to the table. "Take your place, young man," said he. Simon cut the bread, crumbled it into the broth, and they began to eat.

Matryona sat at the corner of the table resting her head on her hand and looking at the stranger. And Matryona was touched with pity for the stranger and began to feel fond of him. And at once the stranger's face lit up; his brows were no longer bent, he raised his eyes and smiled at Matryona.

When they had finished supper, the woman cleared away the things and began questioning the stranger. "Where are you from?" said she.

"I am not from these parts."

"But how did you come to be on the road?"

"I may not tell."

"Did some one rob you?"

"God punished me."

"And you were lying there naked?"

"Yes, naked and freezing. Simon saw me and had pity on me. He took off his coat, put it on me and brought me here. And you have fed me, given me drink, and shown pity on me. God will reward you!"

Matryona rose, took from the window Simon's old shirt she had been patching, and gave it to the stranger. She also brought out a pair of trousers for him. "There," said she, "I see you have no shirt. Put this on, and lie down where you please, in the loft or on the oven." The stranger took off the coat, put on the shirt, and lay down in the loft.

Matryona put out the candle, took the coat, and climbed to where her husband lay. Matryona drew the skirts of the coat over her and lay down, but could not sleep; she could not get the stranger out of her mind. When she remembered that he had eaten their last piece of bread and that there was none for tomorrow, and thought of the shirt and trousers she had given away, she felt grieved; but when she remembered how he had smiled, her heart was glad.

Long did Matryona lie awake, and she noticed that Simon also was awake—he drew the coat towards him. "Simon!"

"Well?"

"You have had the last of the bread, and I have not put any to rise. I don't know what we shall do tomorrow. Perhaps I can borrow some of neighbor Martha."

"If we're alive we shall find something to eat."

The woman lay still awhile, and then said, "He seems a good man, but why does he not tell us who he is?"

"I suppose he has his reasons."

"Simon!"

"Well?"

"We give; but why does nobody give us anything?"

Simon did not know what to say, so he only said, "Let us stop talking," and turned over and went to sleep.

In the morning Simon awoke. The children were still asleep; his wife had gone to the neighbor's to borrow some bread. The stranger alone was sitting on the bench, dressed in the old shirt and trousers, and looking upwards. His face was brighter than it had been the day before.

Simon said to him, "Well, friend, the belly wants bread, and the naked body clothes. One has to work for a living. What work do you know?"

"I do not know any."

This surprised Simon, but he said, "Men who want to learn can learn anything."

"Men work, and I will work also."

"What is your name?"

"Michael."

"Well, Michael, if you don't wish to talk about yourself, that is your own affair; but you'll have to earn a living for yourself. If you will work as I tell you, I will give you food and shelter."

"May God reward you! I will learn. Show me what to do."

Simon took yarn, put it round his thumb and began to twist it. "It is easy enough — see!"

Michael watched him, put some yarn round his own thumb in the same way, caught the knack, and twisted the yarn also. Then Simon showed him how to wax the thread. This also Michael mastered. Next Simon showed him how to twist the bristle in, and how to sew, and this, too, Michael learned at once. Whatever Simon showed him he understood at once, and after three days he worked as if he had sewn boots all his life. He worked without stopping and ate little. When work was over he sat silently, looking upwards. He hardly went into the street, spoke only when necessary, and neither joked nor laughed. They never saw him smile, except that first evening when Matryona had given them supper.

Day by day and week by week the year went round. Michael lived and worked with Simon. His fame spread till people said that no one sewed boots so neatly and strongly as Simon's workman, Michael; and from all the district round people came to Simon for their boots, and he began to be well off.

One winter day, as Simon and Michael sat working, a carriage on sledge-runners, with three horses and with bells, drove up to the hut. They looked out of the window; the carriage stopped at their door, a fine servant jumped down from the box and opened the door. A gentleman in a fur coat got out and walked up to Simon's hut. Up jumped Matryona and opened the door wide. The gentleman stooped to enter the hut, and when he drew himself up again his head nearly reached the ceiling, and he seemed quite to fill his end of the room.

Simon rose, bowed, and looked at the gentleman with astonishment. He had never seen anyone like him. Simon himself was lean, Michael was thin, and Matryona was dry as a bone, but this man was like someone from another world: red-faced, burly, with a neck like a bull's, and looking altogether as if he were cast in iron.

The gentleman puffed, threw off his fur coat, sat down on the bench, and said, "Which of you is the master bootmaker?"

"I am, your Excellency," said Simon, coming forward.

Then the gentleman shouted to his lad, "Hey, Fedka, bring the leather!" The servant ran in, bringing a parcel.

The gentleman took the parcel and put it on the table. "Untie it," said he. The lad untied it. The gentleman pointed to the leather. "Look here, shoemaker," said he. "Do you see this leather?"

"Yes, your Honor."

"But do you know what sort of leather it is?"

Simon felt the leather and said, "It is good leather."

"Good, indeed! Why, you fool, you never saw such leather before in your life. It's German, and cost twenty rubles."

Simon was frightened, and said, "Where should I ever see leather like that?"

"Just so! Now, can you make it into boots for me?"

"Yes, your Excellency, I can."

Then the gentleman shouted at him, "You can, can you? Well, remember whom you are to make them for and what the leather is. You must make me boots that will wear for a year, neither losing shape nor coming unsewn. If you can do it, take the leather and cut it up; but if you can't, say so. I warn you now if your boots become unsewn or lose shape within a year, I will have you put in prison. If they don't burst or lose shape for a year I will pay you ten rubles for your work."

Simon was frightened, and did not know what to say. He glanced at Michael and nudging him with his elbow, whispered, "Shall I take the work?"

Michael nodded his head as if to say, "Yes, take it."

Simon did as Michael advised, and undertook to make boots that would not lose shape or split for a whole year. Calling his servant, the gentleman told him to pull the boot off his left leg, which he stretched out. "Take my measure!" said he.

Simon stitched a paper measure seventeen inches long, smoothed it out, knelt down, wiped his hands well on his apron so as not to soil the gentleman's sock, and began to measure. He measured the sole, and round the instep, and began to measure the calf of the leg, but the paper was too short. The calf of the leg was as thick as a beam. "Mind you don't make it too tight in the leg."

Simon stitched on another strip of paper. The gentleman twitched his toes about in his sock, looking round at those in the hut, and as he did so he noticed Michael.

"Whom have you there?" asked he.

"That is my workman. He will sew the boots."

"Mind," said the gentleman to Michael, "remember to make them so that they will last me a year."

Simon also looked at Michael, and saw that Michael was not looking at the gentleman, but was gazing into the corner behind the gentleman, as if he saw someone there. Michael looked and looked, and suddenly he smiled, and his face became brighter.

"What are you grinning at, you fool?" thundered the gentleman. "You had better look to it that the boots are ready in time."

"They shall be ready in good time," said Michael.

"Mind it is so," said the gentleman, and he put on his boots, wrapped his fur coat round him, and went to the door. But he forgot to stoop and struck his head against the lintel. He swore and rubbed his head. Then he took his seat in the carriage and drove away.

When he had gone, Simon said, "There's a figure of a man for you! You could not kill him with a mallet. He almost knocked out the lintel, but little harm it did him."

And Matryona said, "Living as he does, how should he not grow strong? Death itself can't touch such a rock as that."

Then Simon said to Michael, "Well, we have taken the work, but we must see we don't get into trouble over it. The leather is dear, and the gentleman hot-tempered. We must make no mistakes. Come, your eye is truer and your hands have become nimbler than mine, so you take this measure and cut out the boots. I will finish off the sewing of the vamps."

Michael did as he was told. He took the leather, spread it out on the table, folded it in two, took a knife and began to cut. Matryona came and watched him cutting, and was surprised to see how he was doing it. Matryona was accustomed to seeing boots made, and she looked and saw that Michael was not cutting the leather for boots, but was cutting it round. She wished to say something, but she thought to herself: "Perhaps I do not understand how gentleman's boots should be made. I suppose Michael knows more about it — and I won't interfere."

When Michael had cut up the leather, he took a thread and began to sew not with two ends, as boots are sewn, but with a single end, as for soft slippers. Again Matryona wondered, but again she did not interfere. Michael sewed on steadily till noon. Then Simon rose for dinner, looked around, and saw that Michael had made slippers out of the gentleman's leather.

"Ah," groaned Simon, and he thought: "How is it that Michael, who has been with me a whole year and never made a mistake before, should do such a dreadful thing? The gentleman ordered high boots, welted, with whole fronts, and Michael has made soft slippers with single soles, and has wasted the leather. What am I to say to the gentleman? I can never replace leather such as this."

And he said to Michael, "What are you doing, friend? You have ruined me! You know the gentleman ordered high boots, but see what you have made!"

Hardly had he begun to rebuke Michael, when "rat-tat" went the iron ring that hung at the door. Someone was knocking. They looked out of the window; a man had come on horseback, and was fastening his horse. They opened the door, and the servant who had been with the gentleman came in.

"Good day," said he.

"Good day," replied Simon. "What can we do for you?"

"My mistress has sent me about the boots."

"What about the boots?"

"Why, my master no longer needs them. He is dead."

"Is it possible?"

"He did not live to get home after leaving you, but died in the carriage. When we reached home and the servants came to help him alight, he rolled over like a sack. He was dead already, and so stiff that he could hardly be got out of the carriage. My mistress sent me here, saying, 'Tell the bootmaker that the gentleman who ordered boots of him and left the leather for them no longer needs the boots, but that he must quickly make soft slippers for the corpse. Wait till they are ready and bring them back with you.' That is why I have come."

Michael gathered up the remnants of the leather, rolled them up, took the soft slippers he had made, slapped them together, wiped them down with his apron, and handed them and the roll of leather to the servant, who took them and said, "Goodbye, masters, and good day to you!"

Another year passed, and another, and Michael was now living his sixth year with Simon. He lived as before. He went nowhere, only spoke when necessary, and had only smiled twice in all those years—once when Matryona had given him food and a second time when the gentleman had been in their hut. Simon was more than pleased with his workman. He never now asked him where he came from, and only feared lest Michael should go away.

They were all at home one day. Matryona was putting iron pots in the oven; the children were running along the benches and looking out of the window; Simon was sewing at one window, and Michael was fastening on a heel at the other.

One of the boys ran along the bench to Michael, leant on his shoulder, and looked out of the window. "Look, Uncle Michael! There is a lady with little girls! She seems to be coming here. And one of the girls is lame." When the boy said that, Michael dropped his work, turned to the window, and looked out into the street. Simon was surprised. Michael never used to look out into the street, but now he pressed against the window, staring at something. Simon also looked out, and saw that a well-dressed woman was really coming to his hut, leading by the hand two little girls in fur coats and woolen shawls. The girls could hardly be told one from the other, except that one of them was crippled in her left leg and walked with a limp.

The woman stepped onto the porch and entered the passage. Feeling about for the entrance she found the latch, which she lifted, and opened the door. She let the two girls go in first and followed them into the hut.

"Good day, good folk!"

"Pray come in," said Simon. "What can we do for you?"

The woman sat down by the table. The two little girls pressed close to her knees, afraid of the people in the hut. "I want leather shoes made for these two little girls for spring."

"We can do that. We never have made such small shoes, but we can make them; either welted or turnover shoes, linen lined. My man, Michael, is a master at the work."

Simon glanced at Michael and saw that he had left his work and was sitting with his eyes fixed on the little girls. Simon was surprised. It was true the girls were pretty, with black eyes, plump, and rosy-cheeked, and they wore nice kerchiefs and fur coats, but still Simon could not understand why Michael should look at them like that—just as if he had known them before. He was puzzled, but went on talking with the woman, and arranging the price. Having fixed it, he prepared the measure. The woman lifted the lame girl on to her lap and said, "Take two measures from this little girl. Make one shoe for the lame foot and three for the sound one. They both have the same size feet. They are twins."

Simon took the measure and, speaking of the lame girl, said, "How did it happen to her? She is such a pretty girl. Was she born so?"

"No, her mother crushed her leg."

Then Matryona joined in. She wondered who this woman was, and whose the children were, so she said, "Are not you their mother then?"

"No, my good woman; I am neither their mother nor any relation to them. They were quite strangers to me, but I adopted them."

"They are not your children and yet you are so fond of them?"

"How can I help being fond of them? I fed them both at my own breasts. I had a child of my own, but God took him. I was not so fond of him as I now am of them."

"Then whose children are they?"

The woman, having begun talking, told them the whole story. "It is about six years since their parents died, both in one week: their father was buried on the Tuesday, and their mother died on the Friday. These orphans were born three days after their father's death, and their mother did not live another day. My husband and I were then living as peasants in the village. We were neighbors of theirs, our yard being next to theirs. Their father was a lonely man, a woodcutter in the forest. When felling trees one day, they let one fall on him. It fell across his body and crushed his bowels out. They hardly got him home before his soul went to God, and that same week his wife gave birth to twins—these little girls. She was poor and alone; she had no one, young or old, with her. Alone she gave them birth, and alone she met her death.

"The next morning I went to see her, but when I entered the hut, she, poor thing, was already stark and cold. In dying she had rolled on to this child and crushed her leg. The village folk came to the hut, washed the body, laid her out, made a coffin, and buried her. They were good folk. The babies were left alone. What was to be done with them? I was the only woman there who had a baby at the time. I was nursing my first-born—eight weeks old. So I took them for a time. The peasants came together and thought and thought what to do with them; and at last they said to me, 'For the present, Mary, you had better keep the girls, and later on we will arrange what to do for them.'

"So I nursed the sound one at my breast, but at first I did not feed this crippled one. I did not suppose she would live. But then I thought to myself: why should the poor innocent suffer? I pitied her and began to feed her. And so I fed my own boy and these two—the three of them—at my own breast. I was young and strong, and had good food, and God gave me so much milk that at times it even overflowed. I used sometimes to feed two at a time, while the third was waiting. When one had enough I nursed the third. And God so ordered it that these grew up, while my own was buried before he was two years old. And I had no more children, though we prospered.

"Now my husband is working for the corn merchant at the mill. The pay is good, and we are well off. But I have no children of my own, and how lonely I should be without these little girls! How can I help loving them! They are the joy of my life!" She pressed the lame little girl to her with one hand, while with the other she wiped the tears from her cheeks.

And Matryona sighed, and said, "The proverb is true that says, 'One may live without father or mother, but one cannot live without God.'"

So they talked together, when suddenly the whole hut was lighted up as though by summer lightning from the corner where Michael sat. They all looked towards him and saw him sitting, his hands folded on his knees, gazing upwards and smiling.

The woman went away with the girls. Michael rose from the bench, put down his work and took off his apron. Then, bowing low to Simon and his wife, he said, "Farewell, masters. God has forgiven me. I ask your forgiveness, too, for anything done amiss."

And they saw that a light shone from Michael. And Simon rose, bowed down to Michael, and said, "I see, Michael, that you are no common man, and I can neither keep you nor question you. Only tell me this: how is it that when I found you and brought you home, you were gloomy, and when my wife gave you food you smiled at her and became brighter? Then when the gentleman came to order the boots, you smiled again and became brighter still? And now, when this woman brought the little girls, you smiled a third time, and have become as bright as day? Tell me, Michael, why does your face shine so, and why did you smile those three times?"

And Michael answered, "Light shines from me because I have been punished, but now God has pardoned me. And I smiled three times, because God sent me to learn three truths, and I have learnt them. One I learnt when your wife pitied me, and that is why I smiled the first time. The second I learnt when the rich man ordered the boots, and then I smiled again. And now, when I saw those little girls, I learnt the third and last truth, and I smiled the third time."

And Simon said, "Tell me, Michael, what did God punish you for? and what were the three truths? that I, too, may know them."

And Michael answered, "God punished me for disobeying Him. I was an angel in heaven and disobeyed God. God sent me to fetch a woman's soul. I flew to earth, and saw a sick woman lying alone, who had just given birth to twin girls.

They moved feebly at their mother's side, but she could not lift them to her breast. When she saw me, she understood that God had sent me for her soul, and she wept and said, 'Angel of God! My husband has just been buried, killed by a falling tree. I have neither sister, nor aunt, nor mother: no one to care for my orphans. Do not take my soul! Let me nurse my babes, feed them, and set them on their feet before I die. Children cannot live without father or mother.' And I hearkened to her. I placed one child at her breast and gave the other into her arms, and returned to the Lord in heaven. I flew to the Lord, and said, 'I could not take the soul of the mother. Her husband was killed by a tree; the woman has twins, and prays that her soul may not be taken. She says, "Let me nurse and feed my children, and set them on their feet. Children cannot live without father or mother." I have not taken her soul.'

"And God said, 'Go. Take the mother's soul, and learn three truths. Learn: What dwells in man, What is not given to man, and What men live by. When thou has learnt these things, thou shalt return to heaven.' So I flew again to earth and took the mother's soul. The babes dropped from her breasts. Her body rolled over on the bed and crushed one babe, twisting its leg. I rose above the village, wishing to take her soul to God; but a wind seized me, and my wings drooped and dropped off. Her soul rose alone to God, while I fell to earth by the roadside."

And Simon and Matryona understood who it was that had lived with them, and whom they had clothed and fed. And they wept with awe and with joy.

And the angel said, "I was alone in the field, naked. I had never known human needs, cold and hunger, till I became a man. I was famished, frozen, and did not know what to do. I saw, near the field I was in, a shrine built for God, and I went to it hoping to find shelter. But the shrine was locked, and I could not enter. So I sat down behind the shrine to shelter myself at least from the wind. Evening drew on. I was hungry, frozen, and in pain. Suddenly I heard a man coming along the road. He carried a pair of boots, and was talking to himself. For the first time since I became a man I saw the mortal face of a man, and his face seemed terrible to me and I turned from it. And I heard the man talking to himself of how to cover his body from the cold in winter, and how to feed wife and children. And I thought: "I am perishing of cold and hunger, and here is a man thinking only of how to clothe himself and his wife, and how to get bread for themselves. He cannot help me. When the man saw me he frowned and became still more terrible, and passed me by on the other side. I despaired, but suddenly I heard him coming back. I looked up and did not recognize the same man; before, I had seen death in his face; but now he was alive, and I recognized in him the presence of God. He came up to me, clothed me, took me with him, and brought me to his home.

"I entered the house; a woman came to meet us and began to speak. The woman was still more terrible than the man had been; the spirit of death came from her mouth; I could not breathe for the stench of death that spread around her. She wished to drive me out into the cold, and I knew that if she did so she would die. Suddenly her husband spoke to her of God, and the woman changed at once.

And when she brought me food and looked at me, I glanced at her and saw that death no longer dwelt in her; she had become alive, and in her, too, I saw God.

"Then I remembered the first lesson God had set me: 'Learn what dwells in man.' And I understood that in man dwells Love! I was glad that God had already begun to show me what He had promised, and I smiled for the first time. But I had not yet learnt all. I did not yet know What is not given to man, and What men live by.

"I lived with you, and a year passed. A man came to order boots that should wear for a year without losing shape or cracking. I looked at him, and suddenly, behind his shoulder, I saw my comrade—the angel of death. None but me saw that angel; but I knew him, and knew that before the sun set he would take that rich man's soul. And I thought to myself: 'The man is making preparations for a year, and does not know that he will die before evening.' And I remembered God's second saying, 'Learn what is not given to man.' What dwells in man I already knew. Now I learnt What is not given him. It is not given to man to know his own needs. And I smiled for the second time. I was glad to have seen my comrade angel—glad also that God had revealed to me the second saying.

"But I still did not know all. I did not know What men live by. And I lived on, waiting till God should reveal to me the last lesson. In the sixth year came the girl-twins with the woman; and I recognized the girls, and heard how they had been kept alive. Having heard the story, I thought: 'Their mother besought me for the children's sake, and I believed her when she said that children cannot live without father or mother; but a stranger has nursed them and has brought them up.' And when the woman showed her love for the children that were not her own, and wept over them, I saw in her the living God and understood What men live by. And I knew that God had revealed to me the last lesson and had forgiven my sin. And then I smiled for the third time."

And the angel's body was bare, and he was clothed in light so that eye could not look on him; and his voice grew louder, as though it came not from him but from heaven above. And the angel said, "I have learnt that all men live not by care for themselves but by love. It was not given to the mother to know what her children needed for their life. Nor was it given to the rich man to know what he himself needed. Nor is it given to any man to know whether, when evening comes, he will need boots for his body or slippers for his corpse.

"I remained alive when I was a man, not by care of myself, but because love was present in a passerby, and because he and his wife pitied and loved me. The orphans remained alive not because of their mother's care, but because there was love in the heart of a woman, a stranger to them, who pitied and loved them. And all men live not by the thought they spend on their own welfare, but because love exists in man.

"I knew before that God gave life to men and desires that they should live; now I understood more than that. I understood that God does not wish men to live apart, and therefore He does not reveal to them what each one needs for himself;

but He wishes them to live united, and therefore reveals to each of them what is necessary for all.

"I have now understood that though it seems to men that they live by care for themselves, in truth it is love alone by which they live. He who has love is in God, and God is in him, for God is love."

And the angel sang praise to God, so that the hut trembled at his voice. The roof opened, and a column of fire rose from earth to heaven. Simon and his wife and children fell to the ground. Wings appeared upon the angel's shoulders, and he rose into the heavens. And when Simon came to himself the hut stood as before, and there was no one in it but his own family.

Endnotes

1. Sara Newton Carroll, *The Search: A Biography of Leo Tolstoy* (New York: Harper & Row, 1973), frontispiece.
2. Leo Tolstoy, *Sevastopol* (Ann Arbor, MI: University of Michigan Press, 1996), xiii.
3. Carroll, *The Search*, p. 95.
4. Ibid., p. 96.
5. As printed in Carroll, *The Search*, p. 109.
6. Anne Edwards, *The Life of Countess Tolstoy* (New York: Simon and Schuster, 1981), p. 229.
7. Carroll, *The Search*, pp. 111–112.
8. Ibid., p. 147.
9. Henri Troyat, *Tolstoy* (New York: Dell, 1965), p. 169.
10. Ibid., p. 550.
11. This version of "Love, What Men Live By" appears in *The Works of Leo Tolstoi* (New York: Walter J. Black, Inc., 1928), pp. 4–18. This story sometimes has the title "Love" and at other times "What Men Live By."

Bibliography

Carroll, Sara Newton. *The Search: A Biography of Leo Tolstoy*, New York: Harper & Row, 1973.

De Courcel, Martine. *Tolstoy, The Ultimate Reconciliation*, New York: Charles Scribner's Sons, 1980.

Edwards, Anne. *The Life of Countess Tolstoy*, New York: Simon and Schuster, 1981.

Tolstoy, Leo. *Anna Karenina*, New York: Modern Library, 1950.

_____. *Master and Man and Other Stories*, New York: Penguin, 1979.

_____. *Sevastopol*, Ann Arbor, MI: University of Michigan Press, 1961.

Troyat, Henri. *Tolstoy*, New York: Dell, 1965.

Wasiolek, Edward. *Tolstoy's Major Fiction*, Chicago: University of Chicago Press, 1978.

CHAPTER 9

Fyodor Mikhailovich Dostoyevsky (1821–1881)

If one wants to understand Russia and the Russian people, one must read Dostoyevsky. There is no better source. He is Russia.[1]

– Manuel Komroff

The life and work of Dostoyevsky are inseparable. He "lived in literature." It was his life's concern and his tragic fate. In all of his works he resolved the enigma of his personality; he spoke only of those things which he himself had personally experienced. Dostoyevsky was always drawn to confession as an artistic form. His works unfold before us as one vast confession, as the integral revelation of his universal spirit.[2]

– Mochulsky

Childhood

Fyodor Mikhailovich Dostoyevsky was born in Moscow on October 30, 1921. His brother Mikhail was one year older, and his sister Varvara one year younger. His grandfather was a priest. His father was a physician, a temperamental, suspicious, and, at times, depressed man, given to outbursts which tyrannized the family. His mother, a gentle, sickly woman, came from a merchant family. This patriarchal family lived in isolation, as no guests visited, nor did they do visiting. There was a lonely feeling in the family interaction.

When Dostoyevsky was three years old, his nanny taught him to pray. His father took him on long walks to the Trinity-Saint Sergius Monastery. Through these experiences, the Orthodox Church left a strong impression on him.

Dostoyevsky loved literature from an early age, and at ten, he developed a passionate interest in Schiller's work. He and his brother Mikhail idolized sentimental heroes and medieval knights, and they knew Pushkin by heart. Fyodor was a voracious reader of histories and narratives, and with his excellent memory, he knew the entire Bible.

When Dostoyevsky was sixteen, his mother died. Her death had dire consequences for the children as their father, who was already tyrannical and cold-hearted, retreated into his sullenness, began to drink, squander money, live a low life, and torture his peasants. He moved to their country estate and enrolled Fyodor in the School of Engineering in St. Petersburg. Fyodor had a rather introspective personality and did not get along well with classmates. He hated the strict discipline and the depressing atmosphere of the school, but he found solace in literature.

In his literary enthusiasm he delved into the works of the Romantic writers. "Man is the means through which the sublime will become manifest in humanity; but the body, the pitcher, will sooner or later be smashed to pieces."[3]

At age seventeen on a trip to St. Petersburg, Fyodor was riding in a coach and saw out of the window a courier beating a driver. This became a symbol for him of the ruling class exploiting the peasants. "That disgusting picture has always lingered in my memory. I can never forget that courier, and somehow unwillingly, and for a long time afterward, I was inclined to explain—from what was, of course, already too one-sided a viewpoint—much that is shameful and cruel in the Russian people."[4]

His father's behavior became more extreme, especially in the way he mistreated the peasants. When Dostoyevsky was eighteen, fifteen peasants attacked his father and suffocated him with a pillow. His father's violent death precipitated an onset of epilepsy in Fyodor. The trauma of the murder left him feeling guilty of his father's death because he did not love him and had wished for his death. He wondered if he were guilty of the murder. This theme would arise in Ivan's thoughts in *The Brothers Karamazov*. Dostoyevsky became more withdrawn and suspicious of others. He was determined to find purpose in life, to find meaning in man. He said, "Man is a mystery. One must solve it. If you spend your entire life trying to puzzle it out, then do not say that you have wasted your time. I occupy myself with this mystery because I want to be a man."[5]

Dostoyevsky attended army-engineering school for two years in St. Petersburg and was promoted to the rank of sub-lieutenant. However, he was constantly in financial trouble, and, although his sister Varvara, as the trustee of the estate, sent him his share of the income each month, his extravagances kept him constantly in debt. In the morning he attended lectures for the officers. Evenings he spent at the theater, or playing cards with his fellow officers, or spending money on lavish banquets. And then there were the times when he kept to himself and showed no interest in anyone else.

He passed his exams and worked as a draftsman in the Engineering Corps, but at twenty-three he set his course to become a professional writer. He was usually a loner, easily depressed, and self-absorbed. He admired Western writers and found refuge in German and French Romantics. He read Goethe voraciously, feeling that Goethe had probed the depths of the human soul.

At twenty-five, one of his first works, *Poor Folk*, a biographical novel about the influence of poverty and injustice on the lower class, was published. It brought him instant fame and anticipation of future greatness. He went on to write *The Double* about split personality in which he probed the psychology of madness. This book failed, and so did his health.

However, the publication of *Poor Folk* had attracted the attention of Vissarion Belinsky, an eminent critic who believed that social reform starts with the denial of God. Dostoyevsky joined a group of other young writers and thinkers in St. Petersburg who were no longer as interested in the Romantic movement, but were becoming more concerned with those writers who were calling for reform. But in 1848, with political upheaval all over Europe, such ideas were forbidden to be discussed or published. These young people were caught up in the enthusiastic hope that such ideas could spark change in Russia. Of course, the tsar and his spies were determined to smoke out and suppress any such plans. Dostoyevsky read Belinsky's "Letter to Gogol" at one of the meetings. The letter was basically an argument that "the Russian was essentially an atheist by nature, that religion would not change anything, but that salvation would come in the achievements of civilization, enlightenment and humanitarianism to an awakening of a sense of human dignity."[6] He then read Gogol's answer to Belinsky, which was to defend the existing structure of Russia, including serfdom, as God-given and sacred.

A spy who was present sent in a report that these young men were radically opposed to the existing order and under the influence of western European Utopians, that they imagined that they were called upon to bring about a rebirth of the social life. There is evidence[7] that although most of the people attending the meetings were harmless, Dostoyevsky was part of a small group who did have a revolutionary goal. Upon their arrest, they spent nine months in prison waiting for their sentence.

Dostoyevsky's health had already begun to deteriorate before the arrest, and his nervous condition only got worse in prison. The combination of poor conditions, solitary confinement, boredom, hypochondria, worry, and fear depressed him further. Yet he managed to pull on his reserves of strength to get through this time. When the prisoners were allowed to receive reading materials, he began to delve into the Bible as well as history and literature. He also began to jot down notes for future books. During at least four interrogations, Dostoyevsky stood firmly in his convictions, did not divulge the names of others, and attempted to defend his actions by arguing the meanings of such words as "liberal" and "freethinker." We need to remember that, at this point, Dostoyevsky was a published writer, and, although he had written about the squalid and unjust conditions of the poor, he had not taken sides with either of the letters he had read.

Along with fourteen others, Dostoyevsky was condemned to death by firing squad. Others were given lesser sentences of hard labor and exile. The case was closely followed by the public, and the government wanted to be sure it had conducted its process carefully so as not to incite further rebellious activity. Although the highest military court recommended that all prisoners be freed for lack of evidence, Tsar Nicholas sent the case to the General Auditoriat which ruled more harshly and stated that all the prisoners should be condemned to death by execution. The Auditoriat further asked the Tsar for mercy because of the young age of the prisoners and their confessions. However, the Tsar had his own plan for showing these young rebels that he was still in charge. On December 22, twenty-nine year old Dostoevksy and the other prisoners were led out of their prison cells, given the clothing which they had worn when arrested, told to get dressed and to hurry. They were driven thirty minutes by carriage to the snow-covered Semenovsky Square, where they saw scaffolding hung with black crepe. For the first time since their arrest, the comrades were together again, and despite the joy they felt at their reunion, they also saw how emaciated and ill they all were.

They were led before a line of soldiers, ordered to take off their hats in the biting cold, and hear their punishment—death by firing squad. They were given white peasant shirts and white nightcaps as funeral shrouds, and told to make their confession before God. However, none repented their actions.

The men were then seized and tied to wooden posts, the caps were pulled over their heads. As the men were preparing for the moment of death, a rider galloped across the square carrying a letter from the Tsar, sparing their lives and issuing a new sentence. The white shirts and caps were taken off and the prisoners had to kneel while two soldiers broke their swords over their heads, a sign that they were to be excluded from civilian life. They were then given the clothing of convicts— sheepskin coats and boots. This close encounter with death left Dostoyevsky soul-shaken, and he never forgot it. He was exiled to Siberia for four years of hard labor, to be followed by five years as a common soldier in a penal battalion.

During the next six years, he suffered terrible conditions in the prison camps in Siberia. All the anger he had felt earlier while observing a peasant being beaten was now intensified by the cruelty he saw meted out by those in command as well as by fellow prisoners who were hardened criminals. He was surprised by the hostility the peasants felt toward anyone who had been of a higher class. He began to realize that the peasants would not follow intellectuals into revolution because they despised them.

In the midst of this terrible situation, Dostoevksy regained his religious faith. Although he had lost much of this in his connection with liberal-thinking groups, he had never turned away from Christ. At this time he focused on his memory of the serf Marei who had been kind to him when, as a little boy, he had been terrified that he would be attacked by wolves. As he recalled the love in Marei's eyes, Dostoyevsky's attitude toward his fellow convicts changed, his contempt toward them vanished, and in its place he felt he could see through the coarseness, vulgarity and cruelty to the beauty that lay behind the barbaric behavior. His became a faith in the Russian people as the human image of Christ. He saw in each peasant now someone who, in different circumstances, could be Marei. His belief in the Russian peasant was connected with the Orthodox faith which he had shared during the Easter rituals. In those moments he had experienced a purity in their souls.

Dostoyevsky emerged with a prophetic belief in the sacred mission of Russian people—the salvation of the world by the Russians who through their suffering would purify man's soul. He came face to face with "the people" because he was never alone in prison. Whereas aristocrats and those influenced by Western ideas such as democracy had no real idea what the people were like, he learned to understand them and from them he was led to the "people's" God. Through his experiences he came to feel one with criminals, and he realized that crime follows a pattern of hurt pride. When the convicts read the Bible and celebrated the festivals, they felt an equal part of the whole world. In the company of these criminals he came to realize that reason was not strong enough to overcome impulses of human will. This was his birth into faith, the birth of his belief that the Russian people were the Christ-bearers.

One of the questions Dostoyevsky was struggling with was how to preserve personal freedom yet restrain its destructiveness. He felt that freedom was a destructive force if not committed to the principles of Christianity. From his Siberian experiences he came to see how powerful and personal evil was. Yet he saw that it was also a part of the human condition. It could not be extinguished. It could only be stood on its head and become humility. He came to feel that evil was the absence of God, and if a person were to connect himself with crime, it meant that God was absent from him. The four years he spent in the prison camp allowed him the opportunity to observe the human soul under the most extreme and oppressive conditions, and he recorded these observations in *Notes from the House of the Dead*.

In 1854 Dostoyevsky was released from prison camp and had to serve five years as a common soldier in the Russian army. He was very lonely, and in 1857, at the age of thirty-six, he married. Shortly after the wedding, he suffered another epileptic attack, which scared his wife terribly. To complicate matters, Dostoyevsky was diagnosed with epilepsy and told that it was quite possible he would be suffocated by a spasm of the throat and die. Although he and his wife loved each other, they were not happy together, and there were rumors of her having an on-going affair. During these years Dostoyevsky finished *Notes from the House of the Dead* and also wrote *The Humiliated and the Wronged*. He became conservative and an outspoken tsarist supporter and a practicing member of the Russian Orthodox Church.

After much negotiation, at age thirty-nine, Dostoyevsky was permitted to resign from the penal battalion and return to St. Petersburg. There he founded a magazine called *Vremya* [*Time*] in which he hoped to reconcile all European ideas as part of the Russian ideal. His brother Mikhail acted as editor, and Dostoyevsky handled the artistic and critical work. During the two years he worked on the magazine, he overexerted himself, which brought on a series of epileptic attacks.

It was the year 1861, and serfdom was abolished. At the close of the eighteenth century there had been thirty-four million serfs and two million non-serfs. In other words, serfs accounted for ninety-four percent of the population. In contrast, in the pre-Civil War South in the United States there were four million slaves, nine and a half million free. So in the United States slaves were about fifty percent of the population. Dostoyevsky was ecstatic with the freeing of the serfs, and it further exemplified for him the uniqueness of the Russian nation.

In 1862 Dostoyevsky, now forty-one years old, traveled to Europe for the first time. He had been so excited to go, but due to his experiences of air pollution in France, extreme poverty in London, and atheism and socialism in the place of religion, he felt Europe was in decline and had nothing to offer Russia, that, in fact, European civilization was actually detrimental to Russia's national development. He characterized these impressions in "Winter Notes on Summer Impressions" which he wrote for Vremya.

At age forty-three he wrote *Notes from Underground* which dealt with freedom and suffering. Instead of reason, he said, we should cultivate emotion, intuition, and imagination. For Dostoyevsky, *Notes* was the turning point in his creative work. This book is an exploration of philosophy of the underground man, a composite picture of the human consciousness of the nineteenth century man, a man who is split within himself. Dostoyevsky states that the Fallen Adam cannot be saved through human powers, but out of the shadow of death is revealed a way to God through faith and Christ. *Notes* prepared the way for a five-act tragedy of novels *Crime and Punishment*, *The Idiot*, *The Devils*, *A Raw Youth*, and *The Brothers Karamazov*.

Dostoyevsky made a second trip to Europe, this time developing an addiction to gambling and losing everything. Upon his return, his wife was dying and he stayed with her through to the end. A few months after she died, his brother Mikhail also died, which left the forty-four year old Dostoyevsky heartbroken. He assumed control of the magazine, but as hard as he worked, he was not successful, and he ended its publication. He assumed his brother's debts and the responsibility to support Mikhail's widow and four children. But he was destitute and headed for debtor's prison unless he could come up with the money.

He fled his creditors to Europe, and within five days gambled away whatever money he had with him. Desperate, he tried to borrow money and get advances on books he would write. Boarding in a German hotel in Wiesbaden, he was humiliated when the management refused to give him meals or even a candle for light. All they would give him was tea, and poor tea it was. Living in an awful hotel, with no money, food, or light, Dostoyevsky began to write *Crime and Punishment*. Some friends sent him money, and after almost three months of wretched living, he returned to St. Petersburg. What was to be a short tale in payment for money advanced grew into a full novel. In *Crime and Punishment*, Raskolnikov views himself as a superior being, free to determine his own destiny according to his own laws. He kills to prove his freedom only to find out he is unable to exist without relating to his fellow human beings. To escape his loneliness he finally confesses his crime. With creditors banging on the door, it was difficult for Dostoyevsky to gain the quiet to concentrate on his writing, so he withdrew to his sister's home to write at full speed, working on one novel in the morning and another in the evening. However, he could not sustain the schedule and a friend suggested that he engage the help of a stenographer, as shorthand was a new technique taught at the university.

Dostoyevsky took his friend's advice and dictated *The Gambler* to Anna Grigoryevna Snitkina. In this way he met that deadline and could then return his attention to *Crime and Punishment*. He wrote and rewrote, struggling with the characters and struggling with himself. This novel is a passionate examination of the relationship between believing in God and feeling one is beyond God.

Dostoyevsky fell in love with Anna and proposed to her (he was forty-six, she was twenty-one). She accepted his proposal and became a devoted wife, a true companion for this last part of his life. Although she did not understand much of his ideas, she brought calm and beauty to their lives. She managed the household, took care of the budget, cared for the children, and devoted her life to him.

As had occurred with his first marriage, after the wedding he had a particularly dramatic epileptic seizure. When the doctor advised him to go abroad for treatment, his wife pawned her dowry, and they moved to Dresden. Dostoyevsky worked at night, slept until late morning, spent afternoons and evenings with Anna, and then dictated his copy to her. They had the opportunity to visit the art museum in which he especially loved Raphael's *Sistine Madonna* and the Claude Lorraine landscapes. But as wonderful as Dresden was, Dostoyevsky grew tired of German order and longed for Russia. He gambled and lost everything, including his wedding ring. His compulsion for the extreme worried his wife as she tried to get used to his changing moods. Yet in this half-madness, he continued to write.

They moved to Baden where Dostoyevsky continued to gamble and craft his thoughts about Russia and the West. He developed the plot for a new book, *The Idiot*. The death of their three-year-old daughter Sonya caused him terrible suffering, and for years after he would ask, "Where is Sonya?" In his suffering he identified with Job and neither he nor Anna could be consoled in their grieving at the death of their first child.

When he discovered that the secret police were reading his letters and spying on him, Dostoyevsky and Anna moved to Italy where he began to gain some inner peace. He felt healed by Raphael's paintings which he visited over and over again. He continued to write *The Idiot*, the story about a positively beautiful individual. Although other authors had tried to describe such a person, no one had been successful because only Christ could fulfill this role. Dostoyevsky sought to create the image of the perfectly good man who was misunderstood and abused.

While Dostoyevsky was struggling with this book, they moved back to Dresden where their daughter Lyubov was born. A cold reception to *The Idiot* left him feeling desperate again for money, and he began to plan future books. His obsession with gambling came to an end when, at age fifty, he had a mystical experience. He had gone to Wiesbaden to play roulette and had lost everything. He ran desperately through the streets to what he thought was an Orthodox church, but it was actually a synagogue. He has left no description of the actual experience except to say that he was morally reborn and would never gamble again.

After this experience, Dostoyevsky concluded his four-year exile in Europe and returned to Russia where, soon after, their son Fyodor was born. Dostoyevsky continued to write feverishly: short stories and plots for long novels. He struggled with trying to portray the results of atheism and the alternate consequences of a Christ-centered belief. He wrote *The Devils*, another novel in the new narrative form, the novel-tragedy, which he created. In the midst of his literary struggles, Dostoyevsky discovered that all Anna's possessions and his entire library had been sold by his stepson Pavel to pay creditors. Illness and family problems haunted them. And on top of all this, the reception to his novel *The Devils* was lukewarm.

Upon completion of the novel *A Raw Youth*, which has seven or eight novels within it, the family moved to a small town and a life that was more orderly and peaceful than living in a city. Here Dostoyevsky was able to settle in to a reasonable routine. For example, he would get up at eleven, do gymnastics, and wash. He was a fastidious dresser even when he was at home. After prayer he would drink glasses of strong tea and then go into his study to work. After lunch he would dictate the chapters he had written the previous night to Anna, who would take it down in shorthand, recopy it, hand it to Fyodor to make corrections, transcribe it and send it to the printer. Anna made very few suggestions; she might offer something about the clothes his characters were wearing. When the dictation was done, Dostoyevsky would give the children treats. At four o'clock he would go for his daily walk, head bowed, deep in thought, often giving out alms without even looking. At six o'clock the family had dinner, and at nine o'clock supper. Then he blessed the children, prayed with them, and settled down to work, often smoking during that time.[8]

Dostoyevsky was very close to his children. "Every evening the father would come into the children's room, book in hand, and read to them. The children were about to enter school and he instructed them in Russian, history and geography. When the children could not see him, they wrote notes and shoved them under the doors of the study where he worked. In the Dostoyevsky Museum in St. Petersburg there is a note displayed by young Fyodor: 'Daddy, give me a candy. Fedya.' "

When Dostoyevsky was fifty-four, his son Alexei was born. With *A Raw Youth* finished, the family returned to St. Petersburg where he published it in short installments. He began work on *Diary of a Writer*, which was also serialized. Readers from all over Russia responded warmly to this.

When Dostoyevsky was fifty-five years old, he began writing *The Brothers Karamazov*. Themes that had arisen in his past works came to fruition in this work. For the next three years he was immersed in the thoughts that climaxed in his declaration of love and brotherhood. While he was focused on writing *The Brothers Karamazov*, he also wrote a letter "to the students of Moscow" in which he told them that they had inherited the lie of two whole centuries of history. Two paths lay open to the young Russian generation, and each young person must choose. The first was a false path of following European ideas. The second was a true path which focused on God.

Also while he was working on this novel, his three-year-old son Alexei died from epilepsy. Dostoyevsky felt guilt over the fact that his little son had inherited his disease. To try to ease some of his pain, Anna encouraged Vladimir Solovyov to invite Dostoyevsky on a pilgrimage to Optina Pustyn. This suggestion was taken up, and the family went to the country house while Dostoyevsky and Solovyov made their pilgrimage. He put much of his grief into the novel, naming one of the characters Alexei (Alyosha is his nickname). At age fifty-nine Dostoyevsky finished all of *The Brothers Karamazov* except the last book, "The Boys," and sent it to his editor in January 1880.

He put aside the ending to work on the Pushkin Speech to be delivered in June 1880. Into this speech he poured his thoughts about the unique Russian gift to the world. "To become a real Russian, to become fully a Russian, perhaps, means only to become brother of all men, a completely universal man, if you want. . . . Russia was called to 'utter the ultimate word' of great common harmony, of the brotherly definitive accord of all races following Christ's evangelical law! … Let our land be poor, but through this poor land 'in the likeness of a slave, Christ has gone forth, bestowing His blessing.' "[9]

Dostoyevsky praised Pushkin as the first to depict in his character Onegin the historical Russian wanderer, torn away from his native soil, oppressed and suffering. In Pushkin was the faith in the Russian character, its spiritual power, and therefore hope for the Russian man.

After great acclaim and appreciation for his speech, Dostoyevsky returned home to complete the last book. When asked about his experience of writing his novel, Dostoyevsky replied by letter:

In your last letter you asked me about the state of mind in which I found myself during those days in which I planned the writing of *The Brothers Karamazov*. I feel that this book tells so much of my life purpose, and is the result of an experience so unusual, that even now I am moved by the force of it … It was in the late autumn of 1876 that one day I lay down for a little rest in the late afternoon. To this moment I am not certain that I did not fall asleep, yet the state of my mind was so clear that I believe truthfully I was awake. Yet, I cannot say positively whether my experience was one of dream in sleep or vision in wakefulness. All that I beheld stood before me clearly and sharply — no part of it was indistinct, as is so often in dreams … I saw a great space before me: a great void. At once great loneliness passed before my soul … Everything stood balanced between heaven and earth, and a feeling of timelessness hung over all … Earth there was, but in an unearthly sense. I could find no place I had ever seen before. Only emptiness and loneliness … I remained in this condition for a long time, and I felt then a loneliness and a longing I have never experienced before, even in my darkest hours. Yet, a sweetness and love filled this place too, which made it, otherwise unbearable, at least endurable for me … When I was completely lost in contemplation of this strange place and the silence of it nearly carried me away by its own invisible power, I became aware of an onrushing breath — a warmth which came from far away. It did not come all at once with force, but gently and softly, it swept about me, rising ever more and more. I was wrapped in it, and felt it warm upon my face. But nothing in it changed the feeling of loneliness, which grew stronger … The light grew brighter now, ever broadening and rising within itself, dividing and subdividing — breaking forth all about me. Then I felt all round me, but did not hear, those words of earliest divine direction, "Let there be light!" — and for the first time I knew the majesty and the depth in the meaning of those words.

Fresh music sounded from the space now, while the light grew ever brighter. I was bathed in tears which flowed freely down my face. Yet I did not weep with sadness, but with strange joy. I saw this purposefulness and the insufficiencies of my life, and the destiny of my soul … Bright Beings stood before me, and in their midst was One with fair face and clear gaze. The face shone with light from within, while golden streams poured from the eyes. The eyes held me, for with pity and wonder and wisdom infinite they gazed far beyond me upon the world of man.

In that Face was a warmth of wonder, a glow of love, a beauty fresh with a freshness to which nothing earthly can be compared … All at once, without words to tell me, I knew: This is the Christ! And with this knowledge the music I heard sounded forth with pure, unearthly beauty … The vision stayed with me clearly for a long time, then faded gently from my sight. To the last, those wonderful, miraculous eyes looked out through the rising and falling light, with expression of sorrow and joy mingled … Then all disappeared, and I was left alone.[10]

During 1881 Dostoyevsky made plans to begin Part II of *The Brothers Karamazov* which would take place about twenty years later with Alyosha as the hero. But his health began deteriorating until he began coughing blood. During his illness, he was visited by Countess Tolstoy. He had lived with epilepsy, tuberculosis, and probably lung cancer, and when he realized his death was near, he called his family together. His love for Anna had grown deeper and more beautiful over the twelve years they had been together. She had been a true partner to him, and he was as much or more in love with her at this point than even earlier in their relationship. He asked to have the parable of the Prodigal Son read aloud. He said, "Children, never forget what you have just heard here. Preserve an unbounded faith in the Lord and never despair of His forgiveness. I love you very much, but my love is nothing in comparison with the Lord's infinite love for all men, whom He has created."[11]

Fyodor Mikhailovich Dostoyevsky died on January 28, 1881. Thirty-two thousand people accompanied the coffin to its resting place, and his friend and confidant, the philosopher and poet Vladimir Soloviev honored the great writer by speaking at his grave.

Themes from *The Brothers Karamazov*

In planning the Russian literature main lesson block, I considered each of Dostoyevsky's novels, and I decided to require *The Brothers Karamazov* as student reading over the summer before senior year. Since implementing this in 1978, I have reconsidered each year, and time and again I come back to this book as the one to serve as the major theme in the course.

What is it about *The Brothers Karamazov* that I find so meaningful? Certainly *Crime and Punishment* or *The Idiot* would be grist for excellent class discussions. I think it is because woven through the chapters is a complex set of themes, each theme in itself like a book and rich in literary themes.

The Three Brothers

The obvious theme is that of the three brothers themselves. Dmitri, Ivan, and Alyosha each represent a part of the human being, but none is complete in himself. Dmitri is the impulsive brother who lives passionately in his feelings, never stopping long enough to think. Ivan is the intellectual brother who lives in his thinking and is paralyzed by it. He is trying to find ideas that he can live by.

Alyosha is like the third brother in the fairy tales who exemplifies the heart and will. His actions are selfless. In the beginning, he seems naïve, following the advice of Father Zossima. Over time he begins to take responsibility for his beliefs and act out of his own resources. Throughout, Alyosha is on the move, the constant messenger between all the other characters.

The brothers also each represent a stage in Dostoyevksy's life. Dmitri is the young hot-headed Dostoyevsky who gambles, spends money erratically, and acts impulsively while he is in engineering school. Ivan the reformer, is the cold intellectual, needing proof before he can believe. He is fascinated with rationalist Western ideas and only trusts logic as a way of proving God's existence. This is the Dostoyevsky of the group of young intellectuals exploring Western thought. Alyosha is the man of faith, the Dostoyevsky after his experience in the labor camp.

Each brother undergoes a transformation. Dmitri begins to take responsibility for his actions, experiences love rather than lust, and awakens his heart through his dream of the wee babe. Dmitri comes to embrace Father Zossima's teaching that all are responsible to all. In typical Russian fashion, he looks forward to suffering as a sign that God is giving him an opportunity to redeem his sins.

Ivan realizes that, although in deed he did not kill his father, in truth he wanted his father dead. Smerdyakov tells him, "You murdered him; you are the real murderer, I was only your instrument, your faithful servant, and it was following your words I did it."[12] As Ivan confronts his deeper feelings, he finds that he does have a moral responsibility. At that point, Ivan has hallucinations as he faces the Devil accusing him of his complicity in the murder of his father, and then conflicted with guilt, he is overcome with brain fever.

Alyosha suffers temptation after the death of Father Zossima whose corpse gives off a smell showing he was not a saint. He experiences doubt until he regains his faith and can then stand up for his beliefs out of his own efforts. His ability to see the Higher Self in each human being allows other characters to transform.

The Fourth Brother

We must not forget the fourth brother, Smerdyakov. It has been speculated that Smerdyakov is the son of Fyodor Karamazov and Stinking Lizaveta, but it has not been completely proven plausible. Smerdyakov is a picture of the forgotten child, born in shameful circumstances, unacknowledged, resentful, and hostile. Reared by the servants Grigory and Marfa, he never feels accepted by Fyodor Karamazov. He is asocial and lacks empathy. He is clever but lacks a heart. He is influenced by other people's arguments but lacks moral development. Yet we can sympathize with him.

Fatherhood

What a vile character is Fyodor Pavlovich Karamazov! His character is distasteful—a sensualist, a buffoon, a selfish egoist, a man who lives for lust. He is physically repulsive, and, even more importantly, he is morally repulsive. He has no understanding or sympathy for either of his wives and mistreats them. He lacks any sense of responsibility for the upbringing of his sons. Yet he is the father. Through him, the theme of parricide enters the plot. Aside from Alyosha who loves and trusts everyone, the other brothers, for different reasons, detest their father and wish him dead.

In our time the father-son relationship is a very delicate one. Many boys in our society are living separated from their fathers. Being able to discuss the complex relationship that is described in the book offers seventeen–eighteen-year-olds a chance to explore their thoughts without being personal.

Questions that often arise in class discussions include: How can Alyosha still love such a vile person? Why is Ivan so arrogant and cool? Is this his way of handling his feeling that his father mistreated his mother? Can't Dmitri see that he is so much like his father? How does Dmitri break the cycle of not repeating his father's mistakes?

Women in *The Brothers Karamazov*

There are four main women characters—Katerina, Grushenka, Lisa, and Madame Hohlakov. Whereas the book focuses on the men, it is clear that Ivan and Dmitri are aided in their transformations by the behavior of Katerina and Grushenka. Lisa is not well developed in the plot, although Alyosha indicates that he understands her temperamental nature and that he plans to marry her. She is sixteen years old and quite hysterical. In some ways she mirrors an adolescent girl's emotional ups and downs. Madame Hohlakov is the typical village busybody; she knows everyone and wants to know each person's secret. She lacks faith and seeks it in her meeting with Father Zossima. She creates a backdrop in which the other characters can meet and interact. Yet we don't really get to know what she thinks and feels.

The major activity circles around Katerina and Grushenka. Both women are connected to the brothers and are confused about their true feelings.

Katerina is tied to Dimitri emotionally because she feels she owed him sexual favors since he protected her father from being arrested for embezzlement. Because he does not take advantage of her, she feels she owes him something. Her sometimes arrogant and aloof attitude is connected with her not wanting to face her real feelings for Ivan.

At first Grushenka does not seem like a sympathetic character. She teases people and changes her mind often. She is suffering because her Polish lover has left her and promises to return. She has worked hard to make herself financially independent, although rumors fly that her relationship with her merchant mentor is more than platonic. She becomes the object of desire for both Dmitri and Fyodor, and enjoys teasing them both. She becomes more clear about her feelings for Dmitri when her Polish lover returns and shows himself to be a cad. After the murder of Fyodor, she comes very ill and begins to realize she also has some guilt in relation to it. Her faithfulness to Dmitri and her inner strength become clear at the end of the book.

As we follow Grushenka and Katerina through the novel, we see not only their immature aspects but also their noble sides. This is especially contrasted in the scene between Grushenka and Katerina in Madame Hohlakov's house, a magnificent portrayal of feminine wiles.

The Schoolboys

One could ask the question, why did Dostoyevsky include the scenes involving the schoolboys? In some ways, the plot itself did not need these scenes. Yet the book is made deeper and richer because of them. The interactions among the schoolboys are not much different from those found in other countries and even among our own boys of this age in contemporary America. They tease, challenge, torment, sympathize, brag, and fight with each other. They gang up on the most vulnerable; when they awaken to their conscience, they are sweet and innocent. The Snegirov family becomes the backdrop for the reader to enter into the home of a poor family with disabled members. Yet honor and dignity are necessary aspects of their life.

After Ilusha's funeral, Alyosha tells the boys, "Let us never forget how good we once felt here, all together, united by such good and kind feelings as made us, too, for the time that we loved the poor boy, perhaps better than we actually are. . . . You must know that there is nothing higher, or stronger, or sounder, or more useful afterwards in life, than some good memory, especially a memory from childhood, from the paternal home. . . . And even if only one good memory remains with us in our hearts, that alone may serve some day for our salvation. . . . Let us first of all and before all be kind, then honest, and then—let us never forget one another. . . . Ah, children, ah, dear friends, do not be afraid of life! How good life is when you do something good and rightful!"[13]

Father Zossima

Father Zossima is one of the elders, a very special small group of monks who are considered holy and saintly. Zossima's insights and teachings show a man of remarkable wisdom and understanding and form an important part of the book. They foreshadow what Rudolf Steiner describes as the Sixth Epoch, or the time of *Philadelphia*, Brotherly Love. He teaches forgiveness and love, that God lives in Nature as well as in every human being, that prayer should not be for oneself, and that masters should become servants.

Father Zossima's teachings act as counterpoint to the Grand Inquisitor scene where Christ is accused of giving man freedom rather than happiness. Throughout the novel, characters act out of free choice and realize the role of suffering in their lives. As they freely choose to love and forgive, they offer the answer to Ivan's deepest questions about God, morality, and suffering.

Freedom and Happiness

The Grand Inquisitor scene presents students with very profound questions about the nature of freedom and the consequential danger of making choices. It is helpful to review the Three Temptations of Christ from the New Testament or to have a student present them. This scene is quite difficult to understand at first reading, but for the more philosophical student, it offers much on which to chew. Some students have found this to be the most interesting part of the book.

Student writing:

Excerpt from "The Nature of Man as Explored through The Brothers Karamazov*"*

Emerson tells us that the only gift one gives is a part of oneself. In this sense Dostoyevsky has given us a true gift in *The Brothers Karamazov*, and yet it is not only himself whom he illuminates but also all of mankind. Through the main characters he explores the nature and personality of Man as well as Man's relationship to the Divine. As Dostoyevsky did himself, the characters all search for the meaning of happiness, love, forgiveness, and ultimately, life. The Karamazov brothers — Dmitri, Ivan, and Alyosha — can be seen as the collective personality of mankind as well as the different stages in man's development.

The first idea I would like to introduce is that the characters in *The Brothers Karamazov* represent a spectrum of mankind's spirituality. It is a spectrum between the polarities of light and dark, God and devil, noble and base. Each of us is at a certain level of spirituality within the spectrum, and when we learn our lessons on earth we rise to a new level until we are ready to become one with God. The father, Fyodor Karamazov, is immersed in sensuality and spiritual darkness, and thus he represents the lowest, darkest level of spiritual attainment. The highest level is represented in Father Zossima.

Man may be seen as a brilliant gem with many facets, and by studying each Karamazov brother we come to a better understanding of man from different perspectives as seen through light and darkness. – A.G.

Excerpt: Father Zossima

The first pleasant surprise about the course was back in the summer when I was reading about Father Zossima from *The Brothers Karamazov*. I am somebody who does not necessarily believe that there is a God, but I also do not have a good reason why God should not exist, so I cannot say that I agree with Zossima's teachings because I was taught them or because I learned them in church and agree. To me, there was something about what Zossima said that very much paralleled my agnostic views of the world. There seemed to be a quality about him that was truly enlightened, and if I were able to have a conversation with anybody about religion or God, I think I would put him at the top of my list of people to talk to. – A.S.

What points in the Grand Inquisitor scene are most convincing to you and why?

The most important point of the Grand Inquisitor scene is at the very end when Christ kisses the Grand Inquisitor, forgiving him. After everything the Grand Inquisitor has said and done, although Christ is clearly saddened by it, even though he knows it to be wrong, he still forgives the Grand Inquisitor. In that way he has proved his ultimate point. All he ever wanted was for humans to be free, to make their own destiny. Where he could have stuck down the Grand Inquisitor, or in some other way thwarted him, he forgives him and lets him continue on his path. The kiss is not just for the Grand Inquisitor. Christ has kissed mankind, and in doing so he has forgiven all men as only he can. Though we may stray from the path and fall from the eyes of God, we are not met with contempt, but instead with pity. We are free in that we are not obliged to follow God. Jesus will not cast miracles to aid us or command our belief; it falls to us to make our own decisions, whether they are right or wrong. That kiss is the ultimate blessing and our greatest curse. We are free to do as we please and will be forgiven if we should stray, yet at the same time we must come up with our own faith. We as individuals can only believe because we choose to, not because we must, and in that we are free.   – J.B.

The Grand Inquisitor scene brings up a very credible point: freedom is inherently dangerous. During the scene, the Grand Inquisitor tells Jesus that Jesus was wrong in giving people free choice of religion. He tells Jesus that it is his fault that so many people die at the hands of religious cleansings and so forth. The Grand Inquisitor says that if Jesus had given only one way by which people would have to follow him, the world would be a much better place.

Whether it is correct or not, this theme is very prevalent in literature. The concept that most humans don't know what is best for themselves is widely accepted as truth. That is part of the reason why there are no countries anywhere in the world that technically practice anarchy. Besides the fact that governmental anarchy is an oxymoron, humans just do not have the ability, at this point in their evolution, to safely coexist without some form of limitation on their actions.

The idea that the Grand Inquisitor brings is, to me, a very practical one. I am someone who thinks he is unique, but I am also fully aware of the fact that most people believe themselves to be that way. We are conditioned to believe that in much the same way as the church in the Grand Inquisitor scene kept the people under a shroud of ignorance. Here in the United States, our "Grand Inquisitor" is the media. We bow before it because we know no better. What we are told is true is what we believe, and therefore, whether it is intentional or not, the media keeps most of the people of the United States in a relatively blissful cocoon of ignorance.

I agree with the Grand Inquisitor on a purely intellectual basis, because, whether or not I like the idea of having my truth spoonfed to me by the media, humanity is not ready for independence yet. I would much rather live with the peace and happiness I have had for all my life than be pulled out of the matrix and shown that my existence is only fictional. I guess that does not sound like the statement of a unique person, but how can I be unique if I am unique in the same way as everybody else? – A.S.

There are many convincing points in the Grand Inquisitor scene, and yet morally I do not agree with most of them. I do believe the Grand Inquisitor is correct in knowing that most people will sacrifice their beliefs and comfort of the afterlife for the chance of being happy in the present. He is also right in thinking people want to have someone to help direct them in what is wrong and forgive them for their offenses. These three facts allow the Grand Inquisitor to be able to erect a strongly supported church.

The Grand Inquisitor proves his point of the desire for immediate satisfaction with the story of bread. The people would rather have the bread that the church can provide them to feed their families than wait for the divine bread that Jesus may never produce. Jesus did offer the people free will, but the people still chose the tangible. The Grand Inquisitor says the people do this because they are weak, and I agree. I think they are weak in their beliefs, but not in their souls. They are unsure if Jesus will provide for them and so take what is offered to them.

The church that gives them the bread also provides directions for what is ethical. Although people want freedom, they also need this guidance and a sense of unity in it. The Grand Inquisitor speaks clearly on this topic of people all wanting to believe in the same source of moral leadership. The church has used this humanistic tendency to strengthen the faith of their followers. They have also used the tool of forgiveness. People do not like to take responsibility for their wrongdoings and don't like the burden of guilt. The church offers to fully expunge all sins and release people from their shame and asks only for loyalty in return. – *L.D.*

In the Grand Inquisitor chapter, the Grand Inquisitor tells Christ that he cannot do his work on earth because Christ's work is at odds with the work of the Church. The point that I find most convincing is when the Grand Inquisitor tells Christ that by rejecting the three temptations, he gave free will to human beings. The Grand Inquisitor goes on to state that free will is a devastating burden to mankind, because Christ has given the people the freedom to choose whether or not to follow him, and he says that most humans do not have the strength to be faithful to Christ. The Grand Inquisitor says that Christ should have taken the ability to choose away from the people, and should have instead taken the temptation of power, and therefore not given humanity the freedom.

This is not a point I agree with, but I do find it most convincing. I believe that all human beings deserve the freedom to choose what they do and whom they follow, but the Grand Inquisitor does have a point. By choosing to have power over all of humanity and taking away the freedom of the people, Christ could have offered happiness and security to all people while they remained on earth, and could have made all moral decisions for them. The Grand Inquisitor says that the church is making up for what Christ did not do, by offering people security in their spiritual lives.

The Grand Inquisitor justifies his choice to place Christ in prison through all that I have already said. If Christ were allowed to go free, he might undo all the work of the Church in keeping the ability of free will away from humanity. – *L.J.*

Endnotes

1. Manuel Komroff, in his Foreword to *The Brothers Karamazov* by Fyodor Dostoyevsky (New York: Penguin, A Signet Classic, 1957), xvii.
2. Konstantin Mochulsky, *Dostoyevsky, His Life and Work* (Princeton, NJ: Princeton University Press, 1973), xix.
3. Ibid., p. 12.
4. Ibid., p. 11.
5. Ibid., p. 17.
6. Ibid., p. 123.
7. Joseph Frank, *Dostoyevsky: The Years of Ordeal 1850–1859* (Princeton, NJ: Princeton University Press, no date), p. 19.
8. Mochulsky, *Dostoyevsky*, pp. 483–484.

9. Ibid., p. 641.
10. Reprinted in *Journal of Anthroposophy*, unclear date, pp. 11-12. The note with this quotation cites that this extract is from a letter Dostoyevsky wrote to S. P. Katkov, editor of the *Russian Messenger [Russkaya Missyl]* and his lifelong friend. It was published in a Russian newspaper in 1900 with permission of his widow.
11. Mochulsky, *Dostoyevsky*, p. 647.
12. Fyodor Dostoyevsky, *The Brothers Karamazov* (New York: New American Library, 1980), p. 565.
13. Fyodor Dostoyevsky, *The Brothers Karamazov*, newly translated by Richard Pevear and Larissa Volokhonsky (New York: Random House, 1991), p. 774. This is a very readable translation.

Bibliography

Banerjee, Maria N. *Dostoyevsky, The Scandal of Reason*, Great Barrington, MA: Lindisfarne Books, 2006.

Dostoyevsky, Fyodor. *The Brothers Karamazov*, New York: Vintage Books, Random House, 1991.

_____. *Crime and Punishment*, New York: Norton Critical Edition, 1975.

_____. *Diary of a Writer*, Santa Barbara: Peregrine Smith, Inc., 1979.

_____. *Notes from Underground*, New York: Bantam Books, 1976.

Frank, Joseph. *Dostoyevsky: The Years of Ordeal 1850–1859*, Princeton, NJ: Princeton University Press, no date.

Mochulsky, Konstantin. *Dostoyevsky, His Life and Work*, Princeton, NJ: Princeton University Press, 1973.

Wasiolek, Edward, ed. *Dostoyevsky: The Notebooks for* The Brothers Karamazov, Chicago: University of Chicago Press, 1971.

Zenkovskii, V.V. *Russian Thinkers and Europe*, Ch. IX, Ann Arbor, MI: American Council of Learned Societies, J.W. Edwards, 1953.

Red Square, Moscow

Street in Moscow

CHAPTER 10

BORIS PASTERNAK (1890–1960)

Poet, keep watch, keep watch,
You must not fall asleep —
You are eternity's hostage
A captive of time.[1]

– Boris Pasternak

Boris Pasternak's life offers us a way of connecting with twentieth century history in Russia and the Soviet Union. His life was dramatic and touched on issues of courage and truth.

Childhood and Youth

Boris Pasternak was born in Moscow on February 10, 1890. At that time Moscow was a city of stark contrasts: elegant palaces and wooden huts, golden domed churches and dark alleyways. His parents were of Jewish lineage from the Odessa area. His father, Leonid Ossipovich, wanted to be a doctor, but gave up his studies to be a painter. He had to renounce Judaism in order to live in Moscow. His mother, Rosalia Isidorovna Kaufmann, was a talented pianist who gave up her career to devote herself to her family.

When Pasternak was two, his father was invited to contribute some illustrations for Tolstoy's *War and Peace*. After that he was offered the post of Director of the Moscow School of Painting, Sculpture and Architecture, and the family situation was much improved. They lived in one of the wings of the school in a comfortable apartment with large windows facing a tree-lined avenue. From the balcony, Boris could see the fashionable coaches and elegantly dressed students who came to study with his father. From this balcony, he experienced such historic occasions as the funeral procession of Alexander III, and two years later the procession of the crowning of the new Tsar Nicholas II.

The Pasternaks were a happy family. His mother was a warm smiling woman who handled the business arrangements for her husband's work and ran the house efficiently. His father, although sterner, was also devoted to his family. Boris looked back at his childhood as a happy time, with evening concerts and peasant women invited in to pose for paintings. Leonid was given additional commissions to illustrate a number of Tolstoy's books, and the two families became very good friends. Leonid often took Boris with him to the Tolstoy estate, Yasnaya Polyana, and at Tolstoy's death, Countess Tolstoy asked Leonid to paint his death portrait.

Leonid had become Christian, and at an early age Boris was taken to church by his nanny to be baptized. Over the years, Boris experienced Christian imagery very deeply as is evident in his poetry.

Boris was a serious boy, sensitive, and fastidious. He did not have his father's gift for painting, but after meeting the composer Schriabin, he decided to study music. Later, when he learned he did not have perfect pitch, he gave up music.

As a youngster, he was thrown by a horse. Because his leg was not set properly, making one shorter than the other, he had a slight limp and later was denied acceptance into the military.

When Boris was fourteen, his protected world was shattered by Russia's loss of the war to Japan. This was followed by strikes. One night railway workers marching through the streets were attacked by dragoons. Boris ran out, and a Cossack struck him across the shoulder and left him lying in the snow. The political situation intensified, and like most liberal intellectuals, his family sympathized with the revolutionaries.

By the time Pasternak was sixteen, he had met the three great heroes who were to influence his life—the writer Leo Tolstoy, the poet Ranier Maria Rilke, and the musician Alexander Schriabin. Boris had actually seen Rilke years earlier when he and his father were traveling on a train to Tolstoy's estate. Now he discovered Rilke's poetry and his thoughts turned to poetry rather than composing.

Pasternak had learned German from his father and at this time, he began to read the German philosophers Kant and Hegel. In his classes at university, he was attracted to the Russian poets Andrei Biely and Alexander Blok.

At nineteen, Pasternak joined a group of young poets at the University of Moscow. This was an exciting time as he became interested in symbolism and in questions of immortality. A powerful experience during this time was accompanying his father when he was painting Tolstoy's death portrait. As Boris gazed at the dead Tolstoy, he felt Tolstoy's great soul and his capacity to penetrate the lives of the peasants as no one else had. In fact, in the moment, Tolstoy's face seemed more like a peasant's.

As exciting as Moscow was at this time, Boris began to yearn to experience the medieval cities of Europe as his father had in Munich, but he was a penniless student. His readings in philosophy had led him to think about studying in Marburg where Professor Hermann Cohen was the center of a new school of philosophy. To his surprise and joy, his mother presented him with two hundred rubles she had saved from giving piano lessons, and she hoped he would spend it on travel. Excited, Boris bought a copy of the summer syllabus courses at Marburg University and a month later was on the train to Germany.

The experience in Marburg was everything he had hoped it to be—lectures, cafes, studying, meetings with students from all over the world, and even a first love. The experience led to a decision to give up philosophy in favor of poetry, and Boris took off for Italy, especially Pisa and Venice. He devoured the artwork, and he was especially fascinated by how the artists of the Renaissance adapted the Biblical themes of spirituality and sensuality. From this experience he began to contemplate the theme of resurrection.

Pasternak returned to Moscow determined to be a poet. But how to make a living? He passed his finals at Moscow University, and since his parents could no longer support him, he found work as a tutor. He published his first book of poetry, *A Twin in the Clouds*, which he later regretted.

Pasternak Finds His Style as a Poet

World War I broke out, and Pasternak was given draft clearance because of his leg. He went to work in the factories to help with the war effort. He was working in the Urals when the Revolution broke out, and he tried to get back to Moscow as quickly as possible, by horse-drawn sled over the snow and through the forests.

In 1917, he found himself observing the world through the eyes of a poet; he was interested in nature and in the human condition. He did not agree with the Symbolist poets who were stretching the language and inventing new words. He felt the Russian language was so rich he did not have to invent new words. His style was simple and direct. He wrote *My Sister Life* and *Themes and Variations*. During this time he worked as a librarian or assistant in a bookshop. The revolutionary time was a time of great suffering, and it was difficult to get enough food. He was refining his writing to try to capture the subtleties of the human soul. He used everyday objects to create powerful images. In four short stories he wrote of his concerns with large philosophical concepts: the nature of the self, the nature of poetry and the nature of war. In his idealism, he supported the aims of the revolutionaries, and he wanted to write poems to honor the revolution.

During the Civil War from 1918–1921, Pasternak was forced to sell some of his valuable books in order to buy bread. It became impossible to publish, so the ways to make one's work known were to give poetry readings and circulate one's work illegally through carbon copies that were retyped and passed around the country. This underground system was known as *samizdat* and became the main way writers made their work known through the period of Soviet power. The situation eased for a few years after the war; publishing became possible again, and travel outside of Russia. During this time, Pasternak's parents traveled to Berlin and then later on moved to England; they never returned to Russia.

By this time, Pasternak was considered one of the three major Russian poets, along with Sergey Essenin and Vladimir Mayakovsky. These two poets lived brief and very tormented lives, while Pasternak continued to deepen his insights and poetic skills. He was unhappy being alone and yearned for a family. Despite his father's advice that a true artist should avoid marriage, in 1923 Pasternak married a young painter, Eugenia Vladimorovna Muratova, whom he had known from before the war. He was hopelessly in love with her, and they enjoyed traveling through Germany together. They returned to Russia, had a son, and settled down in Moscow. Boris received advances for his books and translation and worked as a researcher in a library. He wrote a number of narrative poems but never finished them. The situation in the country was becoming unstable again, and writers especially did not know how long they could continue to write freely.

By 1929 his marriage had fallen apart. In his cousin Olga's diary, she describes the situation: "At this time Boris and Zhenya were going through a period of strained relations. Each of them was an artist and each had an artist's egoism. Zhenya dreamed of Paris and thought that her marriage to Borya would relieve her of all worldly cares. She was deeply disappointed. He was used to the Tolstoyan standard: a daily life based on lofty ideas and family life such as that depicted in *War and Peace*. Zhenya offered him a Bohemian life. He was not to be tempted by a Puccini libretto or convinced that art required a loosening of the reins. His father was a painter, his mother a musician, he himself a poet. He was convinced of something quite different: that art binds and constrains, concentrates and crystallizes the family."[2]

During this time Boris fell in love with Zinaida Neuhaus, the wife of a famous painter and teacher at Moscow Conservatory of Music. They ran away together to the Caucasus Mountains where the Georgian poet Paolo Yashvili had invited them. Pasternak developed a special love for the dramatic landscape of this area. He began translating the work of Georgian poets, especially Titsian Tabidze and Yashvili, with whom he had become very close friends.

After the couple moved back to Moscow, Boris had times when he was ill, times when he was depressed, and times of hope. He wrote *The Second Birth*, a collection of poetry.

Surviving the Dangerous Years

By the time Pasternak was forty, he was well known as a talented poet. He was invited to join the Writers Union, published *Georgian Lyrics*, and was invited to give poetry readings. Unfortunately, he was not an effective speaker and stumbled over lines or forgot them. To his joy and appreciation, listeners would call out the forgotten lines when he needed them. In his writing, he kept to his own style, refusing to obey the governmental standard for poetry. Where others were writing to support Marxism and extol the glorious victory of Communism, he kept his work more in line with classical Russian writers. This would cause serious problems for him in the future, but for a few years in the 1930s, special situations were provided for members of the Writers Union, such as very nice apartments and dachas (summer houses) in the wooded area of Peredelkino. Boris and Zinaida married in 1934, and two years later they moved into a dacha there which became their home for the rest of Pasternak's life.

However, as the State began exercising more control over what writers could write, it became a difficult, dangerous time for writers in the Soviet Union. Pasternak published very little. Around him well-known writers were being sent off to labor camps, being shot by the secret police, and committing suicide. Stalin wanted complete obedience and acknowledgement of the regime, and he would tolerate no deviation from his orders. It has never been clear how Pasternak survived these years when his contemporaries met such tragic ends.

An example of how tense the times were is a telephone call between Stalin and Pasternak. There are two different versions of this call. As described by Payne,[3] one version begins with a group gathering in Pasternak's Moscow apartment. The poet Osip Mandelstam recited some verses he had written mocking Stalin. This was a dangerous act, and those gathered agreed not to discuss them. However, news of the verses reached Stalin, and he ordered Mandelstam arrested. Nadezda Mandelstam begged Pasternak to do what he could to save her husband from arrest. He agreed to do so. Where Pasternak was staying at a friend's country house, the phone rang and it was Stalin. How could Stalin have found him? Pasternak assumed he was to be arrested. Stalin asked Pasternak why he had tried to intervene to help Mandelstam. Pasternak answered that he was always concerned with the fate of a brother poet from whom he had learned a great deal. Stalin asked, "Is he a great poet?" Unsure of how to answer, Pasternak said that one cannot measure greatness just as one cannot measure beauty in a woman. A second time Stalin asked. A second time Pasternak was evasive. When Stalin demanded an answer, Pasternak said Mandelstam was a great poet deserving of protection. Stalin was quiet. To Pasternaks's relief, Mandelstam was not executed, but banished to a provincial town. A few years later he was allowed to return to Moscow, then was later exiled to Vladivostok, where he died in a Siberian labor camp in 1940.

A second version is that Stalin phoned Pasternak to let him know that he had listened to his pleas and also to those of Anna Akhmatova on behalf of Mandelstam. After an exchange Pasternak said he wanted to meet Stalin and talk with him. "About what?" Stalin asked. "About life and death," Pasternak replied. Stalin hung up, and that was the end of the conversation. Pasternak had thought he might be able to open Stalin's eyes to what was going on. But Stalin was not interested. Different authors place this phone call in 1932 and in 1934.[4]

Another strange incident involved Stalin and Pasternak. Stalin's wife had died mysteriously (shot in the abdomen, possibly by herself, possibly by Stalin in a drunken rage). Thirty-three well-established Soviet writers wrote a rather formal and cold letter of condolence, and it was printed in the newspaper. Pasternak had not signed it but had added a short note indicating that, although he had read the letter, he preferred to make his own statement. He wrote that he had had a deep intuition about this death as if he had been present. Did Stalin think Pasternak might have second sight? Was Pasternak a genius of a poet with special qualities? Some scholars surmise that because of this feeling, Stalin, while he was willing to send other writers to labor camps or to be shot, may have protected Pasternak. From Pasternak's point of view, life was very dangerous and he never knew if he would be arrested.

The years between 1930 and 1940 were particularly dangerous because Stalin ruled with an iron hand, demanding complete obedience. In 1934 at the First Congress of All Soviet Writers, Stalin laid out the requirements of Socialist Realism in which all literary works were to support the State and honor the accomplishments of Communism. Pasternak alone stood up and spoke of the need for writers to have independence, and he asked other writers not to be afraid. Because of this challenge, he became the target of hostility. His poetry was banned, and his books could not be published or sold. He supported himself doing translations of Shakespeare, Goethe and Rilke. Not able to sleep at night, he became exhausted mentally and physically. In 1935, at the age of forty-five, Pasternak had a heart attack.

The Situation Worsens

During the 1936 Reign of Terror, numbers of "enemies of the people" were exiled, imprisoned, and executed. In 1937 both Yashvili and Tabidze perished. Tabidze "vanished" in the manner familiar of those years and was executed soon after his arrest, although news only reached his family in 1955. Yashvili committed suicide. Pasternak wrote to his widow: "Just as one moves away from something very, very big, his outlines began to take shape only at the fateful distance of his loss."

Up to this point Pasternak had considered literature to be separate from society. However, with the Stalinist arrests, he decided to resist the government. Communist ideology focused on collectivism, changing all aspects of Russian life. Pasternak stood firmly against it by stating a philosophy based on the individual. He no longer wrote only about feelings and emotions, but began to use his writing to stand up for individualism and Christianity, knowing that by referring to the political situation, he was risking not only his reputation but his life. He was still not able to publish freely and spent much of 1940 translating Shakespeare's *Hamlet*. During these years he felt suffocated, and when World War II began, Pasternak and many others greeted it with relief.

As fighting drew near Moscow, Pasternak, his wife, and four-year-old son were evacuated along with other members of the Writers Union to a village in the Urals, the same area where he had lived during World War I. He returned to Moscow and acted as a fire-watcher. These were savage times as the war became intense. He lived in a ruined building, fending for himself, and survived on occasional gifts of food that admirers left for him. In 1943, when the German offensive was broken, he returned to Peredelkino. He had hoped that with the Soviet victory, the situation would lighten, and he would be free to publish again. As a result of the difficulties during the war years, he was exhausted, in ill health, and still in imminent danger of being arrested. Rather than liberalizing, Stalin celebrated his victory by intensifying his hold on the people, and on writers in particular.

In 1945 Pasternak decided to use the only weapon he had against Stalin. He began to write a novel that would describe the true conditions during the Revolution and Civil War. It was during this time that he met Olga Ivinskaya, an editor and translator, who became his collaborator on this new book. Their relationship continued for the rest of his life.

He continued writing, and occasionally he read a chapter of the book at a gathering of friends. In 1948 he was attacked again in the Congress of Writers, declared an enemy of the state, as he had written no poems in praise of Stalin or the Red Army. Since he could not publish, he continued working on his translations, including the complete set of Shakespeare's tragedies, and on his book which would be titled *Dr. Zhivago*. He was determined not to retreat from confrontation.

That same year, an evening of poetry on the theme "Down with the Warmongers! For a Lasting Peace and People's Democracy" was announced. The names of poets listed to take part included Boris Pasternak. It seemed strange that he would be invited since he was continually under attack in the press. As the evening began, the large hall was jam-packed. Twenty-two poets sat in chairs on stage, but one chair remained empty, and Pasternak's absence was noted. The audience looked around as the first poet spoke his verse denouncing NATO, Western warmongers, and Churchill. Was Pasternak going to come? Halfway through the first poet's last line, the audience burst into applause. Ah! Pasternak had arrived and slipped into a seat in the back row. The audience burst into applause despite Pasternak's attempts to quiet them. The recital continued, as each poet stood up and recited poetry denouncing NATO. When Pasternak's name was called, the audience went wild with clapping and shouting. Pasternak smiled shyly, and the audience calmed down. Instead of walking up to the microphone, he came down some steps, stood below, facing the audience directly and gestured for the audience to stop clapping. A tense silence followed. Pasternak spoke: "Unfortunately, I have no poem on the theme of the evening, but I will read you some things I wrote before the war." Pasternak recited several well-known poems. After each poem, the audience burst into tremendous applause. At one moment when he forgot a line, the audience filled it in. People began to shout out requests for particular poems, including some that had been published illegally. Someone shouted, "Give us the Sixty-sixth."[5] (The sixty-sixth Shakespearean sonnet includes the words, "And art made tongue-tied by authority.") The moderator did everything to try to restore order and keep the meeting from getting out of hand. When nothing else worked, he called for intermission, and Pasternak did not get to speak the sixty-sixth sonnet.

In 1949 Olga Ivinskaya was arrested, held in a Lubyanka prison, headquarters of the secret police, and sentenced to five years in labor camp. Pasternak was shaken by this and tried to get them to take him in her place, but they were able to mentally torture him more effectively by keeping his mistress imprisoned.

In 1952 Pasternak had a second heart attack and was rushed to hospital in an ambulance. He had expected to die, but was delighted that he had survived. Although he was willing to accept death, he was so happy to be alive and to be able express his joy of life. He recuperated, and continued writing.

In 1953 Stalin died. Olga was released, and they were reunited. No longer did Pasternak need only to translate, although he had just completed the first translation of *Faust* in the Soviet Union. A year later Pasternak announced that he had completed the book, *Dr. Zhivago*, "the most important and most difficult work I have ever accomplished in my life."[6] Doctor Zhivago is the eternal rebel. Although he was idealistic at the beginning of the Revolution, he comes to hate the

Soviet state. He is a poet and a doctor, and he is unable to fight the state directly. All he can do is suffer the powers of evil and bear witness through his poetry.

In 1956 Pasternak submitted the manuscript of *Dr. Zhivago* to the editors of *Novy Mir* (*New World*) for publication. The manuscript was returned with a thirty-page reply attacking the novel. The letter from *Novy Mir* accused Pasternak of being anti-democratic, unjust to the revolution, unfair to the Russian people, inaccurate in his portrayal of events, too personal and self-indulgent, and championing a return to the Russia of the tsars. The letter follows:

From *Novy Mir*: An Attack on Pasternak's *Dr. Zhivago* (1954)

Your heroes, and particularly Dr. Zhivago, spent the years of the Revolution and the Civil War in search of relative well being and tranquility of soul, and this amid all the vicissitudes of struggle, amid general devastation and ruin. Physically they are not cowards, and you as the author go to great pains to stress this aspect of their characters even though they have only one goal — to preserve their own lives. This desire to preserve their lives guides them in all their actions, and the knowledge that their lives remain insecure during the tribulations of the Revolution and the Civil War leads them to an ever-increasing resentment. Of course, they are not property grabbers, gourmets, or sybarites. They do not need comfort for its own sake, but as a means to continue the enjoyment of the spiritual life.

And what is this spiritual life they are always seeking? It is the life they lived in the past, for nothing enters their spiritual life and nothing changes it. They regard the possibility of continuing to live without outside interference as the greatest possible blessing, not only for themselves but for all mankind. Because the Revolution steadfastly requires them to take sides, they turn in self-defense from a feeling of alienation from the Revolution to a feeling of active hostility toward it.

You have written a novel which is essentially a political sermon, and you have conceived it as a work to be placed freely and unreservedly at the service of certain political concepts, and, of course, we have had to focus attention on this aspect of it, if only because you yourself have paid so much attention to these ideas.

However painful it is for us, we must call a spade a spade. We find your novel profoundly unjust and lacking in historical objectivity in its portrayal of the Revolution, the Civil War and the years following the Revolution. We regard it as a profoundly anti-democratic work and without benefit to the people. We come to these conclusions in the light of your position as a man attempting to prove that the October Revolution, far from possessing a great significance for mankind, brought only hardship and evil into the world.

Our position is diametrically opposed to yours, and therefore we believe that the publication of your novel in the columns of *Novy Mir* is undesirable.[7]

About the same time a copy of the corrected typewritten manuscript was given to an agent of the Italian publisher Feltrinelli and taken to Milan. Other copies typed by students in Moscow University were also in circulation. From some accounts it seems that an abridged version was going to be published, but then Pasternak fell ill and spent the winter of 1956 in the Kremlin clinic reserved for eminent politicians, scientists and artists. Pasternak was pressured to get the Italian edition postponed by six months, but Feltrinelli did not agree. When the novel began to appear in the Italian magazine *Espresso*, the excerpts concentrating on the failure of the Bolshevik Revolution gave a distorted view of the novel. This distortion convinced Moscow that Pasternak had written this as a political attack on all that had happened since 1917. Despite pressure from Soviet Communists who had gone to Italy to stop the book from being published, the Italian edition appeared on November 15, 1957. The first six thousand copies sold out immediately, and more copies were printed. Pasternak insisted that this was not a political novel. Rather, he had written it in his heart's blood, celebrating the genius of the Russian people.

Pasternak spent his days writing, tramping through the pinewoods with his dog, visiting with his three sons and many friends, and trying to find peace from the political pressures. But the storm was coming. When his novel appeared in Great Britain and the United States in September 1958, it received more acclaim than any novel in twenty years. What could the Russian government do? They could not arrest or kill him, but they could make his life miserable. They could not threaten his income because thousands of dollars in royalties were going into foreign banks. Exile would be the worst fate, and that is what they were preparing.

By the time Boris Pasternak was sixty-seven, he had lived in so much turmoil. He felt he had the duty to bear witness to the truth, not as a politician, but as an artist. He continued working despite the storms, and he gave readings of his poems. Although he was officially watched all the time, his appreciative audiences let him know how much they valued his stance. A year after publication of Dr. Zhivago, in 1958, he was awarded the Nobel Prize in Literature. Invited to come to Stockholm to receive the medal and prize, he replied to the telegram in English: "INFINITELY GRATEFUL TOUCHED PROUD ASTOUNDED CONFUSED." He was told sternly by the Kremlin to refuse the prize. In the press he was called a pig, a snake and a traitor.

Although forbidden to speak with Western journalists, he resisted the order and spoke openly about the prize. The new Russia was coming to birth; it could not be stopped. "In our age, people are moving towards a new attitude towards life. Let me point out one thing. During the nineteenth century it was the bourgeoisie that ruled. Our own literature tells you about this. Mankind sought security in money, land, and things. Man's dream of security was heaviness and stability. This applies not only to Russians. In this age of world wars, in this atomic age, the values have changed. We have learned that we are the guests of existence, travelers between two stations. We must discover security within ourselves. During our short span of life we must find our own insights into our relationship with the existence in which we participate so briefly. Otherwise, we cannot live! This means, as I see it, a departure from the materialistic view of the nineteenth century. It means a reawakening of the spiritual world, of our inner life—of religion. I don't mean religion as a dogma or as a church, but as a vital feeling. Do you understand what I mean?"[8]

But Pasternak was forced to telephone the Nobel Prize Committee and tell them he had to decline the award. He was ousted from the Union of Soviet Writers under the most horrifying circumstances in which a crowded auditorium of hacks screamed and yelled that he should be arrested, shot, or at least exiled. Loss of his membership meant he could no longer publish. Hounded by the KGB, he was threatened with exile and loss of citizenship. He asked not to be exiled, saying that to be out of Russia would also be a death. Although he performed the act of recantation and apologized for his actions, the attacks continued.

He wrote the poem "Nobel Prize" in which he described how impossible his life had become. His health deteriorated as he had lung cancer and heart disease. Over fifteen days, the government harassed him and taunted him to the point of his considering suicide. He died quietly in an oxygen tent, his last words addressed to his wife.

Boris Pasternak died on May 30, 1960. The government did everything it could to downplay the event. In another situation there would have been newspaper announcements of the funeral, but in this case, only a handwritten scrap of paper was posted next to the ticket window at the Kiev Station in Moscow. It was taken down, but mysteriously replaced several times. The paper said: "Comrades! On the night of May 30–31, 1960, one of the great poets of modern times, Boris Leonidovich Pasternak, passed away."[9]

Last rites of the Orthodox Church were performed at his house. The next morning the funeral was held. Outstanding pianists took turns performing. Among the pallbearers who bore the coffin out were Andrei Sinyavsky and Yuki Daniel (later to be persecuted for their dissident writing), and Lev Kopelev. They emerged to a sea of grieving faces—friends, students, workers, and peasants. A Writers Union official stepped out of a large black limousine and attempted to take charge of the coffin, but the students shouted him down. The people insisted on carrying the coffin to the cemetery.

There were plainclothes agents pretending to mourn, while eavesdropping and clicking their cameras; and there were foreign journalists just doing a job. All the rest of the four or five thousand crowding into Peredelkino's cemetery were there out of love and respect. Someone shouted: "He loved the workers." Another cry: "He spoke the truth." Yet another: "The poet was killed." And the crowd responded: "Shame! Shame! Shame!" In an anguished voice, a young physicist read the poem "Hamlet" from *Doctor Zhivago*, its final line the Russian proverb: "To live your life is not as simple as crossing a field."[10]

Members of the crowd spoke softly and lovingly as they bade Pasternak farewell. At one point an official tried to end the funeral, but the crowd would not obey. One young man spoke, "God marks the path of the elect with thorn, and Pasternak was picked out and marked by God. He believed in eternity and he will belong to it. . . . We excommunicated Tolstoy, we disowned Dostoyevsky, and now we disown Pasternak. Everything that brings us glory we try to banish to the West … but we cannot allow this. We love Pasternak and we revere him as a poet."[11]

As the coffin was lowered, the cemetery became one blaze of flowers, passed from hand to hand over the heads of the crowd, toward the grave. Afterward, the people refused to leave. Poems were read or quoted by heart, on into the candlelit night. People's lips could be seen moving silently, in unison. Rain fell, but still the readings went on.

His membership in the Union of Soviet Writers was posthumously reinstated. In 1987 *Dr. Zhivago* was published in the U.S.S.R. Soon after, the KGB raided Olga Ivinskaya's home, seized notes, letters, papers of Pasternak, and she and her daughter were sentenced to the Gulag (labor camp) again, this time for four years.

Winter Night[12]

It snowed and snowed, the whole world over,
Snow swept the world from end to end.
A candle burned on the table;
A candle burned.

As during summer midges swarm
To beat their wings against a flame,
Out in the yard the snowflakes swarmed
To beat against the windowpane.

The blizzard sculptured out the glass
Designs of arrows and of whorls.
A candle burned on the table;
A candle burned.

Distorted shadows fell
Upon the lighted ceiling:
Shadows of crossed arms, of crossed legs —
Of crossed destiny.

Two tiny shoes fell to the floor
And thudded.
A candle on a nightstand shed wax tears
Upon a dress.

All things vanished within
The snowy murk — white, hoary,
A candle burned on the table;
A candle burned.

A corner draft fluttered the flame
And the white fever of temptation
Upswept its angel wings that cast
A cruciform shadow.

It snowed hard throughout the month
Of February, and almost constantly
A candle burned on the table;
A candle burned.

Nobel Prize (1959)[13]

Like a beast in a pen, I'm cut off
From my friends, freedom, the sun,
But the hunters are gaining ground,
I've nowhere else to run.

Dark wood and the bank of a pond,
Trunk of a fallen tree.
There's no way forward, no way back.
It's all up with me.

Am I a gangster or a murderer?
Of what crime do I stand
Condemned? I made the whole world weep
At the beauty of my land.

Even so, one step from my grave,
I believe that cruelty, spite,
The powers of darkness will in time
Be crushed by the spirit of light.

The beaters in a ring close in
With the wrong prey in view.
I've nobody at my right hand,
Nobody faithful and true.

And with such a noose on my throat
I should like for one second
My tears to be wiped away
By someone at my right hand.

Holy Week[14]

The murk of night still prevails.
It is yet so early in this world
That the sky even now flaunts its countless stars,
And each star is radiant as the day.
And if the earth could really have its way
It would sleep through all of Eastertide
To the droning of the Psalms as a lullaby.

The murk of night still prevails.
The Creation's hour is yet so early
That the square extends like eternity
From one corner to the other,
And there is still a millennium
Until the dawn and warmth come.

The earth is stark-naked yet:
It hasn't got a stitch to wear of nights
To ring the bells, or to chime in
Of its own accord, with choirs singing.

From Maundy Thursday right up to
The very eve of Easter the waters gnaw
At riverbanks, and are busy weaving
Their currents, whirlpools, and eddies.

The forest, too, is stripped, exposed,
And all through Passiontide
The trunks of pines stand in a throng
Like worshippers aligned in prayer.

While in the town, not too far off,
The trees stand mother-naked too,
As if about to enter church
And peering within its gratings.

Their gaze is overcome with awe,
Nor is their panic hard to fathom:
The gardens leave their boundary walls,
The laws that govern the earth are shaken —
A god is being interred.

They see a glow about the altar screen,
And the black pall, and tapers in a row,
And faces all in tears. . . .
And a procession suddenly emerges
Bearing the Cross and Shroud,
And comes toward them. Two birches
Guarding the portals have to step aside
And yield the right of way.

The procession makes a circuit of the church grounds,
Walking along the very curb of the pavement,
And brings in from the street within the portals
The spring, and all the murmurings of spring,
And air that has about it the tang of consecrated wafers
And of the heady fumes of spring.

And March scoops up the snow on the porch
And scatters it like alms among the halt and lame —
As though a man had carried out the Ark,
And opened it, and distributed all it held.

The singing lasts until the glow of dawn.
The voices, having sobbed their fill,
Are more subdued. Their chanting of the Psalms and Gospels
Floats out more and more faintly
Until it reaches wastelands under lonely lamps.

And when the midnight comes
All creatures and all flesh will fall silent
On hearing spring put forth its rumor
That just as soon as there is better weather
Death itself can be overcome
Through the power of the Resurrection.

Parting[15]

The man is staring across the threshold
And cannot recognize his home.
Her going had been like a flight.
Havoc has left its traces everywhere.

Chaos prevails in all the rooms.
He cannot judge the devastation.
Because his eyes are blurred with tears,
Because his head is pounding.

Ever since morning his ears have been ringing.
Is he awake or having a bad dream?
And why do thoughts about the sea
Persist in coming to his mind?

When one no longer sees the day
Because of hoarfrost on the panes,
The hopelessness of grief redoubles
Its likeness to the sea's vast desert.

He drew her every trait to him,
Even as the sea draws near it
Each of the many littorals
Throughout the stretch of the incoming tide.

Even as reeds go down beneath
The rough seas following a storm,
So every line of her had gone
To the bottom of his soul.

In years of hardships, in the days
Of an unthinkable existence,
She had been cast up from the depths
By a high wave of destiny.

Amid innumerable perils,
Avoiding every reef and shoal,
The wave had borne her on and on
And brought her close.

And now, this flight of hers, perhaps
It had been forced upon her.
This parting will consume them both
And grief gnaw clean their bones.

His eyes take in the whole scene.
At the moment of her going
She had upset the contents of
Every compartment in her dresser.

He paces aimlessly and till dark comes
Keeps putting back inside a drawer
The scattered scraps of cloth,
The crumpled sample patterns.

And having run into his hand
A needle left in some unfinished sewing
He suddenly sees all of her
And falls to sobbing. Softly.

Recollections of Pasternak by Andrei Voznesensky

When Andrei Vozensensky was fourteen, he made contact with the fifty-seven-year-old Pasternak to show him his poems. Pasternak treated the boy with respect and shared his own poems. The following are excerpts from *I Am Fourteen*.[16]

He stood in the doorway. Everything swam before my eyes. The surprised, elongated dusky flame of his face looked out at me. A wax-yellow sweater clung to his sturdy torso. A breeze ruffled the hair on his forehead. . . .

I was astonished by the asceticism, the impoverished expanse of his unheated study ... Muller's *English-Russian Dictionary*, he was chained to his translation then. My school copybook cowered on the desk — probably prepared for the conversation. A wave of horror and adoration passed over me. But it was too late to flee. . . .

Why did he get in touch with me?

He was lonely in those years, tired from many troubles; he wanted sincerity, an honest relationship, he wanted to break out of the encirclement — but it was more than that. Perhaps this strange relationship with an adolescent, a schoolboy, this friendship that was not quite a friendship, explains something about him. It was not friendship between a lion and a dog, it was more like that of a lion and a puppy.

Perhaps what he liked in me was himself, who had run to Schriabin as a schoolboy.

"The artist," he used to say, "is by nature optimistic. The very essence of creative activity is optimistic. Even when you write tragic works, you must write powerfully; despair and whining do not create works of strength." His speech flowed in an uninterrupted, breathless monologue. There was more music than grammar in it. His speech was not divided into sentences or sentences into words — everything flowed in a stream of consciousness, a thought was uttered, only to return and enchant. His poetry had the same kind of flow.

Later, the boy was invited to readings in Peredelkino.

The readings took place in his semicircular bay-windowed study on the second floor. People gathered. Chairs were brought up from downstairs. Usually there were about twenty guests. . . . Through the wall of windows one could see the September woods. The trees were ablaze. . . . The air over the field shimmered. And the same agitated trembling was in the air of the study. It vibrated with anticipation. . . .

We quieted down. Pasternak took his place at the table. He wore a light silvery jacket, of military cut now popular again. That time he read from *Dr. Zhivago*, and the poems—"White Night," "Nightingale," "Fairy Tale"—his whole notebook of that period. "Hamlet" came at the end. As he read, he stared at something above our heads, visible to him alone. His face grew longer and thinner. And his jacket was a reflection of the white night.

... Did he help me find my voice?

He simply told me what he liked and why. For instance, he spent a long time explaining the meaning of my line: "The epaulets' big hands gripped you by the shoulders." Besides precision of imagery, he wanted poetry to breathe, to have tension and the added ingredient that he called "force."

... He was buried on June 2.

I remember the terrible feeling of emptiness that engulfed his dacha, filled to overflowing with people. . . . Everything swam before my eyes. Life had lost its meaning. . . . He was carried by pallbearers (they had refused to use the hearse), carried from the house, the haven of his life, circling the famous field he loved, carried to the hillside with the three pines, at which he used to stare. . . . The unneeded hearse moved slowly ahead of him. Back down the hill was the grieving nonliterary crowd—locals and out-of-towners, witnesses and neighbors of his days, sobbing students, the heroines of his poems. His features surfaced desperately on the face of his eldest son, Zhenya. . . . Cameras clicked. The trees came out from behind their fences, the melancholy dirt road, which he had taken so often to the station, bitterly threw up dust.

Someone stepped on a red peony, fallen by the roadside.

I did not return to the dacha. He was not there. He was not anywhere anymore.

Personal Comments

On my second trip to Moscow I was determined to visit Boris Pasternak's house. I was no longer paranoid about being arrested by the KGB. But I had to be clever as well. I researched what train station would be our starting point for a train to Peredelkino, the writers' village where he had lived. I had read an article in the *New York Times* about the transformation of his house into a photographic museum, and a photograph of his house accompanied the article. I approached our guide and said, "IF we were to go to Peredelkino, would we go to such and such a train station?"

She replied, "No, IF you were to go to Peredelkino, you would go to the Kiev station." This response kept her out of trouble since it was all based on IF. Armed with this information, I offered the opportunity to the group, explaining that I did not know how much the train would cost or how long it would take.

About ten students decided to come with me. At the train station we purchased pink roses and paid for our tickets which cost all of thirteen cents each. As we rode to Peredelkino (about half an hour), we were jammed between people carrying chickens and those carrying baskets of recently picked mushrooms. The cityscape soon gave way to birch forest, and the train stopped at Peredelkino. Armed with the roses and copies of *Dr. Zhivago*, we found our way to the cemetery. Students started at the four corners eagerly searching for his tombstone, and one by one, we all gathered at the gravesite of Boris Pasternak. We took turns reading his poem "Resurrection" and putting roses on his grave. It was an awe-inspiring moment.

Filled with self-confidence, we asked, *"Gdye doma Pasternaka?"* and a woman beckoned us to follow her on a narrow path through the forest. Soon the familiar site of the brown country house (*dacha*) was seen, and we continued on our own. We knocked on the door, and a caretaker came out, but he would not let us in. We hung around, sharing snacks of raisins and nuts. Meanwhile a woman came through the forest, walking arm in arm with a gentleman on either side. The students offered them snacks and we began speaking. It turned out that the woman was the widow of Nazim Hikmet, a Turkish poet who had been favored by the Soviet regime. One of the men was a French filmmaker, and the other a Russian. Upon learning that Hikmet had been her husband, my son George who had majored in poetry at Brown University then spoke some lines of his poetry by heart.

Not only was she deeply moved that this young American had done that, but the caretaker, who had been lingering on the porch, then beckoned to us that we could have five minutes in the house. We actually had over an hour in the house, looking at photographs of Pasternak's life, experiencing the room where he died which had been kept exactly as it had been at that time. It was a glorious experience. Filled with self-confidence, we buoyantly retraced our steps through the forest back to the train station. What a wonderful day we had had.

Student writing:

Describe your thoughts on how historical events affected Pasternak's work.

In many ways, Pasternak has been defined by historical events and his reaction to them. He would have been a completely different writer if he had been born in a different era. Many of his poems are topical, and his pen was his greatest weapon against the Communist Russian government.

One of the greatest struggles in Pasternak's life was trying to get his work approved and published by the government. His status with the Russian Writers Union (the arm of the government that dealt with the approval and publishing of literature) was constantly changing, and this made for an extremely unpredictable and tense life. He went from being officially recognized and given a country house to write in, to not being allowed to accept the Nobel Prize he had won and having his mistress forced to work in a labor camp for four years. He later wrote poems about both of these events, entitled "Nobel Prize" and "Parting." His funeral was a microcosm of his life: It was attended by thousands of common people who loved his work and a few suspicious government agents.

What is truly amazing about Pasternak is that throughout his life and all of his trouble and torment by the government, he never stopped writing, and he never turned his critical eye away from the government. His story is that of a man who never wavered in his views and told the world about the injustices of the world. – *L.S.*

Passages from *Dr. Zhivago*

Following are a few selections from the book that lend themselves to interesting class discussions.

Chapter 1

Nikolai Nikolaievich (a former priest and Yuri Zhivago's uncle) and Ivan Ivanovich are having a conversation.

"What you don't understand is that it is possible to be an atheist, it is possible not to know whether God exists, or why, and yet believe that man does not live in a state of nature but in history, and that history as we know it now began with Christ, and that Christ's Gospel is its foundation. Now, what is history? It is the centuries of systematic explorations of the riddles of death, with a view to overcoming death. That's why people discover mathematical infinity and electromagnetic waves, that's why they write symphonies. Now, you can't advance in this direction without a certain faith. You can't make such discoveries without spiritual equipment. And the basic elements of this equipment are in the Gospels. What are they? To begin with, love of one's neighbor, which is the supreme form of vital energy. Once it fills the heart of man it has to overflow and spend itself. And then the two basic ideals of modern man—without them he is unthinkable—the idea of free personality and the idea of life as sacrifice. Mind you, all this is still extraordinarily new. There was no history in this sense among the ancients. They had blood and beastliness and cruelty and pockmarked Caligulas who do not suspect how untalented every enslaver is. They had the boastful dead eternity of bronze monuments and marble columns. It was not until after the coming of Christ that time and man could breathe freely. It was not until after Him that men began to live toward the future. Man does not die in a ditch like a dog—but at home in history, while the work toward the conquest of death is in full swing; he dies sharing in this work. Ouf! I got quite worked up, didn't I? But I might as well be talking to a blank wall."

"That's metaphysics, my dear fellow. It's forbidden by my doctors, my stomach won't take it."

"Oh well, you're hopeless. Let's leave it. . . . "[17]

Chapter 2

Nikolai Nikolaievich is trying to explain his ideas about Tolstoyan doctrines to a follower of Tolstoy.

"Up to a point I am with you, but Tolstoy says that the more a man devotes himself to beauty the further he moves away from goodness. . . .

"And you think it's the other way round—the world will be saved by beauty, is that it? Dostoyevsky, Rozanov, mystery plays, and what not?

"Wait, let me tell you what I think. I think that if the beast who sleeps in man could be held down by threats—any kind of threat, whether of jail or of retribution after death—then the highest emblem of humanity would be the lion tamer in the circus with his whip, not the prophet who sacrificed himself. But don't you see, this is just the point—what has for centuries raised man above the beast is not the cudgel but an inward music: the irresistible power of unarmed truth, the powerful attraction of its example. It has always been assumed that the most important things in the Gospels are the ethical maxims and commandments. But for me the most important thing is that Christ speaks in parables taken from life, that He explains the truth in terms of everyday reality. The idea that underlies this is that communion between mortals is immortal, and that the whole of life is symbolic because it is meaningful." [18]

Chapter 3
Throughout November 1911, Anna Ivanovna stayed in bed with pneumonia.

They wanted to give me the last sacraments. . . . Death is hanging over me. . . . It may come any moment. . . . When you go to have a tooth out you're frightened, it'll hurt, you prepare yourself. . . . But this isn't a tooth, it's everything, the whole of you, your whole life … being pulled out …And what is it? Nobody knows. . . . And I am sick at heart and terrified."

She fell silent. Tears were streaming down her cheeks. Yuri said nothing. A moment later Anna Ivanovna went on. "You're clever, talented. …That makes you different …You surely know something. . . . Comfort me."

"Well, what is there for me to say?" replied Yuri. He fidgeted on his chair, got up, paced the room, and sat down again. "In the first place, you'll feel better tomorrow. There are clear indications—I'd stake my life on it—that you've passed the crisis. And then—death, the survival of consciousness, faith in resurrection. . . . You want to know my opinion as a scientist? Perhaps some other time? No? Right now? Well, as you wish. But it's difficult like that, all of a sudden." And there and then he delivered a whole impromptu lecture, astonished that he could do it.

Resurrection. In the crude form in which it is preached to console the weak, it is alien to me. I have always understood Christ's words about the living and the dead in a different sense. Where could you find room for all these hordes of people accumulated over thousands of years? The universe isn't big enough for them; God, the good, and meaningful purpose would be crowded out. They'd be crushed by these throngs, greedy merely for the animal life.

But all the time, life, one, immense, identical throughout its innumerable combinations and transformations, fills the universe and is continually reborn and you rose from the dead when you were born and you didn't notice it.

Will you feel pain? Do the tissues feel their disintegration? In other words, what will happen to your consciousness? But what is consciousness? Let's see. A conscious attempt to fall asleep is sure to produce insomnia, to try to be conscious of one's own digestion is a sure way to upset the stomach. Consciousness is a poison when we apply it to ourselves. Consciousness is a light directed outward, it lights up the way ahead of us so that we don't stumble. It's like the headlights on a locomotive—turn them inward and you have a crash.

So what will happen to your consciousness? Your consciousness, yours, not anyone else's. Well, what are you? There's the point. Let's try to find out. What is it about you that you have always known as yourself? What are you conscious of in yourself? Your kidneys? Your liver? Your blood vessels? No. However far back you go in your memory, it is always in some external, active manifestation of yourself that you come across your identity—in the work of your hands, in your family, in other people. And now listen carefully. You in others—this is your soul. This is what you are. This is what your consciousness has breathed and lived on and enjoyed throughout your life—your soul, your immortality, your life in others. And what now? You have always been in others. And what does it matter to you if later on that is called your memory? This will be you—the you that enters the future and becomes part of it.

And now one last point. There is nothing to fear. There is no such thing as death. Death has nothing to do with us. But you said something about being talented — that it made one different. Now, that does have something to do with us. And talent in the highest and broadest sense means talent for life.

There will be no death, says Saint John. His reasoning is quite simple. There will be no death because the past is over; that's almost like saying there will be no death because it is already done with, it's old and we are bored with it. What we need is something new, and that new thing is life eternal.[19]

Chapter 5

Zhivago is talking with Lara Antipov before she leaves the field hospital.

Just think what's going on around us! And that you and I should be living at such a time. Such a thing happens only once in an eternity. Just think of it, the whole of Russia has had its roof torn off, and you and I and everyone else are out in the open! And there's nobody to spy on us. Freedom! Real freedom, not just talk about it; freedom, dropped out of the sky, freedom beyond our expectations, freedom by accident, through a misunderstanding.

It was partly the war, the revolution did the rest. The war was an artificial break in life — as if life could be put off for a time — what nonsense! The revolution broke out willy-nilly, like a sigh suppressed too long. Everyone was revived, reborn, changed, transformed. You might say that everyone has been through two revolutions — his own personal revolution as well as the general one. It seems to me that socialism is the sea, and all those separate streams, these private, individual revolutions, are flying into it — the sea of life, the sea of spontaneity. I said life, but I meant life as you see it in a great picture, transformed by genius, creatively enriched. Only now people have decided to experience it not in books and pictures but in themselves, not as an abstraction but in practice.[20]

Zhivago is on his way home from the Front.

His thoughts swarmed and whirled in the dark. But they all fell clearly into two distinct groups, as it were, two main threats that kept getting tangled and untangled.

One group of thoughts centered around Tonia, their home, and their former, settled life where everything, down to the smallest detail, had an aura of poetry and was permeated with affection and warmth. The doctor was concerned about this life, he wanted it safe and whole and in his night express was impatient to get back to it after two years of separation.

In the same group were his loyalty to the revolution and his admiration for it. This was the revolution in the sense in which it was accepted by the middle classes and in which it had been understood by the students, followers of Blok, in 1905.

These familiar, long-held ideas also included the anticipations and promises of a new order which had appeared on the horizon before the war, between 1912 and 1914, which had emerged in Russian thinking, in Russian art, in Russian life, and which had a bearing on Russia as a whole and on his own fortune.

It would be good to go back to that climate, once the war was over, to see its renewal and continuation, just as it was good to be going home.

New things were also in the other group of his thoughts, but how different, how unlike the first! These new things were not familiar, not led up to by the old, they were unchosen, determined by an ineluctable reality, and as sudden as an earthquake.

Among these new things was the war with its bloodshed and its horrors, its homelessness and savagery, its ordeals and the practical wisdom it taught. So, too, were the lonely little towns to which the war washed you up, and the people you met in them. And among these new things too was the revolution — not the idealized intellectuals' revolution of 1905, but this new upheaval, today's, born of the war, those professional revolutionaries, the Bolsheviks.[21]

Chapter 9
From Yuri Zhivago's journals written in Varykino

What I have come to like best in the whole of Russian literature is the childlike Russian quality of Pushkin and Chekhov, their modest reticence in such high-sounding matters as the ultimate purpose of mankind or their own salvation. It isn't that they didn't think about these things, and to good effect, but to talk about such things seemed to them pretentious, presumptuous. Gogol, Tolstoy, Dostoyevsky looked restlessly for the meaning of life, were absorbed in the current, specific tasks imposed on them by their vocation as writers, and in the course of fulfilling these tasks they lived their lives, quietly, treating both their lives and their work as private, individual matters, of no concern to anyone else. And these individual things have since become of concern to all, and their works, like apples picked while they are green, have ripened of themselves, mellowing gradually and growing richer in meaning.[22]

Chapter 13
Yuri Zhivago has returned from being a hostage at the front, frostbitten and shaken by the loss of his family, amazed that he has survived. He and Lara are aware of the danger he is in and that each day they survive is a precious gift.

A spring evening. The air punctuated with scattered sounds. The voices of children playing in the streets coming from varying distances as if to show that the whole expanse is alive. And this vast expanse is Russia, this incomparable mother; famed far and wide, martyred, stubborn, extravagant, crazy, irresponsible, adored, Russia with her eternally splendid and disastrous, and unpredictable adventures. Oh, how sweet to be alive! How good to be alive and to love life! Oh, the ever-present longing to thank life, thank existence itself, to thank them as one being to another being.

All customs and traditions, all our way of life, everything to do with home and order, has crumpled into dust in the general upheaval and reorganization of society. The whole human way of life has been destroyed and ruined. All that's left is the naked human soul stripped to the last shred, for which nothing has changed because it was always cold and shivering and reaching out to its nearest neighbor, as cold and lonely as itself.

Lara speaking about her husband, Pasha Antipov

We were married two years before the war. We were just beginning to make a life for ourselves, we had just set up our home, when the war broke out. I believe now that the war is to blame for everything, for all the misfortunes that followed and that hound our generation to this day. I remember my childhood well. I can still remember a time when we all accepted the peaceful outlook of the last century. It was taken for granted that you listened to reason, that it was right and natural to do what your conscience told you to do. For a man to die by the hand of another was a rare, an exceptional event, something quite out of the ordinary. Murders happened in plays, newspapers, and detective stories, not in everyday life.

And then there was this jump from this peaceful naïve moderation to blood and tears, to mass insanity, and to the savagery of daily, hourly, legalized, rewarded slaughter.

I suppose one must always pay for such things. You must remember better than I do the beginning of disintegration, how everything began to break down all at once—trains and food supplies in towns, and the foundation of the family, and moral standards.

It was then that untruth came down on our land of Russia. The main misfortune, the root of all evil to come, was the loss of confidence in the value of one's own opinion. People imagined that it must be out of date to follow their own moral sense, that they must all sing in chorus, and live by other people's notions, notions that were being crammed down everybody's throat. And then there arose the power of the glittering phrase, first the tsarist, then the revolutionary.

This social evil became an epidemic. It was catching. And it affected everything, nothing was left untouched by it. Our home, too, became infected. Something went wrong in it. Instead of being natural and spontaneous as we had always been, we began to be idiotically pompous with each other. Something showy, artificial, forced, crept into our conversation—you felt you had to be clever in a certain way about certain world-important themes.[23]

Endnotes

1. Max Hayward, *Writers in Russia, 1917–1978* (New York: Harcourt, Brace, Jovanovich, 1983), p. 194.
2. Elliot Mossman, ed., *The Correspondence of Boris Pasternak and Olga Friedenberg, 1910–1954* (New York: Harcourt, Brace, Jovanovich, 1982), pp. 132–133.
3. Robert Payne, *The Three Worlds of Boris Pasternak* (Bloomington: Indiana University Press, 1961), pp. 149–150.
4. Hayward, *Writers in Russia*, p. 199.
5. Ibid., pp. 204–207.
6. Payne, *Three Worlds*, p. 188.
7. Ibid., pp. 193–194.
8. Ibid., p. 202.
9. Olga Ivinskaya, *A Captive of Time* (New York: Doubleday, 1978), p. 326.
10. Ibid., p. 331.
11. Ibid., pp. 331–332.
12. Boris Pasternak, *Dr. Zhivago* (New York: New American Library, 1958), pp. 445–446.
13. Following are two sources for this poem: Ivinskaya, pp. 298–299, and Payne, p. 216. However, the translation I have used for over twenty years, and include here, is slightly different.
14. Pasternak, *Dr. Zhivago*, pp. 434–434.
15. Ibid., pp. 446–447.
16. Andrei Voznesensky, *An Arrow in the Wall, Selected Poetry and Prose* (New York: Henry Holt, 1987), pp. 255–286.

17. Pasternak, *Dr. Zhivago*, p. 13.
18. Ibid., pp. 38–39.
19. Ibid., pp. 59–60.
20. Ibid., pp. 123–124.
21. Ibid., pp. 135–136.
22. Ibid., p. 238.
23. Ibid., p. 325.

Bibliography

Hayward, Max. *Writers in Russia 1917–1978*, New York: Harcourt, Brace, Jovanovich, 1983.

Ivinskaya, Olga. *A Captive of Time*, New York: Doubleday, 1978.

Mossman, Elliot, ed. *The Correspondence of Boris Pasternak and Olga Friedenberg, 1910–1954*, New York: Harcourt, Brace, Jovanovich, 1982.

Pasternak, Boris. *Dr. Zhivago*, New American Library, New York, 1958.

Payne, Robert. *The Three Worlds of Boris Pasternak*, Bloomington: Indiana University Press, 1961.

Thomas, D.M. *Alexander Solzhenitsyn, A Century in His Life*, New York: Saint Martin's Press, 1998.

Voznesensky, Andrei. *An Arrow in the Wall, Selected Poetry and Prose*, New York: Henry Holt, 1987.

Aerial View of Moscow

Moscow University

CHAPTER 11

ANNA AKHMATOVA (1889–1966)

I'm not one of those who have left their land
For enemies to tear apart.
I don't heed their rough flattery
And I will not give them my songs.[1]
                                                – Anna Akhmatova

Anna Akhmatova not only brings a feminine perspective to the experience of the times, but she raises personal themes to a universal level. Her poetry uses everyday items, short fragments, sensory experiences, and a directness that invites us into the scenes to be participants. Whether it is her description of a last meal with a lover or her exhaustion standing on the line outside the prison, we are there with her. We feel her silence, her agony, and her pain. Her work is very accessible to high school students, especially when we read it aloud and discuss each image.

Childhood and Adolescence

Anna Akhmatova was the name she chose when she became a poet. Her birth name was Anna Gorenko. She was born on the Black Sea coast, and although her family would move north when she was eleven months old, this southern region where she would visit for carefree summer days, would always be a place of refuge and freedom in her difficult life. From the date of her birth, she seemed to have a wildness in her soul. She was born on Saint John's Eve, also known as Midsummer Night, when the nature spirits were especially active, when people built fires either on the ground or on a tall pole, and stayed up all night, dancing and singing, waiting for the sun to rise. As the fire died down, they jumped over it either alone or in pairs, and then bathed in the river as they cleansed themselves for a new year.

Her childhood was not a happy one as her parents' marriage was turbulent, and she found it difficult to find peace. Her family was of the upper class, but several members of it were active in a terrorist group, "People's Will." When she was five, she was told that her four-year-old sister Rivka had been sent to stay with an aunt. The truth was that the child had died of tuberculosis. This was one of many secrets that Akhmataova lived with in her childhood.

When her father was transferred to St. Petersburg, the family moved to Tsarskoye Selo (Tsar's Village), the site of the summer palace of the tsars with its beautiful parks and walkways. Here breathed the spirit of Pushkin, who went to school at the summer palace and which would be Akhmatova's inspiration.

Even as a child, Anya, as she was called, was teased about wanting to become a poet. A severe illness when she was ten left her feeling that she had come close to death, and she began seriously writing poetry during this time. Although there were few books in her home, she already began memorizing poems, some in French. When she was fourteen, she met Nikolay Gumilyov, a precocious poet who fell madly in love with her, and who would have a significant impact on her life and work. He saw her as being a mysterious sea nymph, and he convinced a friend to paint the walls of his room as the sea with a mermaid swimming in it. Anya, at that time, seemed oblivious to his affection.

In high school, her teachers considered poetry nonsense. As she looked in vain for women poets to lead the way, she sensed she would have to blaze the trail.

Her time in St. Petersburg added another element to her personality: in contrast to the wildness of the South, she had the coolness of the North. She associated the South with summers where she could run freely and swim in the sea. The North, as she experienced St. Petersburg, was a place of discipline and self-restraint. Both sides of her were active, sometimes in conflict, other times in balance, but always dynamic.

It was during this time that the Russian naval fleet was entirely destroyed by the Japanese, and it shocked her into the outside world of reality. Another shock came when Gumilyov tried to kill himself because she would not take his love seriously. Shocks continued when her father decided to leave the family to move in with his mistress, and her mother took the family of four children back to the South. Anna, at sixteen, was writing poetry. Later she would write, "Stepping out like a sleepwalker, I walked into life and life frightened me."[2] Her feeling of a protected childhood had ended.

In her final years at a high school in Kiev, she changed her name from Gorenko to Akhmatova because her father felt she would bring shame upon the family with her poetry. She chose the name of the last Tatar princess of the Golden Horde and the name of her Tatar great-grandmother. Meanwhile she and Gumilyov began corresponding again and sharing poems. He had continued his obsession with her and asked her to marry him, but she refused. This led to his second suicide attempt. Anna entered the Faculty of Law at the Kiev College for Women. Gumilyov continued to come see her and press her to marry him. At another refusal, he tried to commit suicide a third time. This was the last attempt, although he continued to see her. The shadow of death, which had begun with her little sister, continued with Gumilyov's suicide attempts, and then with her brother Andrey's suicide some years later. Death also stalked with the Revolution of 1905 and would continue with World War I, the Revolution of 1917, the horrors of the Civil War, the Stalinist terror, and World War II. Years later, she wrote,

So that's when we've decided to be born
In order not to miss a single
unprecedented spectacle.[3]

Akhmatova was stunned when she read a manuscript by Innokentiy Annensky, former headmaster of the grammar school that Gumilyov had attended. She knew from that moment that he would her teacher and poetic-mentor.

Adulthood

When Akhmatova turned twenty-one, she finally agreed to marry Gumilyov because she felt it was her fate. He took off to Africa, and then returned for their wedding, which her family did not approve of and did not attend. The couple went to Paris for their honeymoon. While in Paris, Akhmatova developed a close relationship with the artist Modigliani and was swept into the world of the leftwing artists. When the newly-married couple returned to St. Petersburg, they moved in with his mother. Gumilyov was restless and unfaithful, taking off to exotic places, having affairs with other women, and all the while proclaiming Anya was his true love.

When Gumilyov returned from Ethiopia, she met him at the railway station. He demanded to know if she had been writing, and then to read it right there. He proclaimed it, Good! Akhmatova began to have her poems published in journals. Gumilyov, himself a published poet, brought together a group of young poets, who met several times a month eat dinner together, recite their poems, and argue about them. It was here that she first met Osip Mandelstam. The group was breaking away from symbolism, and they adopted a new style which they called "Acmeism" meaning clarity. They steered their poems in a direction more down to earth, rather than escaping to another world. They would search for God through the terrors of their time rather than escape from the world around them.

Many of the forty-six poems in *Evening*, Akhmatova's first collection, deal with a woman who has been left by her lover or is in the midst of a breakup. She uses everyday images as props to support her more universal images of a soul that has lost her mate and is grieving. The book received good reviews. Her poems attracted young people who formed a circle of admirers around her. Similarly, I find that high school students make an easy and immediate connection with these poems, especially the pain of loving as a reflection of their own experiences.

During this time she devoured the writings of Tolstoy and Dostoyevsky as she connected with their desire to understand human nature. She and Gumilyov took an exciting journey in western Europe, during which time she drank in European art. She gave birth to her son, Lev, on October 1. Unfortunately, she and Gumilyov were not the kind of parents who would set up a safe, comfortable life for a child. Their relationship was too stormy. Each was independent. They could not live with each and they could not stay away apart. Each was too big a personality, too passionate about life and relationships to be able to be confined by a conventional one. Akhmatova wrote about the sacrifices a woman had to make to become a poet. This conflict followed her throughout her life in her role as mother and artist. She asked, What is the role of the woman poet in Russian society? While she wrote in her poem, "The Muse," that the Muse takes away from the poet the golden ring, the marriage ring, symbolizing normal family life, she also shared with all other women the torment of love.

Akhmatova stayed home with Lev at the beginning, but then left him to his grandmother to rear. She visited him at holidays and in the summer. Gumilyov, off on his escapes to Africa, was jealous of her success. The two remained legally married, but their relationship was only a formality.

She spent many nights at the Stray Dog, a bohemian café, holding court dressed in her usual black silk dress, and cameo belt. She cut a dramatic figure, reciting her poetry in a musical rhythm. Flanked by her admirers, Akhmatova managed to keep a cool aloofness, protecting her private self from her public one. The subject of many drawings and paintings, she was a mysteriously beautiful woman. Mandelstam wrote of her as a "black angel with the strange mark of God upon her."[4]

Her second collection, *Rosary*, made her one of the most popular poets in Russia. The poems in this volume and from her third one, *White Flock*, capture the images of a woman maturing, surviving the loss of love, and holding out hope. She referred in one of her poems to the touch of God's hand on the poet's closed eyelids, inspiring words uniting the mortal with the divine, harkening back to Pushkin's "The Prophet."

In 1914, when the news arrived that war had broken out, she recognized it as something she had felt coming. Now life in its truest form would begin. The war was a punishment for Russian people because the intelligentsia and the upper class had ignored the suffering of the common people. She felt she was now living the life she had come to live. She wrote:

> For nothing would exchange the splendor
> Of our granite city of fame and misfortune,
> The sparkling ice of its wide rivers,
> Its somber, sunless gardens
> And the barely audible voice of the Muse.[5]

The revolutionary years were difficult for everyone. During this period she continued to visit Lev, and often saw Gumilyev there. When she was twenty-nine, divorce from Gumilyov was finalized, and, despite his behavior during the marriage, Gumilyov took the divorce very hard. Akhmatova had a brief marriage with Viktor Shileiko, a brilliant and eccentric Babylonian scholar, and they moved to Moscow. Akhmatova had thought that this marriage would not be as contentious since they would not be competing poets. But Shileiko wanted a wife, not a poet, and he burned her poetry in the samovar. Akhmatova and Shileiko had a hard time finding enough fuel to keep the apartment warm or get enough food. They lived in such intense poverty that, despite her being an acclaimed poet, they relied on contributions of food from admirers. Anna was reduced to looking like a skeleton, dressed in rags, and under this stress, she suffered a bout of tuberculosis.

In 1921 the Civil War was over in St. Petersburg (Petrograd during the Revolution). Under Lenin's New Economic Policy, the government was nationalizing factories and banks. There was corruption and there was a new energy. When Akhmatova gave poetry readings, the halls were filled. She experienced Shileiko's jealousy as a prison, and they separated. Then she received the news that Gumilyov had been arrested and shot for having joined an anti-Bolshevik conspiracy. Her deep and complex feelings for him aroused in her the sense that she was now a widow in black clothes. She wrote more collections of poetry, particularly about the horror of war and loss of love.

Following the death of Gumilyov came the death of the poet Alexander Block, then her brother and her sister. Death was stalking her again.

The years 1922–1930 were years of intensity and possibility. Similar to the Roaring Twenties in the United States, in Russia this was a time of the Jazz Age. Everything was jumping, business was good, the Black Market was thriving, and interest in the decadent West was growing. This was the age of whiskey and flappers, smoky rooms and experimentation. In her thirties, Anna was in her prime.

In 1924 Lenin died, and Stalin took over. Petrograd became Leningrad. Stalin issued his decree of Social Realism—art could only glorify the new Soviet state. The Stalinist regime cracked down on free expression, and writers began to be arrested and disappear into exile. Many of her intellectual friends were leaving Russia, but she was determined to stick it out, and, in fact, she was hostile to those who left. She declined invitations to go abroad, saying, "Foreign bread tastes like wormwood." Attacks on her intensified, and her work was banned by an unofficial Communist Party resolution.

During this time she was regularly seeing Nikolai Punin, a member of the avant garde movement. Her friends did not approve of the relationship as they still held the image of her as Gumilyov's wife. When divorce from Shileiko came through, she moved in with the Punins. This gave her a roof over her head, but it meant she and Punin were living in one room of the apartment and his wife and daughter in another. They all ate meals together, and Lev moved in with them when he was in high school and university. Anna wrote articles on art, Nikolai reviewed exhibitions. He was under the same pressures as other artists, but when he became head of the Institute of Artistic Culture, he was more protected.

Through her thirties, Anna continued to struggle with illness and was in and out of the sanatorium. When the poet Osip Mandelstam brought his young wife Nadezhda to see her, this was the beginning of a lifelong friendship.

Her forties were the terrible time of the Stalinist Great Terror in the 1930s. Purges and show trials were common. Akhmatova focused on writing articles, particularly about Pushkin. She was recognized for her scholarship, but publishing was dangerous during this time of forced collectivization and deportations. She stopped giving public readings and could get nothing published. She did appear at concerts and was allowed to eat at the dining room of the literary organization, although the only thing there available was kasha and that is what everyone else had. At least she could maintain her connection with other writers.

The relationship with Punin was strained. Friends in Paris sent her money, which was a help, but she had to sell her library to buy food. She worked on a translation of *Macbeth*, but another version was published before hers. She correlated the situation in Russia and Stalinist crimes with the murder by Macbeth.

Akhmatova often stayed with the Mandelstams when she went to Moscow, and they tried to give each other support. Her relationship became tense as Osip could not publish his poetry, and he was convinced he would die soon. When he wrote a poem describing Stalin's "cockroach whiskers" and "fingers fat as worms," he was arrested and soon thereafter went insane. Akhmatova and Boris Pasternak interceded on his behalf, so instead of executing him, the government exiled him to three years in a small town in the Urals.

In 1933 Lev was arrested as a way the government could punish her, a typical experience during this time when many children of those suspected were arrested. He was released after a few days but then rearrested. Punin was also arrested. Akhmatova was so distressed she wrote a letter to Stalin begging him to release Lev. She burned any of her documents that could compromise her. That night she went to the Pasternaks' home. In the morning, she received a telegram from Leningrad that Punin and Lev were home.

During these terrible years of fear, many of the poets felt themselves losing inspiration and going numb. Akhmatova became immune to all the terrible things happening to her: " 'That is what my life, my biography is like. Who can refuse to live his own life?' Her strength lay in her ability to face up to what was before her and master it. . . . It involved an honesty and respect for the word which was fast disappearing in the literary world around her, and her fight was the more remarkable at a time when the truthful representation of fact was most often considered to be a crime against the all-powerful state, punishable by concentration camp and death. For love of a man, for a normal home, Akhmatova had tried more than once to sacrifice her 'ring,' her poetry. She had also offered it up as a sacrifice to help her country. Now in her complete acceptance of her vocation she found a rock on which to build."[6]

Akhmatova began to reach out to her contemporary poets—Mandelstam, Pasternak, Mayakovsky, Tsvetayeva—with ways they could support each other. Together, they read poetry. In 1938 Mandelstam was arrested again and died from "heart failure." Lev was also arrested again, sentenced to ten years, and condemned to be shot. His sentence was then reduced to five years, and he was sent into exile. Akhmatova had called a friend for help to collect warm clothes for him, and she stood on line for hours on a miserable, hot day waiting to hand him the package. Out of exhaustion, she collapsed, and friends took her place in line so she could rest.

Akhmatova referred to the 1930s as having two halves: The first was the "vegetarian years" followed by the "meat- eating" years, which were much more terrible. It is this period that she described in "Requiem."

"Requiem"

All the suffering and anxiety of these years was bearing fruit in Akhmatova's creative powers, and she regained her voice as she began writing her great poem "Requiem" (1935–1940). Through her words and images she bore witness to the

Great Terror. Inspired by Greek tragedies which focused on the suffering of wives and mothers during wartime, she described the "hope, the threat of death, madness, indifference, readiness to accept death."[7] What is it that the Russian people, and especially the women, were being challenged with? The Russian belief is strong that one's experience of suffering is in imitation of Christ, and that to suffer is to be tested. How can one respond to suffering? Out of her Orthodox faith, which had become more and more important to her, she saw three ways to respond. First, to overcome one's doubt and accept the idea that one's suffering is part of a divine plan, whose meaning is known only by a benevolent God. Second, to become immoral, give up one's faith, and turn to demonic forces. Or third, to become totally amoral, in the belief that the individual can decide his or her own destiny.

This dilemma is echoed in the writings of the other Russian novelists and poets. Over and over again, the people have to choose how to respond to the terrible suffering that befalls them. I remember when having conversation with some Russians during Soviet times that they expressed that they must have done something wrong to have warranted Stalin's terrible treatment of their citizens.

Brodsky wrote, "The degree of compassion with which the various voices of "Requiem" are rendered can be explained only by the author's Orthodox faith; the degree of understanding and forgiveness which accounts for this work's piercing, almost unbearable lyricism, only by the uniqueness of her heart, herself, and this self's sense of time. No creed would help to understand, much less forgive, let alone survive this double widowhood at the hands of the regime, this fate of her son, these forty years of being silenced and ostracized."[8]

Akhmatova added this Epigraph to "Requiem" but it was not published until 1961, after her death:

> No, we didn't suffer together in vain.
> No, not under the vault of alien skies,
> And not under the shelter of alien wings—
> I was with my people then,
> There, where my people, unfortunately were.[9]

Introduction to "Requiem"

In 1939 Stalin's daughter had read Akhmatova's poetry and encouraged her father to let her work be published. As soon as it was, long lines formed in front of the bookstore. A few months later, after Stalin himself read her poetry, he stopped publication.

In 1940 England was being bombed. Lev was in prison. Anna was being attacked for her writing. Her health was failing. She was afraid of going mad from the stress. In October, she had a heart attack. As she was recovering she began writing "Poem without a Hero." She would work on it for the next twenty years as a way of describing her century.

"In the terrible years of the Yezhov terror, I spent seventeen months in the prison lines of Leningrad. Once, someone 'recognized' me. Then a woman with bluish lips standing behind me, who, of course, had never heard me called by name before, woke up from the stupor to which everyone had succumbed and whispered in my ear (everyone spoke in whispers there): 'Can you describe this?' And I answered: 'Yes, I can.' Then something that looked like a smile passed over what had once been her face."[10]

After sixteen years of living with Punin, in 1941 she left him. She was very poor, living mainly on black bread and bitter tea. She could barely stand up, yet she was standing in the long lines outside the prison. She would write a verse on a scrap of paper, memorize it, and burn the paper, for if a scrap of paper with such words were found, that would be enough to be arrested. Her friends also memorized the poems to be sure they would safeguard them for the future. Out of these experiences, Akhmatova was able to write directly from "I" and not have to refer to anyone else. She had lived it, she was it. She felt that if she did not write to witness the event, she would be committing a crime. Akhmatova held on to this purpose with all the energy she had, and she became the voice of the people.

She met Vladimir Garshin, a doctor, a professor, and a member of the Academy of Medical Sciences. He was very helpful to her, especially when she became ill, verging on insanity from the stress. At least when she was hospitalized, she received three meals a day.

In 1941 Hitler's armies marched into the Soviet Union. Instead of focusing on who was an enemy and who was not within, the government and the people focused their energy on defeating the enemy without. Akhmatova was able to join the Union of Soviet Writers and have her work published and she had been asked to speak on the radio. In September Nazi and Finnish troops began the siege of Leningrad. For the next eighteen months the city was under constant bombardment, and no food could reach the population. People were reduced to eating bread made from sawdust; trolley cars became morgues. Akhmatova spoke to the women of Leningrad:

> My dear fellow citizens, mothers, wives, and sisters of Leningrad. It is more than a month since the enemy began trying to take our city and has been wounding it heavily. The city of Peter, the city of Lenin, the city of Pushkin, Dostoyevsky, and Blok—this great city of culture and labor is threatened by the enemy with shame and death. My heart, like those of all the women of Leningrad, sinks at the mere thought that our city, my city, could be destroyed. My whole life has been connected with Leningrad: in Leningrad I became a poet and Leningrad inspired and colored my poetry. I, like all of you at this moment, live only in the unshakeable belief that Leningrad will never fall to the fascists. This belief is strengthened when I see the women of Leningrad simply and courageously defending the city and keeping up their normal way of life. . . . We, the women of Leningrad, are living through difficult days, but we know that the whole of the country, all of its people, are behind us. We feel their alarm for our sakes, their love and help. We thank them and we promise them that we will be ever stoic and brave.[11]

The population withstood the siege, although three and a half million people died. During the siege Akhmatova worked with the fire brigade putting out fires across the city. She stood with a gas mask over her face. And, in the midst of all this, she gave poetry readings.

During one of the bombings, she and a friend who came to take her to stay with his family at the House of Writers, ran from courtyard to courtyard, stumbling down stairs, and found themselves in the Stray Dog Café. For the next days she lived in a couch in the hall of the House of Writers. Garshin visited her there, drank tea with her, and brought her food every evening.

Life in Leningrad continued to be very difficult. Ironically, she who had been attacked previously was now considered important enough to keep safe. She was evacuated to Central Asia, on orders from a writer in a high position in the Union of Soviet Writers. Through his efforts and those of others, many artists, writers, musicians and filmmakers were sent to Central Asia and thus survived the war. The trip was arduous, and she had to go by way of Siberia, a journey of three weeks, in which they passed through scenes of terrible devastation. Arriving in Tashkent, she was given a little airless room which became her home for the next eighteen months. Nadezhda Mandelstam was also staying there.

During this time, Akhmatova accepted her role as the "voice of the age." She visited wounded soldiers, gave poetry readings, published and felt the inspiration to reach out to her countrymen and to the Allies. She wrote,

> And we will preserve the Russian tongue,
> The mighty Russian word.
> Free and pure we will carry you on,
> Pass you on to our grandchildren,
> Save you from slavery forever![12]

Not everyone was able to survive these terrible conditions, and Akhmatova discovered that when she was on her way to Tashkent, Maria Tsvetayeva had hung herself.

During the Tashkent years, Akhmatova had bouts of illness, particularly typhus. When she returned to Leningrad, she found that the stress of the war and the loss of his wife had made Garshin mentally ill. At the Punins' invitation, she returned to her old room at their place.

In 1945 the war was over. A new wind was blowing, and Akhmatova felt hopeful. Lev had survived and returned home. She gave poetry readings. But as the Stalinist Terror picked up new momentum, she was under attack again. One evening she was unwrapping fish from newspaper when she looked down and read a Resolution of the Central Committee condemning two journals for publishing her work. She was accused of being a relic of the past, reflecting bourgeoise aestheticism and decadence rather than social awareness. She was a danger to the new generation. Her brief moment of freedom was over, and she became a pawn to warn people to watch their step.

Because Pasternak had refused to attend the meeting in which she was condemned, he was expelled. Akhmatova was penniless, and losing her membership in the Writers Union meant she had no access to food. Pasternak defied the authorities and went to see her and to give her a thousand rubles. Punin arranged for her to eat with his family, even though their relationship had been long over.

The Cold War Begins

Along with Shostokovich and Prokoviev, Akhmatova was named an enemy of the people, and this was published in children's textbooks. Lev was not allowed to get his degree or defend his dissertation even though he had already taken his exams and written the paper. But the punishment was not over. In 1948 Punin was arrested along with eighteen of his colleagues. He never returned from a camp in Siberia and died in 1953.

In 1949 scientists and scholars were hounded constantly, and many died of strokes or heart attacks. In 1949 Lev was arrested again and sentenced to ten years in a camp. Although she was ill and in need of care herself, Anna traveled back and forth from Leningrad to Moscow. Every month she sent a parcel to give Lev an allowance; as long as it was accepted, it meant he was alive. The stress was too great, and on May 28, she had a serious heart attack and was taken to the hospital. While she was recovering, a friend organized raising the money to send to Lev. Akhmatova was getting translation work. She did not know what to do to save Lev, so she decided to repent and seek favor with the Stalinist regime by writing a poem praising him; this was published in the magazine *Ogonyok*.

The Thaw 1953–1958

On March 5, 1953, Stalin died and a period of power struggles began. Beriya, the head of the secret police, was arrested and shot. Khrushchev survived the secret struggles for power, and achieved the position of First Secretary of the Communist Party. He denounced Stalin in the Twentieth Party Congress, speaking about the cult of Stalin and the terrible crimes he had committed. It looked as if this Thaw would bring better days, but the government could tolerate only so much criticism. There was concern that if people were allowed to criticize the acts of cruelty carried out in the government's name, where would this freedom end? The reins were tightened again but not before Lev was freed on May 14, 1956, and cleared of any crimes.

By this time, sixty-seven-year-old Anna Akhmatova was no longer the tall, slender poet in her stylish black dress. Her hair had turned gray. She had put on weight. She lived in fear and paranoia for what would come next. Isaiah Berlin, leading political philosopher and speaker, wanted to see her again, but she was too frightened to respond, fearing she would be arrested again or that Lev would be rearrested because he was her son. In 1958 her first volume of poetry since the Stalinist period was published.

A significant event in 1962 was the publication of Solzhenitsyn's *One Day in the Life of Ivan Denisovich*. Did this mean things were becoming open again? No, with the ascension of Brezhnev to power in 1964, the next eighteen years would be another time of arrests and expulsions, including that of Brodsky, Solzhenitsyn, and Sakharov.

For now, however, Akhmatova was receiving recognition as a great poet at home and abroad. In 1963, Robert Frost visited her. Mikhail Alekseyev, a Soviet literary scholar and specialist in Pushkin, toasted the two of them, and said he "considered this meeting one of the greatest literary events of the time; each was a leading poet of their country, of an entire national literary culture and tradition. They ate a seven-course dinner, and the conversation turned first to American and English writers, then to the Greek and Roman classics. Asked to recite a poem, Akhmatova chose 'The Last Rose,' which she said referred to 'four powerful, passionate women from world history who directed their passion to serve the integrity of a nation in which they had transcendent faith.' "[13]

The Last Rose
You will write about us on a slant.[14]
 – Joseph Brodsky

I have to bow with Morozova,
Dance with Herod's stepdaughter,
Fly up with the smoke of Dido's fire,
Only to return to Joan of Arc's pyre.

Lord, You see I am tired
Of living and dying and resurrection.
Take everything, but grant that I may feel
The freshness of this crimson rose again.[15]

The Last Years, the 1960s

During her last years, Akhmatova received the acknowledgement and recognition that she well deserved. She continued translating, and she wrote serious works on Pushkin. When she traveled, meeting noted poets around the world, she was treated like royalty with an entourage in attendance.

One of the highlights was a formal poetry recital with over two hundred guests. She recited in Russian. Each of the other poets in turn read poems to her. When she grew weary, she walked out. A curious and yet tender scene occurred in her hotel room after she had received the prize. She had invited the members of the Soviet delegation to celebrate with her. From her trunk she solemnly drew out caviar, jam, all kinds of sweets. "On the table there will be only ours. I brought everything, even black bread, and even this," and she held up a bottle of Stolichnaya vodka. The celebration went on well into the night.[16]

At age 76, Akhmatova went to Oxford to receive an honorary doctorate. There she met Isaiah Berlin, and they filled in for each other of their lives during the many years since they had last seen each other. She went to Stratford to visit Shakespeare's birthplace. (Besides her translations of some of his plays, she had written a book on Shakespeare.) She went to Paris. When she returned to Russia, she continued to write sketches for her autobiography.

In November 1965, she had another heart attack and was kept in the hospital in Moscow for three months and then went to a sanatorium where she died March 5, 1966, in her sleep. When her coffin was returned to Leningrad, the government, afraid of a public demonstration, kept it quiet.

Requiem (1961) [17]

No, not under the vault of alien skies,
And not under the shelter of alien wings –
I was with my people then,
There, where my people, unfortunately, were.

INSTEAD OF A PREFACE

In the terrible years of the Yezhov terror, I spent seventeen months in the prison lines of Leningrad. Once, someone "recognized" me. Then a woman with bluish lips standing behind me, who, of course, had never heard me called by name before, woke up from the stupor to which everyone had succumbed and whispered in my ear (everyone spoke in whispers there): "Can you describe this?" And I answered: "Yes, I can." Then something that looked like a smile passed over what had once been her face.

[The 1st of April in the year 1957. Leningrad]

DEDICATION

Mountains bow down to this grief,
Mighty rivers cease to flow,
But the prison gates hold firm,
And behind them are the "prisoners' burrows"
And mortal woe.
For someone a fresh breeze blows,
For someone the sunset luxuriates—
We wouldn't know, we are those who everywhere
Hear only the rasp of the hateful key
And the soldiers' heavy tread.
We rose as if for an early service,
Trudged through the savaged capital
And met there, more lifeless than the dead;
The sun is lower and the Neva mistier,
But hope keeps singing from afar.
The verdict … And her tears gush forth,
Already she is cut off from the rest.
As if they painfully wrenched life from her heart,
As if they brutally knocked her flat,
But she goes on … Staggering … Alone …
Where now are my chance friends
Of those two diabolical years?
What do they imagine is in Siberia's storms,
What appears to them dimly in the circle of the moon?
I am sending my farewell greeting to them.

[March 1940]

PROLOGUE

That was when the ones who smiled
Were the dead, glad to be at rest.
And like its useless appendage, Leningrad
Swung from its prisons.
And when, senseless from torment,
Regiments of convicts marched,
And the short songs of farewell
Were sung by locomotive whistles.
The stars of death stood above us
And innocent Rus writhed
Under bloody boots
And under the tires of the Black Marusyas.

I

They led you away at dawn,
I followed you, like a mourner,
In the dark front room the children were crying,
By the icon shelf the candle was dying.
On your lips was the icon's chill.
The deathly sweat on your brow … Unforgettable!
I will be like the wives of the Streltsy,
Howling under the Kremlin towers.
[Autumn 1935. Moscow]

II

Quietly flows the quiet Don,
Yellow moon slips into a home.
He slips in with cap askew,
He sees a shadow, yellow moon.
This woman is ill,
This woman is alone.
Husband in the grave, son in prison,
Say a prayer for me.

III

No, it is not I, it is somebody else who is suffering.
I would not have been able to bear what happened,
Let them shroud it in black,
And let them carry off the lanterns …
Night.

IV

You should have been shown, you mocker,
Minion of all your friends,
Gay little sinner of Tsarskoye Selo,
What would happen in your life —
How three-hundredth in line, with a parcel,
You would stand by the Kresty prison,
Your tempestuous tears

Burning through the New Year's ice.
Over there the prison poplar bends,
And there's no sound — and over there how many
Innocent lives are ending now ...

[1938]

V

For seventeen months I have been screaming,
Calling you home.
I've thrown myself at the feet of butchers
For you, my son and my horror.
Everything has become muddled forever —
I can no longer distinguish
Who is an animal, who a person, and how long
The wait can be for an execution.
There are now only dusty flowers,
The chinking of the thurible,
Tracks from somewhere into nowhere
And, staring me in the face
And threatening me with swift annihilation,
An enormous star.

[1939]

VI

Weeks fly lightly by. Even so,
I cannot understand what has arisen,
How, my son, into your prison
White nights stare so brilliantly.
Now once more they burn,
Eyes that focus like a hawk,
And, upon your cross, the talk
Is again of death.

[Spring 1939]

VII
THE VERDICT

The word landed with a stony thud
Onto my still-beating breast.
Never mind, I was prepared,
I will manage with the rest.

I have a lot of work to do today;
I need to slaughter memory,
Turn my living soul to stone
Then teach myself to live again ...

But how. The hot summer rustles
Like a carnival outside my window;
I have long had this premonition
Of a bright day and a deserted house.[18]

[22 June 1939. Summer. Fontannyi Dom]

VIII

TO DEATH

You will come in any case — so why not now?
I am waiting for you — I can't stand much more.
I've put out the light and opened the door
For you, so simple and miraculous.
So come in any form you please,
Burst in as a gas shell
Or, like a gangster, steal in with a length of pipe,
Or poison me with typhus fumes.
Or be that fairy tale you've dreamed up —
So sickeningly familiar to everyone —
In which I glimpse the top of a pale blue cap
And the house attendant white with fear.
Now it doesn't matter anymore. The Yenisey swirls,
The North Star shines.
And the final horror dims
The blue luster of beloved eyes.

                    [19 August 1939. Fontannyi Dom][19]

IX

Madness with its wings
Has covered half my soul
It feeds me fiery wine
And lures me into the abyss.

That's when I understood
While listening to my alien delirium
That I must hand the victory
To it.

However much I nag
However much I beg
It will not let me take
One single thing away:

Not my son's frightening eyes —
A suffering set in stone,
Or prison visiting hours
Or days that end in storms

Nor the sweet coolness of a hand
The anxious shade of lime trees
Nor the light distant sound
Of final comforting words.

                    [14 May 1940. Fontannyi Dom][20]

X
CRUCIFIXION
Do not weep for Me, Mother.
I am in the grave.

1.

A choir of angels sang the praises of that momentous hour,
The heavens dissolved in fire.
To his Father he said: "Why hast Thou forsaken me!"
And to his Mother: "Oh, do not weep for me …"

[1940. Fontannyi Dom]

2.

Magdalena beat her breast and sobbed,
The beloved disciple turned to stone,
But where the silent Mother stood, there
No one glanced and no one would have dared.

[1943. Tashkent] [21]

EPILOGUE
1.

I have learned how faces fall,
How terror can escape from lowered eyes,
How suffering can etch cruel pages
Of cuneiform-like marks upon the cheeks.
I know how dark or ash-blond strands of hair
Can suddenly turn white. I've learned to recognize
The fading smiles upon submissive lips,
The trembling fear inside a hollow laugh.
That's why I pray not for myself
But all of you who stood there with me
Through fiercest cold and scorching July heat
Under a towering, completely blind red wall.

2.

The hour has come to remember the dead.
I see you, I hear you, I feel you:
The one who resisted the long drag to the open window;
The one who could no longer feel the kick of familiar
soil beneath her feet;
The one who, with a sudden flick of her head, replied,
"I arrive here as if I've come home!"
I'd like to name you all by name, but the list
Has been removed and there is nowhere else to look.
So,
I have woven you this wide shroud out of the humble words
I overheard you use. Everywhere, forever and always,
I will never forget one single thing. Even in new grief.

Even if they clamp shut my tormented mouth
Through which one hundred million people scream;
That's how I wish them to remember me when I am dead
On the eve of my remembrance day.
If someone someday in this country
Decides to raise a memorial to me,
I give my consent to this festivity
But only on this condition — do not build it
By the sea where I was born,
I have severed my last ties with the sea;
Nor in the Tsar's Park by the hallowed stump
Where an inconsolable shadow looks for me;
Build it here where I stood for three hundred hours
And no-one slid open the bolt.
Listen, even in blissful death I fear
That I will forget the Black Marias,
Forget how hatefully the door slammed and an old woman
Howled like a wounded beast.
Let the thawing ice flow like tears
From my immovable bronze eyelids
And let the prison dove coo in the distance
While ships sail quietly along the river.

[March 1940. Fontannyi Dom][22]

Poem Notes:

Streltsy is an elite guard which rose up in rebellion against Peter the Great in 1698. Most were either executed or exiled.

Tsarskoye Selo is the imperial summer residence outside St. Petersburg where Akhmatova spent her early years.

The Crosses is a prison complex in central Leningrad near the Finland Station, so named because of the shape of two of the buildings.

Fontannyi Dom is the house in which Akhmatova lived in Leningrad.

Endnotes

1. Amanda Haight, *Anna Akhmatova: A Poetic Pilgrimage* (New York: Oxford University Press, 1976), p. 75.
2. Ibid., p. 12.
3. Anatoly Nayman, *Remembering Anna Akhmatova* (New York: Henry Holt & Co., 1989), viii.
4. Haight, *A Poetic Pilgrimage*, p. 30.
5. Ibid., p. 50.
6. Ibid., p. 94.
7. Roberta Reeder, *Anna Akhmatova, Poet and Prophet* (New York: Saint Martin's Press, 1994), p. 272.
8. Ibid., p. 212.

9. Ibid., p. 213.
10. Ibid.
11. Haight, *A Poetic Pilgrimage*, p. 123.
12. Ibid., p. 125.
13. Reeder, *Poet and Prophet*, p. 373.
14. Ibid.
15. Ibid., pp. 373–374.
16. Ibid., pp. 496–497.
17. Selections from Reeder, *Poet and Prophet*, pp. 213–218.
18. www.poemhunter.com/poem/requiem.
19. Reeder, pp. 218–219.
20. www.poemhunter.com.
21. Reeder, pp. 219–220.
22. www.poemhunter.com.

Bibliography

Haight, Amanda. *Anna Akhmatova: A Poetic Pilgrimage,* New York: Oxford University Press, 1976.

Leiter, Sharon. *Akhmatova's Petersburg*, Philadelphia: University of Pennsylvania Press, 1983.

Nayman, Anatoly. *Remembering Anna Akhmatova*, New York: Henry Holt & Co., 1989.

Reeder, Roberta. *Anna Akhmatova, Poet and Prophet*, New York: Saint Martin's Press, 1994.

Winter Scene

CHAPTER 12

Alexander Isayevich Solzhenitsyn (1918–)

Solzhenitsyn is not an easy writer to introduce to high school students. The exception is *One Day in the Life of Ivan Denisovich* which is very accessible, brief, and to the point. It is used in many schools because of that. His other books tend to be dense. Having said that, I know that some students have enjoyed reading *The First Circle* and *Cancer Ward*. Excerpts from "A World Split Apart" which he gave at the 1978 Harvard University graduation provide provocative subjects for discussion. The address poses the contrast between freedom under tyranny in the Soviet Union and freedom in an open society such as the United States.

Solzhenitsyn is an important writer for the students to know about because he is a passionate and courageous fighter against totalitarianism, and he is a witness to the crimes committed under Stalin. He is a man of extraordinary energy and fierce concentration. He can be challenging and intimidating, and he can be gregarious and warm. Solzhenitsyn's life and personality offer high school students a sense of human complexity, defying simplification.

Childhood and Youth

Alexander Solzhenitsyn was born on December 11, 1918, in Kislovodsk in the Caucasus Mountain region between the Black and the Caspian Seas. His mother was an educated and modern woman of her times, interested in art and culture; his father, of peasant stock, and deeply influenced by Tolstoy's concerns for the plight of the peasant, was the first and only one of his family to attend university. He died on the German front in 1918, six months before Solzhenitsyn was born.

With the burden of a young child and no income, his mother placed Alexander, or Sanya as he was called, with relatives, and she worked as a shorthand typist. His religious life was cultivated by his grandmother who took him to church.

When he was able to go to school, he moved with his mother into a rickety wood house in Rostov, a large cosmopolitan city. He idealized his father and became the man of the family, disciplined and responsible. Since his mother was often ill, he took on many of the chores. Already as a boy, he showed a strong will and self-sufficient nature. He was an avid reader. His mother had decided she would never remarry, but would devote herself completely to the education and rearing of her son.

The extended family lived in a nostalgic bubble of pre-Revolutionary Russia, and through this, Solzhenitsyn was protected in an atmosphere celebrating the beauty of church ritual and voicing strong anti-Soviet ideas. An avid and keen observer, he knew already at the age of nine that he wanted to be a writer. However, although some of his teachers were disappearing, he did not connect that with the secret police. In fact, he did not question it at all. He tried to blend the two worlds by becoming a member of the Young Pioneers and at the same time wearing a cross, which at one point was ripped from his neck, leaving a scar.

As Solzhenitsyn moved into adolescence, he began to rebel against his family, and sought to conform to the Soviet and Communist Party ideals. A strong student in natural science and mathematics, he was well on his way to university studies and a successful career in the Stalinist state. Stalin held mathematics in the highest regard and arranged for financial rewards for university students who excelled in this field. Solzhenitsyn was awarded a Stalin scholarship for his academic achievements, but also for his participation in the Young Communist League. The generous scholarship lightened the financial load for his mother, and the family was able to improve their lifestyle and even take some vacations.

Despite his skill in mathematics and the rewards he gained for it, his real love was literature. He had hoped to attend the University in Moscow, but felt he could not leave his mother alone, especially since her health was not good, so he stayed in Rostov and studied mathematics at Rostov State University. Although he did not have a passion for mathematics, it saved his life in a number of situations. He wrote continuously — especially poetry — although none of it was published at the time.

His university years coincided with the Stalinist horrors — the purges and show trials. Although he believed in the revolution and his country, Solzhenitsyn did not believe in Stalin and distrusted anything Stalin said. He decided he had to write a series of novels that would examine the events and movements at the basis of the Revolution and Soviet society. He began to research historical documents; he read the philosophical basis of Marxism and Leninism. He could not share the results of his research, as Stalinist teachers kept a careful eye on their students, searching for any hint of questioning or disagreement with the regime.

Solzhenitsyn had an active circle of friends, especially a classmate referred to as X or NV, who shared countryside excursions as well as philosophical and political views, and Natalia, a classmate at the university and his future wife.

Adulthood — the War Years

Solzhenitsyn married a former classmate, Natalia Alekseevna Reshetovskaia, in 1940, divorced in 1950, remarried in 1957, and divorced again in 1972. A central issue between them was that he wanted to give his attention to writing and did not want children.

In addition to his university studies in math and physics, he and his friends studied at the Moscow Institute of Humanities. On the day he came to Moscow to take those exams, World War II broke out with a declaration of war between Russia and Germany (June 22, 1941). He graduated from the Department of Physics and Mathematics at Rostov University. Although he wanted to enlist, he was not accepted and began work as a teacher. But as the war progressed, in October the situation had worsened, and as Moscow was threatened, all available reserves were mobilized. Solzhenitsyn was twenty-three years old and he never dreamed that when he went to war, he would not return for fifteen years.

Because of weak health, he was sent to serve as a driver of horse-drawn vehicles during the winter of 1941–1942. He was the butt of jokes because he had no knowledge of horses. But he was persistent and besides cleaning out the stables, he learned to be an able rider. He wanted to get to the Front where the action was, but his requests went unanswered. Feeling that his skills in mathematics were not being put to good use, he talked his way into officer-training school where he trained in instrumental reconnaissance. He continued his writing, and as a symbol of that, he kept his briefcase with him.

This was a particularly difficult time in terms of Solzhenitsyn's political ideas. He had lost his idealism about Stalin and Stalinism. He felt right about fighting for the liberation of Russia from Nazi occupation, but the constant police-type surveillance even in the army was disheartening. He was in a situation to observe the poor facilities and training of the troops, as well as the purges of the Red Army, and this caused him to lose faith in Stalin as commander-in-chief. Because of his refusal to join the Communist Party, he had a hard time. Due to his mathematical knowledge, he was transferred to an artillery school where he was put in command of an artillery-position-finding company, and in this capacity, he served, without a break, right on the Front line.

With the victory at Stalingrad, Russians experienced a surge of patriotic appreciation of Stalin and took great pride in the Russian victory, but Solzhenitsyn and NV stayed firm in their analysis of Stalin. Through a stroke of luck he found that his friend NV was stationed nearby and the two of them met regularly and resumed their political discussions. They drafted a political manifesto, "Resolution, No. 1," citing the difficulties and suggesting changes. They copied the text of the resolution and swore to each other to keep it with them as long as they were in the military. This was to cause him grief later.

The twenty-five-year-old Alexander Solzhenitsyn was promoted to first lieutenant for his performance in helping drive the Germans toward the Dnieper River. He used any spare time to continue writing both in his journal and in developing short stories and novels. He enjoyed being an officer, but by 1943, the tide had turned, and German forces sent tanks and infantry divisions to penetrate the Russian lines. At twenty-six, he was promoted to captain. He continued writing his impressions as the war continued.

When the situation worsened, Natalia was evacuated. Solzhenitsyn received a ten-day leave, during which he learned his mother had died. Her last years had been those of poverty and illness, which touched Solzhenitsyn very deeply.

Upon his return to the trenches, he hoped Natalia would visit him there. She did come, but things did not go well. In addition to the other tensions between them, Natalia refused to salute him when she entered the trench, which he felt undermined his authority. She returned to Rostov. The issue about having children reemerged, and Solzhenitsyn confirmed that his commitment was to writing, and that children were not part of his vision of his life.

As the war was drawing to a close in January 1945, Russian troops headed toward Berlin. Stalin's message to the troops was that they could take anything they wanted and treat the Germans as cruelly as they wished.[1] There were no limits. The soldiers raped and burned, pillaging and plundering to such a degree that Solzhenitsyn was disgusted and embarrassed. Many of the stories about post-War Russian barbarism and primitivism can be traced to Stalin's message. (I had heard many of these stories, but I had not realized that these actions were approved of or even encouraged by high Soviet officials.)

At age twenty-seven, Solzhenitsyn continued his correspondence with NV, and in one letter, he referred to Stalin as the "mustachioed one." The censors found the letter, and when the authorities also found "Resolution No. 1" and some stories he had written hidden in his map case, Solzhenitsyn was arrested. Scammel describes the scene:

> On February 9, 1945, Alexander Solzhenitsyn was informed to report at once to Brigidier General Travkin. He had no idea why. The political commissar was there. The general ordered him to step forward and hand over his revolver. Travkin then told him to go. At that point the two officers shouted, "You are under arrest." For what? They ripped his epaulettes from his shoulders and the star from his cap, removed his belt, snatched the map case from his hands, and began to march him from the room.
>
> Travkin barked, "Solzhenitsyn, come back here. Have you a friend on the First Ukrainian Front?"
>
> "That's against regulations. You have no right," shouted the two Smersh officers.
>
> Solzhenitsyn realized the reference to NV was a warning. He also realized why he had been receiving so few letters from NV; they had been intercepted and read. As the counterintelligence men were preparing to lead Solzhenitsyn away, the general slowly rose to his feet behind his desk, leaned across it, and ostentatiously shook Solzhenitsyn by the hand. "I wish you happiness, Captain." [2]

Solzhenitsyn was now an enemy of the people. Confident that his arrest was a mistake, he naïvely thought that he could convince them there needed to be a change in the government, and he would be released. He was taken to Lubyanka prison where he was stripped and humiliated. His writings on "Resolution No. 1" were read and his ideas construed to be part of a conspiracy to overthrow the government. At the beginning of his ordeal, he still believed that the Soviet government was devoted to equality and justice, and that when it realized its mistake in arresting him, he would be released. But once in prison, he learned that Marxism was not what he had thought it was. Through an Estonian cellmate who was a very well educated judge, he learned about democracy. "I listened and listened to his loving stories about twenty free years of that reticent, hardworking, small nation of big men with their slow solid ways. I listened to the principles of the Estonian constitution drawn from the best European experiences and how it had been worked out by their single chamber parliament of a hundred deputies. I did not know why I began to be attracted to it all and to store it away as a part of my experience."[3]

This was the beginning of his years in the Gulag Archipelago—poor food rations, little intellectual stimulation, more interrogations, conversations with prisoners who had a better sense of how the Soviet government was treating war prisoners—Solzhenitsyn began to struggle with his judgments. Had it been right for Russia to go to war against the Germans? Was the Revolution the right change for Russia? What was true and what was false? Could anyone be trusted?

On May 9, 1945, with the capture of Prague, the war in Europe was ended. Merrymaking went on outside the prison, but within the prison more and more prisoners were brought in. These new prisoners were Russians who had been arrested because they had been fighting in Western Europe and had fraternized with British, French, and American soldiers. The government feared they had been tainted with ideas of democracy and would bring nothing but trouble. Despite the fact that they had fought bravely in the Soviet army, they were rewarded with arrest and imprisonment. This happened throughout Soviet Union in the aftermath of the war, and was an expression of Soviet paranoia.

1946: Labor Camp

Solzhenitsyn was sentenced to eight years in labor camps. Natalia had kept his arrest secret so that she would not be branded as being married to an enemy of the people, which would adversely affect her continuing graduate studies at the university. She moved to Moscow where she could bring him packages, but then he was transferred to a camp for political prisoners. Already exhausted by the prison experience, he held the hope that after his sentence was completed (if he survived it), he and Natalia would go live in a remote village, far away from the eyes of the government.

When he was sent to a camp with a clay pit, he tried to bluff his way into being a commander by dressing in his officer's uniform. For a short time, he was the shift foreman, but he lacked experience in managing people and was demoted to manual work. The cruelty within the camp was described in the following incident involving Olga Matronina, a fiercely loyal communist dedicated to the system.

> Her consuming goal in life was to maximize brick production just as in any normal enterprise, regardless of the fact that the work force consisted of half-starved convicts working in abominable conditions with out-of-date equipment. She announced that the number of wagonloads per shift had to be doubled. He could not deliver. The next day the post of foreman was abolished, and he was put on general duty: "Make him sweat."
>
> It was pouring rain. They could not fill the quota, put on punishment rations, the clay pit was drenched, they were stuck in it, the clay would not drop off their shovels, they began scooping the wet clay from beneath their feet and toss it into the wagon. She gave orders that they were to be kept in the pit until they had satisfied her norms. The cruelty of this woman only intensified as the situation continued.

The prisoners were kept in the pit day and night, despite their being soaking wet. She was concerned that someone could escape in the dark so she brought in boards and told the men that was where they would sleep.[4]

Through this experience, Solzhenitsyn felt he had become a Soviet Man, no longer an individual. During his next meeting with Natalia, it was clear he had gone through serious changes. He suggested that they get a legal separation, but they swore to remain faithful to each other.

Back in camp he suffered the most humiliating experience of his whole time in the Gulag: He was told that he had to inform on other people or he would be sent to Siberia. He did not want to sign such a pledge unless the person was a thief. But he was forced to sign and report any plans of escape.

Marfino, the Scientific Institute

When Solzhenitsyn was asked to write down what kind of professional experience he had, he bluffed his way by saying he knew about atomic energy because he had read a book about the American atom bomb. Also, because of his abilities as a mathematician, he was transferred to a scientific research camp, Marfino, rather than being sent to a hard labor camp. His experiences were later described in *The First Circle*.

Life in this camp was very different from the Gulag. Marfino was assigned the task of developing a walkie-talking radio for the police. The camp residents included scientists from all over the Soviet Union, gathered here to conduct research for the government including improving rocket technology and the invention of the liquid-fuel jet engine. Scientists met daily, exchanged information, read, played chess, held concerts. They could send out and receive letters and books. In Marfino, Solzhenitsyn made lifelong friends, and together they discussed Marxism, Leninism, and Stalinism, and shared their passion for literature. During walks in the yard, they surmised how life would have been different if Lenin had lived. During his time at Marfino, Solzhenitsyn began to read Eastern philosophy.

Once a year Natalia could visit him. Finishing her doctoral dissertation in chemistry, she wanted to go on to study music. He encouraged her. One of the things that helped him through this time was that he began to listen to music and shared his impressions with her. These were good years in their relationship.

In 1948 his school friend NV also arrived in the Institute. They had much catching up to do, comparing their arrests and experiences. They continued discussing ideas on the meaning of life and on the Revolution. Solzhenitsyn rediscovered the works of Dostoyevsky and found them much more satisfying. He came to agree with Dostoyevsky on the importance of the spiritual over the material. This was a turning point in his thinking.

On his thirtieth birthday, he met with Natalia and told her that in order to avoid dismissal from the university, she needed to file for divorce, which she did.

Life at Marfino became more intense as the scientists were given the task of developing a scrambler telephone for Stalin and his top aides. In this top-secret environment, discipline tightened and visitors were no longer allowed. They studied the Russian language and determined that it had thirty-five hundred phonetically differentiated sounds. They studied the sound properties of the human voice with the object of breaking it down into quantifiable and analyzable units. A satisfactory encoding system was developed during this time.

As his idealism faded, and he felt that he would not be released, Solzhenitsyn came to distrust everyone and decided he would rather work at manual labor. When he was transferred to work with other mathematicians on cryptology, he did not want to make the change, refused to accommodate the government, and so was sent to a work camp for political prisoners.

Bricklayer in a Labor Camp

After three years in the Institute, thirty-two-year-old Solzhenitsyn was sent to Kazakhstan where he worked as a miner, a bricklayer, and a foundryman. Despite how difficult the work was, he felt better about it than the work at the Institute because he was not betraying his conscience. He began to memorize poetry again, and to write some also. One of his companions was in charge of the machine shop. After a time, he made a warm safe place for Solzhenitsyn inside his shop. "Amid the clattering of iron, unobserved by stool pigeons and guards, Solzhenitsyn rewrote his verses until satisfied, committed the day's work to memory, and destroyed the paper."[5]

In his time in this camp, he developed stomach cancer and underwent surgery. This experience gave him pause to evaluate his life. He realized he had survived terrible conditions, that he had not compromised himself for an extra piece of bread or money, and that he had actually gained in his moral and spiritual development. He felt that his youthful arrogance had given way to humility. "It was on the rotting prison straw that I felt the first stirrings of good in myself. Gradually it became clear to me that the line separating good from evil runs not between states, not between classes, and not between parties—it runs through the heart of each and every one of us, and through all human hearts. This line is not stationary. It shifts and moves with the passing of the years. Even in hearts enveloped in evil, it maintains a small bridgehead of good. And even the most virtuous heart harbors an un-uprooted corner of evil."[6]

Solzhenitsyn began to see that religion had a power over ideology because in religion the person struggles with evil within, whereas revolutions destroy the contemporary carriers of evil, and often become evil themselves afterwards.

During his last years in the camp, his relationship with Natalia was cooling, and she began another relationship. When she wrote him that she had remarried, they stopped writing to each other. One month after serving the full term of his eight-year sentence, there came an administrative decision to the effect that he would not be released but exiled for life to Kok-Terek (southern Kazakhstan).

Exiled for Life

Arriving in Kok-Terek, he felt hope as he experienced his first night under the open sky. A month later, on March 6, 1953, came the announcement on the loudspeakers in the village square that Stalin had died. Solzhenitsyn spent the rest of the day writing a poem, "The Fifth of March."

This area of Kazahkstan was poor and dusty, a place of exile for people of many ethnic groups. He began to teach math and made a special effort to raise the standard of education. He proved to be a very effective teacher, and his students were devoted to him. When he developed cancer again, he was admitted to a clinic in Tashkent, a thousand miles to the west. The pain in his abdomen was intense, and his prognosis was not good. But with a long series of radiation treatments, he began to recover. In this experience of feeling reborn, he developed interest in his fellow patients and renewed his relationship with God in gratitude for life. After years of prison and then life in a small village, being able to walk around Tashkent was exhilarating. He wrote about his experiences in *Cancer Ward*.

Nikita Khrushchev gave his "secret speech" about the cult of Stalin at the Twentieth Congress of the Communist Party on February 26, 1956. This marked the end of labor camps and exile. In April Solzhenitsyn received a letter informing him his sentence had been annulled and his exile lifted. He decided to leave Kazakhstan and move to the Russian heartland. After the school year was over, he journeyed to Moscow a free man.

His visit to Moscow was significant for a number of reasons. He went to the Lubyanka prison and requested to have his stories returned to him. While visiting Natalia who was living with her new husband and caring for his two sons, Solzhenitsyn gave her copies of the poems he had written while in the camps.

Starting a New Life in Freedom

At forty years of age, Solzhenitsyn became a teacher in a provincial town and began writing *One Day in the Life of Ivan Denisovich* based on his experiences in the labor camp. He settled into life in the Russian village, renting a room in the house of a widow. She prepared meals for him, and they developed a routine. He took up teaching and continued writing. However, life changed when Natalia read his poems and was so moved she decided to write him, and they planned to meet. The meeting was intense, and they once again felt the closeness of the earlier years. He told her that if they married again, he expected her to be subservient to his needs. She agreed and told her husband.

Solzhenitsyn and Natalia moved to an area near Ryazan where he taught physics and astronomy. Life was full and, although he loved what he was doing, he used every free hour to write. He was writing *The First Circle* in secrecy and constant fear of discover, for the public was unaware that the scientific institutes had actual labor camps. He had a relapse of cancer, and this time was treated successfully with chemotherapy.

At age forty-two, Solzhenitsyn was exhausted, and he wondered if it would be safe to submit his manuscript of *One Day in the Life of Ivan Denisovich* for publication. Works of Pasternak, Akhmatova, and Zoschenko were being published once again. After Khrushchev publicly denounced Stalin's crimes, Solzhenitsyn decided to approach Alexander Tvardovsky, poet and chief editor of *Novy Mir*, the leading literary magazine. When Tvardovsky began reading the manuscript, he could not get to sleep; he got up, dressed, had a cup of tea and finished reading it. It was his cleverness in figuring how to get Khruschev to approve it that got it through the final leg of the process: He compared Solzhenitsyn to Tolstoy.

The manuscript was accepted and printed the next year in *Novy Mir*. The first Soviet prison-camp literature ever to be published, *One Day in the Life of Ivan Denisovich* landed like an atomic bomb, exploding the lies and telling readers about the political prisoners and the conditions in the labor camps. The book was particularly poignant because Solzhenitsyn spoke through the eyes of a simple man as he described the horror of one day in a labor camp. The book quickly became known all over the world and was compared with Dostoyevsky's novel *House of the Dead*.

Solzhenitsyn was invited into the Writers Union, particularly important because now he could give up teaching and give himself entirely to his writing. However, conservative advisors around Khrushchev were blaming him for allowing too much freedom, saying that it was threatening to Soviet life. They did not want the Stalinist crimes acknowledged. So the Thaw was over, Khruschev was forced into retirement, and Stalin became a hero once again.

One Day warmed the hearts of Soviet readers, and they loved Solzhenitsyn for telling the truth. Many camp survivors felt for the first time that their stories could be told. In 1964, when he was forty-five, he was nominated for the Lenin Prize for *One Day in the Life of Ivan Denisovich*.

In addition to the stress over whether or not he could accept the prize, his personal life was in tension again. The marriage was threatened by his interest in another woman, and Solzhenitsyn justified his behavior by saying he felt a writer was different from other people and that he needed the inspiration of several women.

As the political situation over his book intensified, his own resistance efforts also intensified. During the late 1950s, when writers were again repressed, they circulated their works underground by typing nine carbon copies of a piece and passing them on to others who would receive them and type out nine more copies. This system, known as *samizdat*, allowed expression to spread throughout the country. Solzhenitsyn decided to risk punishment and allowed his work to be published in this manner. As the KGB became stronger after Khrushchev's forced retirement, Solzhenitsyn became more cautious. He was about to send a copy of *The First Circle* to the West. He also began working on what would become *The Gulag Archipelago*.

Solzhenitsyn bought a small plot of land with a ramshackle cabin where he could withdraw and write in privacy. In 1965, the KGB raided the home of a friend and gained access to three copies of *The First Circle* as well as Solzhenitsyn's portfolio of earlier work, some of it unpublished. Literary critics and writers were arrested as fear grew. Solzhenitsyn was crushed by this and expected to be arrested. One solace came from a writer friend at Peredelkino who offered him space to write. And so Solzhenitsyn took refuge in the woods, visiting Pasternak's grave, and enjoying the warmth of the family of Kornei Chukovsky, a well-respected children's book writer.

In 1965, with the stress building, Solzhenitsyn became hardened, more opinionated, and unwilling to listen to others. He trusted only himself. He felt he had to represent all those who were repressed. If his work could not get published in literary magazines, he would have it published in arch-conservative publications. Works by Soviet authors that could not be published in the U.S.S.R. began to be published in other countries. The Soviet government went on the defensive and began putting writers into mental institutions. In response, an organization grew that cited the rights guaranteed by the new Constitution (but had never been meant to be followed.)

Solzhenitsyn began to stand aside from other writers and he became arrogant. All his manuscripts had been censored, but he was not going to give in. He began to lecture and write letters against the government and KGB. He sent a copy of *Cancer Ward* to Slovakia. *The Gulag Archipelago* was in safe hands in a friend's home.

In 1968 on his fiftieth birthday, which was usually a very noted celebration in the Soviet Union, he was basically ignored. He decided to speak his mind, no matter what the consequences. He had two texts already published abroad, which he knew had no chance of being published in the Soviet Union. He wrote an open letter to the Writers Union denouncing the Soviet system of censorship, and said that he considered the Soviet Union to be one great gulag. Before opening day of the Congress, May 18, 1967, the text was circulated via *samizdat*. His letter was copied and posted all over Moscow. In response he was expelled from the Writers Union, which was serious because he lost his pension rights, his right to social security and medical insurance, his right to employ a secretary, and his access to libraries. His sense of alienation increased. After the expulsion, Solzhenitsyn became more strident and sure of his own views. He stated his opinions strongly, embraced Christianity, became friends with Sakharov, although he argued with him, and was sure he was doing God's work.

He smuggled out the manuscript for *The First Circle,* and it was published in the United States. His fame and honor grew even more. However, he was not satisfied with the translations or the publishing arrangements, and from that time on, Solzhenitsyn was embroiled in argument with translators and publishers outside the Soviet Union.

In his personal life he was deeply unhappy. Natalia considered herself to be the wife of a famous author, and she felt she should be included in his life. She resented Solzhenitsyn's attempts to be by himself. In addition, he started a relationship with another woman, Natalia Svetlova; she became his partner and coworker, and the love of his life.

He expressed ideas that set him apart from other dissidents. For example, he disagreed with Sakharov's admiration of Western democracy. Rather, his nationalistic views called for a uniquely Russian approach and warned that Russia should not follow foreign ideas of freedom and democracy.

The Moscow branch of the Writers Union protested his expulsion, and letters of protest appeared in the West. As outspoken writers were put into psychiatric hospitals at that time, Solzhenitsyn was courageously speaking out and was called the conscience of Russian literature.

In 1970 he was awarded the Nobel Prize. He wanted to go to Sweden and accept it, but when Natalia tried to kill herself, he decided not to go. He hoped there could be a ceremony in Moscow. However, the Soviet government boycotted the Nobel Prize ceremony. In retaliation perhaps, Solzhenitsyn sent *August 1914* to the West to be published, a direct challenge to the Soviet government.

He further defied the government by attending the poet Tvardovsky's funeral and internment, even though writers had been forbidden unless they had Writers Union cards. He kissed Tvardovsky in the coffin. This act was a sign to the rest of the world that he was not going to be intimidated. Still thinking he might be expelled or arrested, Solzhenitsyn decided to engage a Western lawyer to protect his literary estate and look after his interests in the West. Chukovsky died and left a bequest to him that would keep him in funds for the next three years.

Life became more tense, and he expected that they would arrest and expel him. At the same time, he saw himself as a teacher of the people, a prophet. He was engaged in a game of time. At what point would the government decide it did not want to deal with him any more? He kept his suitcase packed and the sheepskin coat he had worn in the camp ready by the door.

At this point the divorce was finally completed, but the strain with his exwife continued. Svetlova had borne him two sons, Ermolai and Ignat, but he could not live with her without a residence permit.

The KGB would not let things rest, and in 1973, he found out that it had confiscated a copy of *The Gulag Archipelago*. However, the race was on, as he heard on the radio that *The Gulag Archipelago* had already been published in Paris. Listening to excerpts being read brought him to tears. Now the work was out. What could the government do to him? It did not take long for the plans to be made public. The government wrote an eighteen-hundred-word attack against him. Hundreds of phone calls were made threatening his life and his children's, telling him to leave the country. He put the word out to Western reporters, and supporters in the West began openly calling for the Soviet government to leave him alone. But it was not to be stopped. The KGB intensified threats. Then came the ring of the doorbell, eight men burst in, and took him clad in his sheepskin coat to prison. He was charged with treason. In the morning they gave him new clothes and put him on an airplane to Germany. At fifty-six years old, Alexander Solzhenitsyn was deported.

Exiled Once More

From Germany he moved to Switzerland, and his family joined him. Along with Natalia and their two sons came large numbers of suitcases, his archive and library, and even his desk. It was not easy for him to live in the West. Plagued by reporters, he felt constantly misunderstood. He made pronouncements like a prophet, but felt the West did not understand Russia and what it needed. Feeling more and more isolated, he decided to hold a press conferences so he could speak his own mind. He began to travel to many countries, telling the West not to give in to the Soviets in any way, that Communism was evil. He criticized many of his old friends, disagreeing openly with their viewpoints. During that time, Volume II of *The Gulag Archipelago* was published in many languages. In his messianic pronouncements, he called for a renewal of spiritual over material values.

Solzhenitsyn moved to Vermont on wooded acres surrounded by a chain link fence. This became his first real home. The boys attended school, but he seldom made public appearances. One of the exceptions was at Harvard University's commencement in 1978. In this controversial address, subsequently published as "A World Split Apart," he called upon Americans to safeguard their freedom and not let it be compromised by media and materialism.[7]

> But the persisting blindness of superiority continues to hold the belief that all the vast regions of our planet should develop and mature to the level of contemporary Western systems, the best in theory and the most attractive in practice; that all those other worlds are but temporarily prevented (by wicked leaders or by severe crises or by their own barbarity and incomprehension) from pursuing Western pluralistic democracy and adopting the Western way of life. Countries are judged on the merit of their progress in that direction.
>
> But in fact such a conception is a fruit of Western incomprehension of the essence of other worlds, a result of mistakenly measuring them all with a Western yardstick. . . . I have spent all my life under a Communist regime and I will tell you that a society without any objective legal scale is a terrible one indeed. But a society with no other scale but the legal one is also less than worthy of man. A society based on the letter of the law and never reaching any higher fails to take advantage of the full range of human possibilities. The letter of the law is too cold and formal to have a beneficial influence on society. Whenever the tissue of life is woven of legalistic relationships, this creates an atmosphere of spiritual mediocrity that paralyzes man's noblest impulses.
>
> The press, too, of course, enjoys the widest freedom. . . . But what use does it make of it? Here again, the overriding concern is not to infringe on the letter of the law. There is no true moral responsibility for distortion or disproportion. Hastiness and superficiality—these are the psychic diseases of the twentieth century and more than anywhere else this is manifested in the press.

A fact which cannot be disputed is the weakening of human personality in the West while in the East it has become firmer and stronger. Six decades for our people and three decades for the people of Eastern Europe; during that time we have been through a spiritual training far in advance of Western experience. The complex and deadly crush of life has produced stronger, deeper, and more interesting personalities than those generated by standardized Western well-being.

And yet in early democracies, as in American democracy at the time of its birth, all individual human rights were granted on the ground that man is God's creature. That is, freedom was given to the individual conditionally, in the assumption of his constant religious responsibility. Such was the heritage of the preceding one thousand years. Two hundred or even fifty years ago, it would have seemed quite impossible, in America, that an individual be granted boundless freedom with no purpose, simply for the satisfaction of his whims. Subsequently, however, all such limitations were eroded everywhere in the West; a total emancipation occurred from the moral heritage of Christian centuries with their great reserves of mercy and sacrifice. State systems were becoming ever more materialistic. The West has finally achieved the rights of man, and even to excess, but man's sense of responsibility to God and society has grown dimmer and dimmer.

It has made man the measure of all things on earth—imperfect man, who is never free of pride, self-interest, envy, vanity, and dozens of other defects. We are now paying for the mistakes which were not properly appraised at the beginning of the journey. On the way from the Renaissance to our days, we have enriched our experience, but we have lost the concept of a Supreme Complete Entity which used to restrain our passions and our irresponsibility. We have placed too much hope in politics and social reforms, only to find out that we were being deprived of our most precious possession: our spiritual life. It is trampled by the party mob in the East, by the commercial one in the West. This is the essence of the crisis. . . . Only by the voluntary nurturing in ourselves of freely accepted and serene self-restraint can mankind rise above the world stream of materialism.

His statements caused people to take sides. Some felt he showed no appreciation for the fact that the United States had invited him to live here and work freely. Others said he was right to warn Americans of the dangers.

From age sixty-three to seventy (1981–1988), Solzhenitsyn lived in the United States. He wrote *The Red Wheel* and completed a work on the Russian Revolution. Even with the collapse of the Soviet Union in 1988, he indicated he would not return until his work was published there.

Home Again

At age seventy-five, after twenty years of exile, the treason charges were dropped and his Russian citizenship restored. He was invited to address the Russian Duma. His continued criticism of Western pop culture and the emptiness of Western materialism, linked with his comments about a return to monarchy and the power of the Russian Orthodox religion, made him seem a man out of his time. He said, "The human soul longs for things higher, warmer and purer than those offered by today's mass living habits … by TV stupor and by intolerable music."

Since returning to Russia in 1994, Solzhenitsyn has published short stories, prose poems, a literary memoir of his years in the West (*The Grain between the Millstones*), and a two-volume work on the history of Russian-Jewish relations (*Two Hundred Years Together*). He has been a constant critic of Russia's attempt at democracy and remains totally against Soviet communism. "The writer's task cannot be reduced to defending or criticizing one or another method of distributing the national wealth, to defending or criticizing this or that form of government. The writer's tasks concern more general and eternal questions – the secrets of the human heart and conscience, the clash between life and death, and the overcoming of inner sorrow. They concern the laws of mankind in its uninterrupted course, conceived in the immemorial depths of time and ceasing only when the sun will be extinguished."[8]

Endnotes
1. Michael Scammel, *Solzhenitsyn* (New York: W.W. Norton, 1984), p. 137.
2. Ibid., pp. 142–143.
3. Ibid., p. 157.
4. Ibid., p. 197.
5. David Burg and George Feifer, *Solzhenitsyn* (New York: Stein and Day, 1973), p. 97.
6. Scammel, *Solzhenitsyn*, p. 304.
7. Alexander Solzhenitsyn, "The Harvard Address," as printed in *Solzhenitsyn at Harvard: The Address, Twelve Early Responses and Six Later Reflections*, edited by Ronald Berman, et al. (Washington DC: Ethics and Public Policy Center, 1980), pp. 5–19.
8. Solzhenitsyn, 1967, as printed in Burg, *Solzhenitsyn*, p. 352.

Bibliography

Berman, Ronald, et al. *Solzhenitsyn at Harvard: The Address, Twelve Early Responses and Six Later Reflections*, Washington DC: Ethics and Public Policy Center, 1980.
Burg, David and George Feifer. *Solzhenitsyn*, New York: Stein and Day, 1973.
Frangsmyr, Tore, editor-in-charge. *Nobel Lectures, Literature 1960–1980*, Singapore: Sture Allen, World Scientific Publishing Co., 1993.
Scammel, Michael. *Solzhenitsyn*, New York: W.W. Norton, 1984.
Solzhenitsyn, Alexander. *August 1914, The Red Wheel*, New York: Farrar, Straus and Giroux, 1989.
_____. *The Gulag Archipelago, 1918–1956*, New York: Harper & Row, 1973.
_____. *The Oak and the Calf, Sketches of Literary Life in the Soviet Union*, New York: Harper & Row, 1980.
Solzhenitsyn, Alexander, et al. *From under the Rubble*, New York: Bantam Books, 1976.

CHAPTER 13

ANDREI DMITRIEVICH SAKHAROV (1921–1989)

Such personalities, no matter how few in number, no matter what a rarity they might be, help other people in their everyday lives. They restore one's faith in the beauty of the human soul, that very same beauty which has the power to save the world.[1]

Childhood

Andrei Sakharov was born into a family of intellectuals. A physics teacher and writer of textbooks, his father had a strong influence on Sakharov's childhood interests and education. His mother was devoted to the family. His grandmother was religious and tried to influence him, but his father was not, and at age thirteen, Andrei decided he was not religious either. As a child Andrei was introverted, a problem he had throughout his life. He always felt awkward around people.

University Years

Sakharov studied physics at Moscow University. In 1938 a number of the best teachers were taken away in the Stalinist purges, and when the Germans invaded Moscow in 1941, the university students took on responsibilities in support of the war effort. Because of a medical condition, Sakharov was not accepted into the Air Force, as many of his classmates were. Instead he served on duty during air raids, extinguished incendiary bombs, and unloaded equipment from railroad cars. He began work on a scientific invention to locate shrapnel in horses through a magnetic device. Eventually the entire university was evacuated to Central Asia by freight train. Hunger was constant during the month-long journey through heavy snow.

As the war continued, Sakharov postponed graduate school to help out with routine laboratory work at a cartridge factory. There he met Klavdia Vikhireva, a laboratory technician, who became his wife.

Then came a defining moment. "On the way to the bakery on the morning of August 7, 1945, I stopped to glance at a newspaper and discovered President Truman's announcement that at 8AM the previous day, August 6, an atomic bomb of enormous destructive power had been dropped on Hiroshima. I was so stunned that my legs practically gave way. There could be no doubt that my fate and the fate of many others, perhaps of the entire world, had changed overnight. Something new and awesome had entered our lives, a product of the greatest of the sciences, of the discipline I revered."[2]

After the war, Sakharov decided it was time to go on with graduate studies. He entered FIAN, the Physical Institute of the U.S.S.R. Academy of Sciences. His mentor was Igor Tamm, esteemed head of FIAN's theoretical department.

Career in Physics

In 1946 and 1947, Sakharov, now twenty-five years old, was invited to join the Soviet atomic bomb project. He declined because he wanted to focus on theoretical science, especially under the guidance of Igor Tamm. In 1947 he received his doctoral degree for his work in particle physics. When Tamm was commissioned to join the research team to study the feasibility of a thermonuclear (hydrogen) bomb, Sakharov and a few other students formed a subgroup at FIAN to work on that proposal.

At the same time the Soviet Union wanted to produce an atomic bomb to establish a balance of power with the United States. This was accomplished in 1949 with the first Soviet nuclear test. Meanwhile, research on the H-bomb continued. The Soviets set up the "Installation" in the central Volga region, similar to the U.S. secret Manhattan Project site in New Mexico. Tamm and Sakharov moved there in 1950 and continued to work on it. With Sakharov's ideas for a design, research took a giant step forward, and the first Soviet hydrogen bomb was tested on August 12, 1953. As the tests continued, Sakharov was "seized with an awful sense of powerlessness … it was terrible. After that I was a different man."[3]

Sakharov and Tamm proposed an idea for a controlled thermonuclear fusion reactor which paved the way for international competition to use it for peaceful purposes. After the thermonuclear test of 1953, Tamm returned to theoretical science, his first love. Sakharov was honored for his contribution with many awards including the Stalin Prize and a dacha. When Tamm withdrew, Sakharov took over as head of the "Installation" and went on to be considered Father of the H-bomb, fully-developed and successfully tested in 1955.

Sakharov was deeply concerned about the dangers of radioactive fallout from nuclear explosions, and he made careful calculations about the number of deaths that could occur from ongoing explosions. Despite the assurance that such detonations were safe, Sakharov argued that continuing the testing of nuclear devices was a moral issue, and he refused to participate further.

Sakharov still held an idealistic belief in Soviet ideology and goals. As he became more conscious of the crimes that had been committed by Stalin, he gave up his illusions that Stalin had the good of the country at heart. In his thinking he separated Stalin from the Communist ideals he continued to hold for several years, until he finally decided that those ideals too were actually corrupt and that the authoritarian power of the Communist Party which exerted control over individual's freedom of thought and expression was wrong.

"In 1950 our research was incorporated into a specialized institute. During the next eighteen years I lived in a special world of military designers, inventors, research institutes, committees, academic councils, experimental plants and testing ranges. Every day I saw how much enormous material, intellectual, and nervous energy of thousands of people was invested in creating means of total annihilation capable of destroying the whole of human civilization. I saw that the levers of administration were in the hands of cynical people, although they were talented in their own way. It was Beria who was in charge of the atomic project until the summer of 1952. He wielded power over millions of prison inmates who were virtual slaves, and nearly all of the construction work was done by them. The collective might of the military-industrial complex and its energetic, unprincipled leaders blind to everything except their 'business' had been forming itself more and more clearly since the late '50s. . . . As from 1957 I came to feel responsible for the problem of radioactive contamination during nuclear tests."[4]

Dilemma between Science and Morality

Taking a stand against the suffering of even those not yet born was the beginning of Sakharov's position on human rights. As a result of his questioning the morality of such testing, the Soviet Union announced a moratorium on nuclear tests. Three years later, however, in 1961, Khrushchev revoked the moratorium on bomb tests. Only Sakharov disagreed with this decision. He saw no scientific reasons for renewing tests, and he tried desperately to get Khrushchev to stop, but the carrier plane had already departed with its cargo destined for explosion. When the bomb was tested, it was the most powerful device ever exploded on earth. Sakharov felt helpless and wept.

Sakharov worked hard to facilitate the 1963 Moscow Ban on Testing, agreed to by U.S. President John F. Kennedy and U.S.S.R. Premier Nikita Khrushchev, and signed by the U.S., the U.S.S.R., and the United Kingdom. This treaty banned all nuclear weapons testing in the atmosphere, in outer space and under water, but allowed for testing to take place underground.

In 1965, at age forty-four years, Sakharov moved out of the world of weaponry and turned his work in theoretical science to projects for peace. He began to wake up to the political discrimination and oppression, especially against Jews and those who disagreed with the government. Sakharov preferred to think of these people as "freethinkers," rather than dissidents.

He worked to bring the U.S.S.R. and the U.S. together on a moratorium on anti-ballistic missiles, but when he tried to publish an article on anti-ballistic missile defenses (ABM), he was told it was "unsuitable for publication."

This was the fuse to Sakharov's decision to speak out for himself by himself, and he circulated the article "Reflections on Progress, Peaceful Coexistence, and Intellectual Freedom" through the *samizdat* underground publication method. It was picked up by a Dutch newspaper and by the *New York Times* in July 1968 and soon after became a book of significant influence. His two main points were: l) The divisiveness of mankind threatens it with destruction. . . . Only universal cooperation under conditions of intellectual freedom and the lofty moral ideals of socialism and labor, accompanied by the elimination of dogmatism and pressure of the concealed interests of ruling classes, will preserve civilization, and 2) Intellectual freedom is essential to human society — freedom to obtain and distribute information, freedom for open-minded and undaunted debate, and freedom from pressure by officialdom and prejudices. . . . Freedom of thought is the only guarantee of the feasibility of a scientific democratic approach to politics, economics and culture.[5]

His courageous act caused him to be banned from any military-related research. Around the same time, his wife Klavdia died of cancer, leaving him with three children to rear. With a feeling of relief, he returned to his work in theoretical physics at FIAN and out of the hot seat of public criticism.

Humanitarian Efforts

From 1968 on, Sakharov lived in two worlds—pure theoretical physics and the emerging human rights movement. In 1970 he and two other dissidents founded the Moscow Human Rights Committee. It was in this work that he met Elena Bonner, a doctor, who would become his closest partner in the human rights activities and his future wife. (They were married in 1971.) He began to attend the staged trials of dissidents. He wrote: "I sat in the hall filled with KGB 'trainees' while the friends of the defendants were kept in the corridor of the ground floor throughout the trial." At another trial, he wrote: "We were not allowed into the courtroom, and when the trial began 'unknown persons in plain clothes' used force to push us out of the vestibule into the street. After that a huge barn padlock was put on the entrance door of the people's court. You had to see that senseless and cruel performance with your own eyes to understand fully what it meant."[6]

Sakharov's work to help dissidents gain freedom of expression put him into the limelight. The government could not bear this and began to hound him, writing letters against him in the press, and painting him with Alexander Solzhenitsyn as a traitor. Although Sakharov and Solzhenitsyn did not see eye to eye on every issue, they respected each other. In 1973 Solzhenitsyn nominated Sakharov for the Nobel Prize for Peace. One of Sakharov's defenders, Lydia Chukovskaya, called on the Soviet people to pay attention to what Sakharov was saying, that people of the globe had to speak together, to stop stockpiling bombs and start meeting together to share ideas. In 1974, in retaliation, Chukovskaya was expelled from the Writers Union; Sakharov's daughter-in-law, Tatyana, was expelled from university courses and her husband lost his job; his son-in-law, Alexei, was barred from university and his family was threatened with violence. (Tatyana and Alexei emigrated to the United States in 1977 and 1978 respectively.)

In 1975 Sakharov was awarded the Nobel Peace Prize, the first Russian to receive this honor for his "fearless personal commitment in upholding the fundamental principles for peace..." As were Pasternak and Solzhenitsyn, Sakharov was forbidden to travel abroad to receive the prize. However, his wife Elena was abroad at the time and was able to travel to Oslo to take part in the ceremony.

In his commitment to human freedom of expression, Sakharov spoke about a future universal information system which could give each person maximum freedom of choice through individual miniature-computer terminals. This could break down barriers to the exchange of information across the globe. In this way, he foresaw value in the worldwide web.

When Sakharov strongly protested the Soviet invasion of Afghanistan, this was the final straw for the Soviet government. He and his wife were exiled to

Gorky, a city on the Volga River that was closed to foreigners. He was stripped of his title of Hero of Socialist Labor and all the other awards and decorations. He was not allowed to leave the city, meet with foreigners and other "criminal elements," correspond or have telephone communication with foreigners, or even communicate with his children or grandchildren except by censored mail or telephone. He was followed at all times, and his telephone was bugged.

Sakharov's exile turned out to be a seven-year punishment. Despite his struggle to keep in touch with people, to defend his rights and human dignity, his moments of hope came from secret contacts with Western physicists who had found ways to communicate with him, sending him articles, and protesting to the Soviet government to free him. He used his time in Gorky to write his *Memoirs*. On three different occasions the KGB stole the manuscript and he had to start over. He did not stop protesting Soviet involvement in Afghanistan but wrote letters which were smuggled out of the Soviet Union and printed in the Western press. He was accused by the government of inciting Western countries to nuclear war against the Soviet Union.

Punishment and Protest

As a means of protest when his family members were targeted by the KGB, and especially when the government would not allow his wife to go for medical treatment in the West, Sakharov went on a hunger strike. During the two hundred days he was kept in complete isolation, he wrote an open letter to the president of the Soviet Academy of Sciences describing his situation and explaining that the government had tried to punish him through mistreatment of his wife. The government blamed her for influencing him to be active in human rights initiatives; it was all her fault, and they needed to punish her for it. One of the most painful aspects of his exile was that his children distrusted Elena Bonner and blamed her for his hardships.

Sakharov and Elena survived the years of turmoil in exile, the hunger strikes, the forced feedings, the slander, interrogations and harassment. In 1968 a joint resolution by the U.S. Senate and House of Representatives calling for an end to their punishment paved the way for allowing Elena to make the trip to the West, to receive medical attention and visit her mother and children in Newton, Massachusetts. During that time she wrote a book *Alone Together* to describe their experiences in detail.

One section describes the lengths to which the government went to take away their privacy. "We have no phone in our apartment. Academician Sakharov has been living in Gorky for six years without a telephone. There have been times when I needed urgent medical assistance, not a television repairman. Andrei would have to run outside, even in freezing weather, to look for a phone booth. In winter, still fewer worked properly."[7]

In response to the question, "Do you listen to the radio?" Elena Bonner replied, "Yes, we do. In order to tune in, we travel to the extreme edge of town, to the racetrack or to the cemetery. There we can pick up some Western stations. It isn't bad in spring and summer, but it is cold and windy in winter. The days are short, we don't like to drive at night because the roads are often not clear … and they are slippery. So we seldom listen to the radio in winter."[8]

As a result of Sakharov's many letters and articles claiming that the government was corrupt and illegitimate, members of the Communist Party began to think about these issues and to consider there could be truth in his claims. After Mikhail Gorbachev rose to power in 1985 and resurrected *perestroika*, a time of restructuring, Sakharov was freed from internal exile. Free to return to Moscow and carry out his activities without fear of punishment, he helped to form the first independent legal political organization and became active in political opposition demanding democratic changes that were ever more radical than the reforms proposed under *perestroika*.

Gennadi Zhavoronkov described Sakharov at home[9] — the constant visitors would make their way to the Sakharov's small apartment, and after they were gone, he would do the dishes himself and fill his time with phone calls, interviews, scientific consultations, and work on his Foundation. At times he would long for the peace and quiet of exile in Gorky, but only jokingly so. He would work late at night, often until 3am. He would do the vegetable shopping himself armed with two straw baskets. His diet was of very simple, typical Russian food: sauerkraut, cabbage soup, potatoes, cottage cheese and greens.

The democratic opposition wanted the Communist Party to give up its monolithic power, particularly through abolishing Article 6 of the Constitution which gave the Communist Party the ruling power of Soviet society. Sakharov began drafting a new Constitution. He became a spiritual leader of all those who were trying to turn Russia into a democratic state through non-violent methods.

On December 14, 1989, Sakharov was making a speech when Gorbachev pressed a button to silence him. This was a sign that the Party was still in charge and decided what voices could be heard or not. That night he worked late hours on the Constitution. The next morning the news was brought to the Second Congress of U.S.S.R. People's Deputies that Sakharov had suffered a heart attack and died.

Tatyana Ivanova wrote of her feelings after Sakharov's death:

> Andrei Sakharov is not dead and will never die. His influence on all of us in society is tremendous. We cannot possibly realize how much. We can only observe and draw possible conclusions. In this respect television has given us exceptionally rich material. True, the hall would be in uproar, people would be stamping their feet, even whistling, and the chairman's bell would be ringing and preventing the Academician from speaking up. But those in the hall and in the world as a whole would be seeing him with their own eyes. They would see that he could walk to the rostrum and say what he believed to be the truth. And if his microphone was switched off, he would still be able to speak and move his lips and people would understand him, they would guess and tell one another what he wanted to say, but would not be able to say. . . . We were happy to be alive at the same time as Andrei Sakharov. He displayed heroism before our very eyes; he had absolutely

no fear. Neither his exile, nor hunger strikes lasting for many days, nor the official licentious harassing that went on for many years, nor vile slanderous gossip on a huge scale, nor lies, nor the well-organized "contempt of all the people" from women textile workers with decorations to a well-known writer, nor whistling and foot-stamping—nothing frightened him. Nothing could ever make him betray his conscience, renounce the truth or fail to defend goodness and justice. All this happened before our very eyes.[10]

Though Sakharov's name is universally known, the full impact of his personality on the development of the world's scene is still to be appreciated. We know from history that when new civilizations emerge, it is the saints and prophets who come first; leaders come later. Humanity is in desperate need of a new and more sound basis for the goals and values of the new global civilization that is now in the throes of birth. I see Andrei Sakharov as a prophet of this coming civilization. He demonstrated that the heights of moral strength, courage, and self-sacrifice are not necessarily based on any of the traditional religions which now separate the human race. Nor do they require a belief in the supernatural or life after death. They may take root in the sober and critical but compassionate human thinking so characteristic of Andrei Dmitrievich.[11]

I have several reasons for including the life of Andrei Sakharov in my Russian literature classes. First, I believe he is one of the great cosmopolitan figures of humanity—he stands there with the greatest. (He has been compared to Mahatma Gandhi and to Martin Luther King, Jr.) His commitment to truth and honesty is a model for young people. That he was a scientist is also very important. For students who are planning a career in science, the study of a committed scientist who acknowledged his responsibility for the consequences of technological advances, Sakharov's life is a powerful example. His modesty and sweetness, his courage and steadfastness through difficult times, and his intellectual integrity all point to the spiritual leadership that is necessary in our times. For half of the twentieth century Russia (and the Soviet Union) was considered the enemy, and recognizing the work of Sakharov helps students see the complexity of international relations rather than just simplifying and demonizing the "other."

Further, Sakharov's essay "Progress, Coexistence and Intellectual Freedom" is a worthy literary expression of prose which expresses his clarity and grasp of an essential element of modern civilization. Lastly, the way in which human beings from different cultures courageously reach out and speak with others in the name of Humanity rather than of nations is one of the tasks of our epoch, and of this Sakharov is a perfect example.[12]

Endnotes

1. Andrei Sakharov, *Lessons of Andrei Sakharov* (Moscow: Novosti, 1990), p. 6.
2. Andrei Sakharov, *Memoirs* (New York: Alfred A. Knopf, 1990) p. 92.
3. Edward Lozansky, ed., *Andrei Sakharov and Peace* (New York: Avon, 1985), p. 38.
4. Sakharov, *Lessons*, pp. 8–9.
5. Ibid., pp. 25–39.
6. Ibid., p. 15.
7. Elena Bonner, *Alone Together* (New York, Alfred A. Knopf, 1986), pp. 195–196.
8. Ibid., p. 196.
9. Sakharov, *Lessons*, pp. 85–87.
10. Ibid., p. 101.
11. Valentin Turchin, in Lozansky, *Andrei Sakharov and Peace*, p. 320.
12. For many years I was able to rent the film *Sakharov* with Jason Robards, Jr., and Glenda Jackson. This work spoke strongly to the students. If a copy can be procured to show the class, I believe the teacher would find it helpful.

Bibliography

Bonner, Elena. *Alone Together*, New York: Alfred A. Knopf, 1986.

Lozansky, Edward, ed. *Andrei Sakharov and Peace*, New York: Avon, 1985.

Sakharov, Andrei. *Lessons of Andrei Sakharov*, Moscow: Novosti, 1990.

_____. *Memoirs*, New York: Alfred A. Knopf, 1990.

Sakharov, a film directed by Jack Gold, 1984.

CHAPTER 14

OTHER SPLINTERS OF THE SUN

In addition to the writers and poets included in previous chapters, there are other nineteenth and twentieth century figures who are well worth including in our study. They also had the light and warmth of the Russian sun in their hearts and are inspiring models for high school students. These include the writers Mikhail Lermontov, Ivan Turgenev, and Nikolai Gogol; the dramatist Anton Chekhov; the poets Andrei Biely, Alexander Blok, Osip Mandelstam, Marina Tsvetayeva, and Joseph Brodsky; and three living poets, Irina Ratushinskaya, Andrei Voznesensky and Yevgeny Yevtushenko. For those interested in a play about Chernobyl, *Sarcophagus, A Tragedy* by Vladimir Gubaryey is very interesting. In addition, there is long list of writers who penned memoirs of their experiences under repression; these include Natal Scharansky, Nadezhda Mandelstam and Lev Kopelev.

Osip Mandelstam (1891–1938)

Osip Mandelstam was born in Warsaw, Poland, into a wealthy Jewish family. His father, a tanner, was able to get permission to move his family out of the Pale, where Jews were confined in St. Petersburg. Osip was already writing poetry during his school years. During his university years he studied at the Sorbonne, the University of Heidelberg, and the University of St. Petersburg, but never completed a degree. He converted to Christianity.

After the 1905 Revolution, he began publishing poems and joined, along with Nikolay Gumilyov and Anna Akhmatova, the Acmeist Group, which focused on clear, direct writing rather than symbolism. In 1913 he titled his first book of poetry *The Stone*, to which he continued to add new poems over the years.

Mandelstam married, and with his wife Nadezhda moved to Moscow. His second book of poems, *Tristia*, was published in Berlin. During the 1920s, it was difficult to get his work published. He translated and worked at a newspaper as a day job and at night he wrote, mostly essays and articles. During the terrible Stalin years, he wrote a poem called "Stalin Epigram," sometimes referred to as a "sixteen-line death sentence."[1]

Stalin Epigram (1933)[2]

We live, but we do not feel the land beneath us,
Ten steps away and our words cannot be heard.

And when there are just enough people for half a dialogue,
Then they remember the Kremlin mountaineer.

His fat fingers are slimy like slugs,
And his words are absolute, like grocers' weights.

His cockroach whiskers are laughing,
And his boot tops shine.

And around him the rabble of narrow-necked chiefs —
He plays with the services of half-men.

Who warble, or miaow, or moan.
He alone pushes and prods.

Decree after decree he hammers them out like horseshoes,
In the groin, in the forehead, in the brows, or in the eye.

When he has an execution it's a special treat,
And the Ossetian chest swells.

Shortly after he read his poem at a gathering, his work was brought to Stalin's attention, who had him arrested and exiled with his wife to a town in the Northern Urals. He attempted suicide. He was then banished from big cities, but allowed to choose wherever else to settle. He and Nadezhda moved to Veronezh, where he defiantly continued writing poetry even though he knew of the dangers. This poem was found in 1975 and subsequently printed.

If Our Enemies Took Me (1937)[3]

If our enemies took me
and no one would speak to me
if they took everything, everything —
the right to breathe, to open doors,
to claim that existence will be, will be,
and that the people are judges and judge, they judge;
if they dared to chain me like an animal,
to throw my food on the floor —
it won't make me mute, I won't muffle pain,
I'll write what I'm allowed to write,
and when my nakedness rings like a bell,
and the home of hostile darkness wakes,
I'll yoke ten oxen to my voice
and move my hand like a plow, in the darkness
and then compressed in an ocean of brotherly eyes.
I'll fall with the weight of an entire harvest,
with the exactness of that oath, ripping into the distance.
And deep in the dark sentry night
the earth's unskilled-laborer's eyes
will flare, and a flock of flaming years will flash by,

and like a blind thunderstorm, rustling out, will come — Lenin …
Yes, but that which will endure on this earth,
that which will destroy reason, which will ruin life,
will be — Stalin.

Mandelstam wrote several poems to glorify Stalin, but they did not help his case. During the Great Purge in 1937, he was attacked for anti-Soviet views. While on vacation with Nadezhda, he was arrested and four months later, he was sentenced to hard labor, during which time he died from an unidentified illness, probably typhus.

After his death, Nadezhda went on to write two books about their experiences, *Hope against Hope* and *Hope Abandoned*. Carl Proffer included a very interesting interview with her in his book *The Widows of Russia*.[4]

Mandelstam appears in the biographies of Pasternak and Akhmatova (see those chapters).

Student writing:

The learned poet Osip Mandelstam wrote this untitled poem in 1937. It was most likely composed right before Mandelstam was arrested and moved into a labor camp. In his poem he claims that when they take away all his rights and possessions, he will not stop writing his mind. When the government tries to oppress his voice, he will continue composing and only be more adamant with his pen. He announces against the horrible Stalin and advocates Lenin. Mandelstam does not use rhyming, but he incorporates many metaphors and detailed imagery. One of his most important messages is written in metaphorical form:

and when my nakedness rings like a bell
and the home of hostile darkness wakes,
I'll yoke ten oxen to my voice
and move my hand like a plow …

After he has nothing left and is living in despair, this is what he will do. His "nakedness" is his raw body and soul from living an abusive life in the labor camp. The "hostile darkness" is the deep abyss, into which he will emotionally fall when he has no strength and there is little hope. Even then, when he is frail and weak, he will bring the power of "ten oxen" to his voice and compose his beliefs with gusto and determination.

His remark about Lenin's being "like a blind thunderstorm" brings up images of a man with great energy and force, able to change anything in his way. I believe this is what Mandelstam wanted the reader to believe, that Lenin was a good and vigorous leader who could change things. Mandelstam himself hoped to affect people through his writing. In his poem he stated that with these words: "the earth's unskilled laborer's eyes will flare." I think he speaks of the common person reading his poetry and being sparked by his views. If everything else is taken from him he wants to be able to at least share his thoughts with the public.

This is a poem of determination and Mandelstam expresses the will to survive and hold one's ground. It is also a political statement, one that may have been a reason for Mandelstam's arrest. Mandelstam uses a simple free-verse form for his poem and yet it is perfect for the objective. At first glance, the poem looks rough and meaningless, but when analyzed, it turns out to be a profound piece. Without the reader even knowing the history of Russia, Mandelstam makes it easy to see Russia's despotism, the fortitude of the people and his opinion of the rulers. He does it in such a manner that the poem is clear, but eloquently written. Mandelstam is able to use metaphors like a "flock of flaming years" to make the reader truly image a simple action in the poem. He has a real talent with phrasing and bringing emotion to a subject without being too dramatic.

Mandelstam was taught this method through the Acmeist School of Poetry, where they believed "direct expression through images" was better than symbolism. It was the same group that Anna Akhmatova was affiliated with and they all met in the Stray Dog Café. Twenty-two years after his life as an Acmeist, Mandelstam was arrested for writing poetry against Stalin. He was pardoned and kept out of trouble until 1937 when he wrote this poem of fortitude and others similar to it. That same year he was put into a labor camp and six months later died of disease.

I think his strong will to stand up for what he believed is shown in the intensity of this poem. It demonstrates the passion Mandelstam feels for the right to his voice. He claims that even though the government will cut him down "it won't make me mute, I won't muffle pain." He is a poet who knows that the ability to have free thought and influence the world is more important than to live a long life being constricted and oppressed. Mandelstam speaks of this in his poem, lived by it in his choices, and proved it by continuing to write until he no longer possessed the ability. – L.D.

Marina Tsvetayeva (1892–1941)

Tsvetayeva was born in Moscow and grew up in an intellectual family. The son of a village priest, her father became a distinguished professor of art history at Moscow University. Her mother was a gifted pianist. She published her first book of poems, *Evening Album*, at age seventeen. She married poet Sergei Efron, who was fighting during the Revolution for the White Army. She tried to care for her two children, but her youngest daughter died of starvation. After the Revolution, she emigrated to the West and joined Efron in Paris. She wrote a number of books of lyrical poetry. Much admired by other Russian writers, she has been hailed as one of the leading Russian poets of the twentieth century. However, her life was tragic, and she felt very lonely and abandoned. She returned to the Soviet Union to be with her husband; two months later, their daughter Ariadna was arrested and her husband was arrested soon after and shot as a counter-revolutionary.

Tsvetayeva carried on an active correspondence with Boris Pasternak during the years of her European exile, and these letters have now been published in *The Same Solitude: Boris Pasternak and Marina Tsvetayeva*.

During the Second World War, the government continued to hound her. She was evacuated to Central Asia, but not allowed to publish. Isolated from friends and family, and unable to find work or food for her son, she hanged herself in August 1941.

You Loved Me (1923)[5]

You loved me. And your lies had their own probity.
There was a truth in every falsehood.
Your love went far beyond any possible
Boundary as no one else's could.

Your love seemed to last even longer
than time itself. Now you wave your hand —
and suddenly your love for me is over!
That is the truth in five words.

The Poet (1923)[6]

1.

A poet's speech begins a great way off.
A poet is carried far away by speech
by way of planets, signs, and the ruts
of roundabout parables, between yes and no,
in his hands even sweeping gestures from a bell-tower
become hook-like. For the way of comets
is the poet's way. And the blown-apart
links of causality are his links. Look up
after him without hope. The eclipses of
poets are not foretold in the calendar.

He is the one that mixes up the cards
and confuses arithmetic and weight.
He is the questioner from the desk
the one who beats Kant on the head,
the one in the stone graves of the Bastille
who remains like a tree in its loveliness.
And yet the one whose traces have always vanished,
the train everyone always arrives
too late to catch

for the path of comets
is the path of poets: they burn without warming,
pick without cultivating. They are: an explosion, a breaking in —
and the mane of their path makes the curve of a
graph cannot be foretold by the calendar.

2.

There are superfluous people about in
this world, out of sight, who
aren't listed in any directory; and
home for them is a rubbish heap.

They are hollow, jostled creatures:
who keep silent, dumb as dung, they are
nails catching in your silken hem
dirt imagined under your wheels.

Here they are, ghostly and invisible, the
sign is on them, like the speck of the leper.
People like Job in this world who
might even have envied him. If.

We are poets, which has the sound of outcast.
Nevertheless, we step out from our shores.
We dare contend for godhead, with goddesses,
and for the Virgin with the gods themselves.

3.

Now what shall I do here blind and fatherless?
Everyone else can see and has a father.
Passion in this world has to leap anathema
as it might be over the walls of a trench
and weeping is called a cold in the head.

What shall I do, by nature and trade
a singing creature (like a wire—sunburn! Siberia!)
as I go over the bridge of my enchanted
visions, that cannot be weighed, in a
world that deals only in weights and measures?

What shall I do, singer and firstborn,
in a world where the deepest black is grey,
and inspiration is kept in a thermos?
with all this immensity
in a measured world?

To Boris Pasternak (1925)[7]

Distance: *versts*, miles …
divide us; they've dispersed us,
to make us behave quietly
at our different ends of the earth.

Distance: how many miles of it
lie between us now—disconnected—
crucified—then dissected.
And they don't know—it unites us.

Our spirits and sinews fuse,
there's no discord between us.
though our separated pieces
lie outside
the moat — for eagles!

This conspiracy of miles
has not yet disconcerted us,
however much they've pushed us, like
orphans into backwaters.

What then? Well. Now it's March!
And we're scattered like some pack of cards!

Joseph Brodsky (1940–1996)

Born in St. Petersburg, he was influenced by his father, a newspaper reporter and photographer. He began to write poetry in his teenage years and gained a reputation as a free-thinker. After high school, he began working in many different jobs. Because he was a Jew, he was not allowed admission into the submarine military academy. He taught himself Polish so he could read poetry that had never been translated. He taught himself English so he could read a wide variety of Western authors, and translate them into Russian. By the time he was twenty, he was considered brash but brilliant — a free spirit who did not conform or follow rules.

Because he chose profound themes, Brodsky gained a following from a large public. In one poem he wrote, titled "Pilgrims," he described people walking around aimlessly, realizing that any idea of earthly paradise is an illusion. Although this was not a political poem per se, it was considered a criticism of Communism because it depicted a world without hope.

In 1958 Brodsky began reciting poetry, and students flocked to hear him. His style of recitation was dramatic. In 1960 he participated in a poets' competition in Leningrad, reciting "The Jewish Cemetery." Despite the fact there was no evidence that he planned to overthrow the government or had even spoken against it, his brash, individualistic style was threat enough, and the authorities decided to get rid of him. An article was written against him, filled with inaccuracies, trying to show how dangerous he was by not having a regular job and by writing pessimistic poems, and accusing him of plotting to escape the country to the West. His trial was the beginning of a series of trials against poets. Many people, especially members of the Writers Union, rallied to his cause to protect poets from this unconscionable show of force by the state.

In 1964 Brodsky was advised to get out of Leningrad and give things time to cool off before his trial. He went to Moscow, but when he discovered the woman he loved was having an affair with a good friend, he hastily returned to Leningrad and was arrested and placed in solitary confinement at the same prison in which Anna Akhmatova's son Lev had been. He was labeled as "less than one," a phrase he used later in 1986 as a title for his collection of essays. He smuggled out a collection of poems which was published in the United States.

Because there was an optimism that people would not be treated as they had been during Stalinist times, many people took the risk to come forward in Brodsky's defense. His close relationship with Ahkmatova encouraged leading intellectuals to step forward to defend him by sending letters and signing petitions. Even though the allegations were proved to be false, Brodsky was put on trial a second time. Though very distinguished people testified on his behalf, and it was clear he had committed no crime, he was judged guilty and sentenced to five years of exile to the Archangel region.

The verdict was a depressing blow to those who had believed that truth and honesty were possible, that the climate had changed. It was as if poetry itself was on trial. When Khrushchev was removed from power, there was hope Brodsky might be freed. His case was reviewed and, probably due to the number of influential people pleading on his behalf, in 1965, he was freed. But he was forced against his will to leave the U.S.S.R. With help he made his way to the U.S. where he lived and taught at universities in New York and Massachusetts. In 1987 he was awarded the Nobel Prize for Literature, and his poetry made its way throughout Russia. He had a daughter named Anna after his good friend, Anna Akhmatova.

In 1992 Brodsky was named American Poet Laureate. He wrote numerous essays and contributions to magazines such as the *New Yorker*. He died in New York of a heart attack in 1996.

Irina Ratushinskaya (1954 –)

Irina Ratushinskaya was born in Odessa, educated in Odessa University, and taught school there for three years. She graduated with a Master's degree in physics at age twenty-one. Already at age nineteen she refused to go along with Komsomol activity to become acquainted with foreigners in order to find out their political leanings and report dissidents. However, her superiors may have written "unreliable" in her file, because when her group was scheduled to make a trip to Poland, she was not allowed to go.

When Irina was twenty-three, her Jewish boyfriend, Ilusha, introduced her to the Jewish holidays and to the big four in poetry: Pasternak, Akhmatova, Mandelstam, and Tsvetayeva. She could not believe she knew nothing of them. As she began to read them, she grew angry that she had not met them before, and she devoured their writing. Before Ilusha's family emigrated, he gave her a going-away present of an eighteenth century Bible. After she learned how to read the old style script, she then read the Bible for the first time. She felt she was putting together a puzzle. When she finished, she decided that she was a Christian and believed in God.

At age twenty-five, she and her longtime friend Igor got married. Both became involved in passing *samizdat* copies of Solzhenitsyn's *Gulag Archipelago*, and Irina was also sending her poetry out through the *samizdat* system.

In 1980, the same time that Andrei Sakharov was placed in internal exile, Ratushinskaya and Igor decided to put in applications to emigrate. They were questioned several times as to why they wanted to leave Russia. They sat down and drafted their first letter in defense of human rights. They knew they were doing dangerous things, for the KGB was very clear that if one read or wrote uncensored work, one could be imprisoned or gulaged. As Irina was claustrophobic, they started training themselves so they would not be afraid if such a situation occurred.

During the Moscow Olympics, they tried to pass Irina's poetry to a foreigner to take out of the country, but could find no one who would do it; people were too afraid. Friends were interrogated as to Irina's activities. She and Igor realized they were under surveillance. Igor was questioned about why he wanted to emigrate when he had been working on classified projects: Did he want to share secrets with the West? Since he had not, in truth, been working on such projects, this was just a way of trying to intimidate him.

The KGB told Irina to stop her anti-Soviet activity. She was arrested and taken to prison for ten days. In 1982 she was sentenced to seven years' hard labor and five years' internal exile. She was released after four years, on the eve of the 1986 summit in Reykjavik, Iceland, between President Reagan and Mikhail Gorbachev.

In 1987 she came to the U.S., where she received the Religious Freedom Award and was named Poet in Residence at Northwestern University from 1987–1989. After that she and her husband lived in London, and in the late 1990s they were allowed to return to Russia where they now live with their two children.

Her book *In the Beginning* is about her childhood and the years leading up to her arrest. *Grey Is the Color of Hope* describes her four years in a "strict regime" labor camp at Barashevo, where she lived in the "Small Zone" for female political prisoners. (A number of my students have loved this book.) It is written from a woman's perspective of such imprisonment, focusing on her relationships with the other women prisoners and how she wrote her poems in soap, memorized them, and washed them off. Her latest book *Wind of the Journey* was published by Cornerstone Press, Chicago—her first collection since 1992.

Andrei Voznesensky (1933–)

Andrei Voznesensky was born in Moscow, but he lived part of the time in Vladimir and during the war in the Ural Mountains. His father, a professor of engineering, was involved in evacuating factories during the German blockade of Leningrad. His family had literary interests, and Voznesensky developed a love of poetry as a child.

The family returned to Moscow after the war. Andrei painted, wrote poetry, and studied architecture. Shortly before his graduation from the Moscow Architectural Institute, a fire broke out and destroyed the project he had worked on all year. Relieved that he did not have to take his examinations, he decided to put his energy into becoming a poet instead.

As a boy, he had sent his poems to Boris Pasternak who had become a mentor and a close friend (see Pasternak chapter). Pasternak encouraged him to go on with his writing. Although his early poems had the mark of Pasternak in them, Andrei found his own style. Other poets who influenced him were Pablo Neruda and Vladimir Mayakovsky.

Voznesensky and others of his generation felt they had to bring back real meaning to words that had been corrupted during Stalinism. In 1958 he published his first book of poems, which attracted many young people, and in 1962 fourteen thousand people gathered in a sports stadium to hear him read his poetry. Over half a million people bought his book of poetry, which reflects both the Russian love of poetry and the appeal Voznesensky had to his contemporaries. Until 1963, when the government cracked down on such events, there was a rage for poetry readings in which poets would recite their original works by heart for hours. During the Thaw, Voznesensky not only gave recitals of poetry to large home audiences, but he also traveled to France, Germany, Italy, and the U.S. where he shared his poetry and made contacts with other writers.

The Thaw ended when Khruschev's advisors felt that he was allowing too much freedom. Khrushchev launched a campaign to close down all modern art exhibitions and sentence artists to ten years in prison. He did the same to writers and poets, ending the publication of books of poems, forbidding trips to the West, and chastising their writing.

When Voznesensky was brought up on charges, he responded to Khrushchev, "It has been said at this plenum [of the Union of the Soviet Writers] that I must never forget the stern and severe words of Nikita Sergeyevich [Khrushchev]. I shall never forget them. I shall not forget these severe words but also the advice which Nikita Sergeivich gave me. He said: 'Work.' I do not justify myself now. I simply wish to say that for me now the main thing is to work, work, work. What my attitude is to my country, to communism, what I myself am, this work will show."[8]

His response was accepted, and the attacks became less strident. The writers had won a moral victory, and their work began to appear in print. Poetry readings were rescheduled. However, the attacks had left their mark—Voznesensky's poems became more focused on love than on social commentary, although those began to appear again a few years later.

Voznesensky lives and works in Moscow. He has continued to write not only poetry but also *Juno and Avos* (1979), a very successful rock opera based on the life and death of Nikolay Rezanov. At this time he has written approximately forty volumes of poetry in Russian, two collections of fiction, three plays, and two operas. In 1983 a three-volume collection of his poetry was published in the U.S.S.R., and in 2003, a six-volume set of his collected works appeared. More recently he has written poetry against Russian involvement in Chechnya.

Book Boom[9]

Just try to buy Akhmatova —
Sold out. The booksellers say
Her black agate-colored tome
Is worth more than agate today.

Those who once attacked her —
as if to atone for their curse —
stand, a reverent honor guard,
for a single volume of her verse.

"Print more copies of magazines,"
we beg of the great book gods.
"Give us more copies of our dreams,
release the cranes, vanished birds."

It's rare in our polluted skies
to hear the crane's lonely cries,
while every bookstore's lined with stacks
of monolithic published hacks.

The country demands its birthright,
and maybe that's as well.
Akhmatova will not sell out,
nor Pasternak, although he sells.

The Great Confrontation[10]

Why must two great poet-teachers,
from whom eternal love should flow,
stare unblinking like two pistols?
Rhymes can be friends, but people, no.

Why must two great nations then
freeze on the edge of war also?
Under their fragile oxygen tent
people stay friends, but nations, no.

Two countries like two heavy hands,
guiltily tying non-love's knot,
grasp in terror now earth's head,
Earth that has wrought God knows what.

Student writing:

I think that this poem is fantastic. I chose to memorize it as well. The first time I read it through, I did not even know what it was about, but I thought it spoke of the current time. People seem to be just looking for new creative ways not to have to see each other. They stare unblinkingly at their television sets, ignoring any calls. I felt like it spoke of the receding amount of human contact. I was quite taken aback when I realized what it was actually about. That is what I think makes a good poem—to have multiple layers of which it can be interpreted. This allows people with many different interests to understand and enjoy a poem. – *K.N.*

Yevgeny Yevtushenko (1933–)

Yevgeny Yevtushenko was born in Zima Junction, Siberia in 1933, a fourth-generation descendant of Ukrainians exiled to Siberia. Yevtushenko moved to Moscow as a boy with his mother and attended the Maxim Gorky Literature Institute. In 1948 he accompanied his father on geological expeditions to Kazakhstan. His first poems were published in 1949 when he was sixteen. In 1956 he published his first major poem, "Zima Junction."

During the Khrushchev Thaw in 1961, he wrote "Babiy Yar" (see Chapter 3, Section I, for the complete text), in which he chastised the Soviet government's indifference to the Nazi massacre of tens of thousands of Jews in Kiev in 1941. The government spoke only of the massacre of Soviet citizens, making no mention that these were all Jews. Circulated originally through *samizdat*, it was not published in the U.S.S.R. until 1984, and then recited on the site in 1991 by the author.

Also in 1961 Yevtushenko wrote "The Heirs of Stalin," attacking the remnants of Stalinism that still existed. He warned for people to be on guard. He demanded greater artistic freedom, and young people admired him for his attacks on Stalinism and bureaucracy. His early travels outside the Soviet Union were as a correspondent for *Pravda*, and he visited Cuba.

He and Andrei Voznesensky were part of a group called the Young Poets or The Poets of the Sixties. Their recitals of poetry were very well-attended. During this time, Yevtushenko traveled throughout Europe and the U.S., and in the Amazon Basin, but at the end of the Khrushchev Thaw, from 1963–1965, he was not allowed to travel outside the country.

In 1967 he wrote *Bratsk Station and Other New Poems*, an epic cycle of thirty-five poems about the building of a hydroelectric power station at Bratsk in Siberia. He wrote of his support of the ideals behind the Revolution and of the courageous energy of the Russian people in this project. He paid tribute to "the name of the man dearest to us, Vladimir Ilyich Lenin" and reminded people to keep alive the tradition of the Revolution.

Yevtushenko has been at the forefront of many human rights protest situations, although he has been criticized by some who say he has been careful to toe the party line. He was part of a group that protested Brodsky's sentence; he had a close relationship with Solzhenitsyn and petitioned to the government for the publication of *The Gulag Archipelago*. He wrote asking the Nobel Prize be posthumously granted to Boris Pasternak. In 1968 he protested the Soviet invasion of Czechoslovakia. In 1990 he protested a group of anti-semitic thugs who broke up an independent writers' group. In the years between, he has been banned and threatened, but never imprisoned.

Yevtushenko has written plays (*Under the Skin of the Statue of Liberty*) and novels (*Wild Berries*) and written and directed films (*Kindergarten* and *Stalin's Funeral*). For forty years he has been a public figure promoting the works of former dissident poets, various environmental causes, and the memory of victims of the Soviet gulags. He has been a guest teacher at several American universities. (I heard him speak his poems from memory in Berkeley in 1987.) In 1991 when the Soviet Union collapsed, Yevtushenko was standing next to Boris Yeltsin. Reflecting on the experience of the attempted coup, he wrote "Don't Die Before You're Dead." He was elected a congressman, a People's Deputy from the city of Kharkov, and a co-chairmen with Andrei Sakharov in leading the Memorial Society dedicated to the victims of Stalinism.

The following two poems have been favorites in my classes. "I Would Like" has touched students' hearts and stimulated their feeling of world consciousness. My students have often chosen stanzas of this poem to memorize because they understand and appreciate the humor and the sensitivity that Yevtushenko portrays. This poem epitomizes the theme developed throughout the course—that many Russian writers and poets expressed universal principles and ideals, and at the same time, deeply loved their Russian land. The students are challenged to discuss their own sense of patriotism as they reflect on such thoughts.

I Would Like (1972)[11]

I would like
to be born
    in every country,
have a passport
    for them all
to throw
all foreign offices
    into panic,
be every fish
in every ocean
and every dog
in the streets of the world.
I don't want to bow down
    before any idols
or play at being
an Orthodox church hippie,
but I would like to plunge
    deep into Lake Baikal
and surface snorting
somewhere

why not in the Mississippi?
In my damned beloved universe
          I would like
to be a lonely weed,
             but not a delicate Narcissus
kissing his own mug
             in the mirror.
I would like to be
             any of God's creatures
right down to the last mangy hyena —
but never a tyrant
             or even the cat of a tyrant.
I would like to be
reincarnated as a man
             in any circumstance:
a victim of Paraguayan prison tortures,
a homeless child in the slums of Hong Kong,
a living skeleton in Bangladesh,
a holy beggar in Tibet,
a black in Cape Town,
but never
in the image of Rambo.
The only people whom I hate
             are the hypocrites —
pickled hyenas
in heavy syrup.
I would like to lie
under the knives of all the surgeons in the world,
be hunchbacked, blind,
suffer all kinds of diseases,
             wounds and scars,
be a victim of war,
or a sweeper of cigarette butts,
just so a filthy microbe of superiority
             doesn't creep inside.
I would not like to be in the elite,
and, of course,
in the cowardly herd,
nor be a guard dog of that herd,
nor a shepherd,
sheltered by that herd.
And I would like happiness,
             But not at the expense of the unhappy,
and I would like freedom,
             but not at the expense of the unfree.
I would like to love
             all the women in the world,
and I would like to be a woman too —
             just once …

Men have been diminished
          by Mother Nature.
Suppose she'd given motherhood
          to men?
If an innocent child
stirred
        below his heart,
man would probably
        not be so cruel.
I would like to be man's daily bread —
say,
a cup of rice
        for a Vietnamese woman in mourning,
cheap wine
in a Neapolitan workers' trattoria,
or a tiny cube of cheese
        in orbit round the moon.
Let them eat me,
        let them drink me,
only let my death
be of some use.
I would like to belong to all times,
        Shock all history so much
that it would be amazed
        what a smart aleck I was.
I would like to bring Nefertiti
        to Pushkin in a troika.
I would like to increase
        the space of a moment
          a hundredfold,
so that in the same moment
I could drink vodka with fishermen in Siberia
and sit together with Homer,
        Dante,
        Shakespeare,
drinking anything,
        except, of course,
          Coca-Cola,
        — dance to the tom-toms in the Congo,
        — strike at Renault,
        — chase a ball with Brazilian boys
          at Copacabana Beach.
I would like to know every language,
        the secret waters under the earth,
and do all kinds of work at once.
          I would make sure
that one Yevtushenko was merely a poet,
        the second — an underground fighter
          somewhere,

I couldn't say where
         for security reasons,
the third — a student at Berkeley,
         the fourth — a jolly Georgian drinker,
and the fifth —
         maybe a teacher of Eskimo children in Alaska,
the sixth —
a young president,
         somewhere, say, even in Sierra Leone,
the seventh —
would still be shaking a rattle in his stroller,
and the tenth ...
the hundredth ...
         the millionth ...
For me it's not enough to be myself,
         let me be everyone!
Every creature
usually has a double,
but God was stingy
with the carbon paper,
and in his Paradise Publishing Company
         made a unique copy of me.
But I shall muddle up
         all God's cards —
         I shall confound God!
I shall be in a thousand copies to the end of my days,
So that the earth buzzes with me,
         and computers go berserk
in the world census of me.
I would like to fight on all your barricades,
         humanity,
dying each night
an exhausted moon,
and being resurrected each morning
         like a newborn sun,
with an immortal soft spot
         on my skull.
And when I die,
         A smart-aleck Siberian François Villon,
do not lay me in the earth
         of France
         or Italy,
but in our Russian, Siberian earth,
         on a still-green hill,
where I first felt
         that I was
         everyone.

The following poem introduces the students to a different style of writing. It took a number of readings for them to grasp Yevtushenko's message, but when they did, they commented on his courage and his plea for his generation and future generations to not forget the crimes of Stalin. It reminded some of the students of the line from the cartoon strip Pogo—"We have met the enemy and he is us." Yevtushenko does not accuse directly, but he raises the question whether the heirs of Stalin live among us, although Stalin himself is dead. We can ask the same question of the heirs of Hitler, and we look into our own culture and ask similar questions of those who have brought pain and suffering, as well as those who have brought enlightenment and freedom. What is the role of influence beyond a person's life?

The Heirs of Stalin (1962)[12]

Mute was the marble.
Mutely glimmered the glass.
Mute stood the sentries,
bronzed by the breeze.
But thin wisps of breath
seeped from the coffin
when they bore him
out of the mausoleum doors.
Slowly the coffin floated by,
  grazing the fixed bayonets.
He was also mute—
  he also!—
  but awesome and mute.
Grimly clenching
his embalmed fists,
he watched through a crack inside,
  just pretending to be dead.
He wants to fix each pallbearer
  in his memory:
young recruits from Ryazan and Kursk,
in order somehow later
  to collect strength for a sortie,
and rise from the earth
  and get
   to them,
    the unthinking.
He has worked out a scheme.
  He's merely curled up for a nap.
And I appeal
  to our government with a plea:
to double,
and treble, the guard at this slab,
so that Stalin will not rise again,
  and with Stalin—the past.

We sowed crops honestly.
        Honestly we smelted metal,
and honestly we marched,
        in ranks as soldiers.
But he feared us.
        Believing in a great goal, he forgot
that the means must be worthy
        of the goal's greatness.
He was frightened.
        Wily in the ways of combat,
he left behind him
        many heirs on this globe.
It seems to me
A telephone was installed in the coffin.
To someone once again
        Stalin is sending his instructions.
Where does the cable yet go
        from that coffin?
No, Stalin did not die.
        He thinks death can be fixed.
We removed
Him
        from the mausoleum.
But how do we remove Stalin
        from Stalin's heirs?
Some of his heirs
        tend roses in retirement,
but secretly consider
        their retirement temporary.
Others,
from platforms rail against Stalin,
but,
at night,
        yearn for the old days.
It is no wonder Stalin's heirs,
        with reason today
visibly suffer heart attacks.
        They, the former henchmen,
hate a time
when prison camps are empty,
and auditoriums, where people listen to poetry,
        are overfilled.
My motherland commands me not to be calm.
Even if they say to me: "Be assured ... " —
        I am unable.
While the heirs of Stalin
        are still alive on this earth,
it will seem to me
        that Stalin still lives in the mausoleum.

Student writing:

The first poem that I found that was truly amazing to read was Pushkin's "The Prophet." The poem has a living quality to it, as though it were jumping off the page, and it does not merely paint a picture to view placidly and admire, it became the wasteland and I, as the reader, became the person in the poem. The fiery seraph seemed to accost me and I truly could almost feel it tearing the tongue from my mouth. There is some sort of life and drama that lives between those lines of verse that I connected with that first day I read the poem.

The next poem that truly had an impact on me was Anna Akhmatova's "Requiem." There is a certain matter-of-factness to it that struck me with the same strength as florid prose tends to bore me. There is something about how sad it is—in how it felt sad—that made me love it. She did not have to say she was sad, she merely had to say how she conducted her life and it made me feel sad. For this reason I found Akhmatova's writing to be far more real than so many other lines of verse.

The last bit of poetry that truly and completely grabbed my attention was Joseph Brodsky's work. His poem, "A Song," has a truly Akhmatova-like feeling to the way the events are so matter-of-factly strung together. It seems like a sing-song-y verse about sadness until the last line: "What's the point of forgetting if it's followed by dying?" That last verse somehow has stuck in my mind far longer than the sing-song-y "I wish you were here, dear. I wish you were here." To me it said that the memories of that relationship—of that life—were going to die with the writer of the poem soon enough, so why would it be necessary to spend time trying to kill memories before their time? . . .

In short, this course gave me a reason to read poetry. It let me know that poetry can be more than wilting flowers and the over-stated grievances of life written into rhyming couplets. The poems gave me an experience of Russia and its people that reading history books and listening to lectures could not have done—that understanding is the part, about this course, that I most underestimated.   – *A.S.*

Endnotes

1. Also sometimes called "The Stalin Ode."
2. I have not been able to find the source of this translation which I have used in class. Another translation can be found in *Osip Mandelstam, Poems* by James Greene, p. 78.
3. Carl Proffer, *The Widows of Russia* (Ann Arbor, MI: Ardis, 1987), pp. 13–71.
4. Ibid.
5. www.english.tsvetayeva. com/You-loved-me.
6. Ibid., poet-1-3.
7. Ibid., distance/versts/miles.
8. *Pravda*, March 29, 1963.
9. Andrei Voznesensky, *An Arrow in the Wall, Selected Poetry and Prose* (New York: Henry Holt & Co., 1987), p. 169.
10. Ibid., p. 171.
11. Yevgeny Yevtuschenko, *The Collected Poems 1952–1990* (New York: Henry Holt & Company, 1991), pp. 342–346.
12. Ibid., pp. 113–115.

Bibliography

Brodsky, Joseph. *Less than One, Selected Essays*, New York: Farrar, Straus & Giroux, 1986.

Ciepiela, Catherine. *The Same Solitude: Boris Pasternak and Marina Tsvetayeva*, Ithaca, NY: Cornell University Press, 2006.

Feinstein, Elaine. *A Captive Lion, The Life of Marina Tsvetayeva*, New York: E.P. Dutton, 1987.

Greene, James. *Osip Mandelstam Poems*, London: Granada Publishing, 1980.

Maddock, Mary. *Three Russian Women Poets*, New York: The Crossing Press, 1983.

Meares, Bernard. *Osip Mandelstam: 50 Poems*, New York: Persea Books, 1977.

Proffer, Carl. *The Widows of Russia*, Ann Arbor, MI: Ardis, 1987.

Ratushinskaya, Irina. *Grey Is the Color of Hope*, New York: Vintage International, Random House, 1989.

_____. *In the Beginning*, New York: Alfred A. Knopf, 1991.

Reeder, Roberta. *Anna Akhmatova, Poet and Prophet*, "Joseph Brodsky: Arrest and Exile 1963–1965," New York: Saint Martin's Press, 1994.

Voznesensky, Andrei. *An Arrow in the Wall, Selected Poetry and Prose*, New York: Henry Holt & Co., 1987.

Yevtushenko, Yevgeny. *Bratsk Station and Other New Poems*, New York: Doubleday & Co., 1967.

_____. *The Collected Poems, 1952–1990*, New York: Henry Holt & Company, 1991.

_____. *Fatal Half Measures, The Culture of Democracy in the Soviet Union*, Boston: Little, Brown, and Co., 1991. [This is an extremely moving collection of essays dealing with situations occurring during the critical years of *glasnost* and *perestroika*.]

In Closing

I will end this book with a delightful poem by Vladimir Mayakovsky. This poem presents a modern image of inspiration in contrast to Pushkin's "The Prophet."

A Most Extraordinary Adventure[1]

The sunset flamed, a hundred suns,
Summer had wheeled into July,
The heavens stirred and blurred
with heat,
and it was in the country this occurred.
Pushkino sat
On Mount Akula's hump,
And at its foot
a village writhed, its clump
of roots as warped as bark.
Now off beyond the village was
a hole.
And every day
the sun dropped down into that hole,
as slow as sure.
and every morrow.
the sun, as red
as ever, raised his head
to flood the world.
Dawn after dawn
it was the same
till it began to pall
upon me, till
I just got sore.
One day, in such a rage
that everything grew pale and shook with fear,
I shouted right in the sun's face:
"Climb down! D'you hear?
Stop it—haunting that lousy pit!"
I yelled, right at the sun:
"You loafer!
You've a soft berth in the clouds,
While I must sit,
Not knowing if it's winter, if it's summer,
just painting posters!"
I yelled to the sun
"You wait!
Listen to me, you golden-browed,
instead of setting as you always do,

why don't you come around," I cried out loud,
"and have a glass of tea
with me?"
What have I done!
Now I'm a goner!
Here's the sun
coming to call on me
himself,
and of his own free will!
His beamy legs flung wide,
the sun strides right across the hill.
I beat retreat.
His eyes are in the garden now.
He's tramping through the garden now,
filling
the windows,
filling
doors and cracks.
The burly sun walked in,
just so — dropped in,
and having got his breath,
spoke in a great bass voice:
"I have to hold my fires in check,
the first time since creation.
You've invited me?
Then, poet, get the tea!
And don't forget the jam."
And though I wept with heat
and dripped a flood of sweat,
I got the samovar.
"Well, have a seat, friend luminary."
The devil must have made me shout
my impudence at the sun.
Abashed
I sat on the chair's edge,
afraid of what was going to happen next.
But from the sun
a strange light flowed —
he didn't seem vexed —
And I, forgetting my embarrassment,
no longer scary,
sat
talking to the luminary!
I chat
of this and that,
saying Rosta[2] has got me down
and the sun says,
"Oh, well
don't fret,

Just take it in your stride.
Do you believe that it's a cinch for me
to shine?
You go and try!
But I –
I undertook the job
to light the earth.
Well, then, I shine for all I'm worth."
And so we chat until it's dark —
that is, till when night used to come.
What kind of darkness can there be,
when the sun's there?
Now, having become chummy, we
address each other quite familiarly.
And soon
in open friendship, just like that,
I pat him on the back.
We are a pair!
Let's go, poet.
Let's soar,
and sing to scare
the drabness of the world.
I'll pour out light,
you'll do no worse
in pouring forth your verse —"
At that the sun lets fly a cannonball:
the prison wall
of night falls flat.
Rays and words,
shine for all you're worth!
And when the sun gets tired
and night, the stupid sleepyhead,
wants to drop off,
suddenly I am fired
with zeal, and shine for all I'm worth,
and day rings forth again.
Always to shine
and to the very last
to shine,
and let the rest go hang:
thus runs
my motto and the sun.

Endnotes

1. Subtitled "That befell Vladimir Mayakovsky in the summer at the Rumyantzov Cottage, Mount Akula, Pushkino, on the Yaroslavl Railway"; in *The Bedbug and Selected Poetry* (Indiana: Indiana University Press, 1961), p. 137.
2. *Rosta* is the telephone company.

Ural River

Appendix

CLASS SYLLABUS and COURSE SCHEDULE
for
Russian Literature
Sacramento Waldorf School
October–November
Instructor: Betty Staley

Although Russia is one of the largest countries in the world, many Americans know very little about its history and rich culture. When the United States and the Soviet Union were the two superpowers, Russia (as the largest republic in the Soviet Union) was looked on as the enemy, and stereotypes of communism, the cold north, and vodka were dominant. Twentieth century Russian history and literature are entwined in the culture and events of the former Soviet Union. We will become aware of the former republics although we will mainly focus on Russia.

What lives in the Russian soul is revealed through literature against a background of a complex, chaotic history. In this course we will explore nineteenth and twentieth century Russian literature with emphasis on Fyodor Dostoyevksy's *The Brothers Karamazov*. Additional authors such as Pushkin, Tolstoy, Pasternak, Solzhenitsyn, Akhmatova, Tsvetayeva, Mandelstam, and Yevtushenko will be presented. The study of literature will be augmented with the geography and history of Russia, daily recitation of poetry, and artistic projects.

Important Dates

Monday, Oct. 24: Quiz on *The Brothers Karamazov* based on summer reading
Wednesday, Nov. 2: Quiz on Russian geography
Friday, Nov. 4: Commentary on the daily questions I
Friday, Nov. 11: Commentary on the daily questions II
Monday, Nov. 14: Essay on a Russian poem
Thursday, Nov. 17: Test on the course
Friday, Nov. 18: Art project due. Main lesson book due including concluding essay

Main Lesson Book or Portfolio Contents

- Title page
- Table of contents
- Daily commentaries I and II
- Reflections on a Russian poem
- Explanation of art project
- A copy of the poem you memorized and presented in class
- Concluding essay
- Appendix, including the quizzes and the map

Course Requirements and Evaluation

- Quiz on *The Brothers Karamazov* (5%)
- Map quiz (10%)
- Art project (10%)

> This can be a drawing, painting, sculpture, illustration of a Russian fairy tale, a presentation of Russian music (vocal or instrumental), dance, a memorized scene from a play, or example of Russian cooking with an explanation of its connection with Russian culture. An explanation of your project should be written in your main lesson book.

- Recitation of Russian poem (5%)

> Each student will memorize and present one poem (excluding "Russia My Country"). The poem should be a minimum of twelve lines or two shorter poems. A copy of the poem should be in your main lesson book.

- Oral report (5 to 10 minutes, 10%)

> The oral report should be presented with attention to clarity of speech, eye contact, and grasp of content. Be careful not to rely on *Cliff's Notes*.

- Daily commentaries (10%)

> Each commentary will be based on a question or theme given in class. The commentary is not a summary of the material covered in class, but thoughtful reflections on it. Each day's commentary should include the book number in *The Brothers Karamazov* (if applicable), your name and date on the top of the page, and the question you are addressing. Length: approximately 250 words (one typed page). The commentaries are handed in as final form and may be typed. There are fourteen commentaries. Submit at least three of them November 4 and at least three more on November 11. Your completed main lesson book should have ten of them. Choose what you think are your best ones.

- Reflections on a Russian poem (10%)

> A one- to two-page commentary discussing a Russian poem. This should include the significant imagery, rhythm, and figures of speech (metaphor, simile, personification, alliteration) of the poem. The poem should be beautifully handwritten, and the commentary may be typed.

- Concluding essay (10%)

> This essay should include the key aspects from the course, what has been most significant or interesting for you, and how your perceptions or thoughts have changed. The essay should be a minimum of three pages, and this may be typed.

- Final test (25%)

- Class readiness, preparation, punctuality (5%)

Daily Plan

Mon. Oct. 24: Homework commentary: *How can you imagine that the geography of Russia might influence the character of the Russians?*

Tues. Oct. 25: Homework commentary: *What historical events influenced Russian culture?*

Wed. Oct. 26: History of Russia

Thurs. Oct. 27: Pushkin's biography

Fri. Oct. 28: Homework commentary: *How does learning about Pushkin's life affect your reading of his poetry?*
Finish Pushkin's biography. Discuss *The Brothers Karamazov* books 1 and 2: family relationships

Mon. Oct. 31: No school

Tues. Nov. 1: Homework commentary on books 1, 2 and 3: *How does Dostoyevsky shed light on human behavior?*
Biography of Tolstoy

Wed. Nov. 2: Present book 3: Smerdyakov. *Is there immortality?*
Everyone read "What Men Live By" for discussion on Thursday, Nov. 3.
Map quiz

Thurs. Nov. 3: Homework commentary: *In your opinion, what is the role of suffering in human life? Refer to Tolstoy in your commentary.*
Present book 4: heartache, biography of Dostoyevsky
Discuss "What Men Live By" in class.

Fri. Nov. 4: Homework commentary: *Which is more satisfying, freedom or happiness?*
Present book 5. Give summary and your own thoughts on rebellion. The Grand Inquisitor scene.

Mon. Nov. 7: Books 6 and 7
Homework commentary: *What did you think of Zossima's answer?*

Tues. Nov. 8: Pasternak's biography. Present book 8: Fyodor's murder
Homework commentary: *In what ways could Fyodor's murder be justified or not?*

Wed. Nov. 9: The role of the writer in the twentieth century
Homework commentary: *How did Pasternak respond to historical events?*
Complete Pasternak's biography. Excerpts from *Dr. Zhivago*
Homework commentary: *What did you consider Pasternak's greatest act of courage? Why?*

Thurs. Nov. 10: Solzhenitsyn: witness to the Gulag
Present Solzhenitsyn's biography. Books 9 and 10: Schoolboys
Homework commentary: *How were the schoolboys like contemporary American schoolboys?*

Fri. Nov. 11: Homework commentary: *How does the reader gain a new understanding of Grushenka?*
Recitation of poetry
Present book 11: Grushenka's metamorphosis, Ivan's guilt
Homework: work on poetry reflection

Mon. Nov. 14: *What is the role of youth in transforming society?*
    Recitation of poetry
    Present book 12: Dmitri's trial and verdict, biography of Anna Akhmatova
    Poetry reflection will be checked in class but handed in with the main lesson book on Friday.

Tues. Nov. 15: Poets speak out and take risks
    Recitation of poetry
    Present Epilogue, biography of Marina Tsvetayeva

Wed. Nov. 16: Recitation of poetry
    Biography of Osip Mandelstam, biography of Yevtushenko. Summarizing
    Homework: prepare for open book test
    Work on art project

Thurs. Nov. 17: Main lesson test
    Homework: concluding essay, finish art project

Fri. Nov. 18: Sharing and speaking
    Recitation of poetry
    Art project presented, main lesson book due

Ideas for Research Paper (You may suggest another topic.)

1. History of the Russian peasant
2. Life in a labor camp—reflections on a book, *Grey Is the Color of Hope* by Irina Ratushinskaya
3. Vladimir Soloviev: *The AntiChrist*
4. Vladimir Bukovsky, *To Build a Castle: My Life as a Dissenter*
5. Alexander Solzhenitsyn: *The First Circle* or *Cancer Ward*
6. Solzhenitzyn at Harvard: The Address, *Twelve Early Responses, and Six Later Reflections*
7. A. Anatoli (Kuznetsov), *Babi Yar*
8. Andrei Sakharov, Russian scientist and dissenter
9. A comparison of the book *Dr. Zhivago* and the two films, American-made and European-made
10. The role of Gogol as writer of short stories ("The Overcoat") and model for Russian writers
11. The struggle between Russian writers and the Writers Union during Stalinist times
12. The Letters between Pasternak and Tsvetayeva—a journey into poetry and relationship
13. Images from Akhmatova's "Requiem" and the echoing of her life's issues
14. Two Chekhov plays as commentary on nineteenth century Russian upper class life
15. Dostoyevsky's "Pushkin Address" and a description of the true Russian, using examples from Russian literature
16. Dostoyevsky's *Crime and Punishment* and the Grand Inquisitor scene
17. Exploration of the life and work of a Russian poet not covered in class

Map of Russia

Place the names of the following places on your map. Know the countries that border Russia. Include the map in the Appendix of your main lesson book.

Mountains
1. Tien Shan
2. Ural
3. Altai
4. Caucasus

Bodies of Water
1. Pacific Ocean
2. Arctic Ocean
3. Caspian Sea
4. Baltic Sea
5. Barents Sea
6. Sea of Okhotsk
7. Black Sea
8. Aral Sea
9. Sea of Azov
10. Lake Balkhash
11. Lake Baikal

12. Lake Ladoga
13. Amur River to the Pacific Ocean
14. Dneiper River to the Black Sea
15. Don River to the Black Sea
16. Volga River to the Caspian Sea
17. Amu Darya River in Central Asia
18. Syr Darya River in Central Asia
19. Ob River north to Arctic Ocean
20. Lena River north to Arctic Ocean
21. Yenisey River

Cities

1. Vladivostock
2. Moscow
3. Novgorod
4. Perm
5. St. Petersburg
6. Novosibirsk
7. Omsk
8. Volgagrad
9. Murmansk

Bordering Countries (some are part of the Russian Federation)

1. Latvia
2. Georgia
3. Estonia
4. Lithuania
5. Poland
6. Ukraine
7. Belarus
8. Kazakhstan
9. Moldova
10. Tadjikistan
11. Uzbekistan
12. Finland

Do you see any others on the map?

Quiz: *The Brothers Karamazov* **by Dostoyevsky**

    Name _____

1. Who is the hero of the book and why?

2. Contrast Dmitri and Alyosha in personality and life goals.

3. How does Ivan play a significant role in the plot?

Personal questions: These are not part of the quiz but serve to help me make the block important and relevant to you. Use the back of the paper.

1. What are your personal aims regarding this block?

2. Do you have any special interests you would like me to include in the block?

3. Is there anything I should know about you as a student in order to teach you more effectively?

[Note: *The maps in this book are approximate and simplify the information and it is assumed that the teacher will use a detailed, up-to-date map in the classroom.*]

Location:	Northern Asia (that part west of the Urals is included with Europe), bordering the Arctic Ocean, between Europe and the North Pacific Ocean
Area:	total: 17,075,200 sq km land: 16,995,800 sq km water: 79,400 sq km
Area comparison:	approximately 1.8 times the size of the United States
Land boundaries:	total: 20,017 km
Coastline	37,653 km

Maritime claims:	territorial sea: 12 nm exclusive economic zone: 200 nm continental shelf: 200-m depth or to the depth of exploitation
Climate:	ranges from steppes in the south through humid continental in much of European Russia; subarctic in Siberia to tundra climate in the polar north; winters vary from cool along Black Sea coast to frigid in Siberia; summers vary from warm in the steppes to cool along Arctic coast
Terrain:	broad plain with low hills west of Urals; vast coniferous forest and tundra in Siberia; uplands and mountains along southern border regions
Elevation extremes:	lowest point: Caspian Sea 28 m highest point: Gora El'brus 5,633 m
Natural resources:	wide natural resource base including major deposits of oil, natural gas, coal, and many strategic minerals, timber note: formidable obstacles of climate, terrain and distance hinder exploitation of natural resources
Land use:	arable land: 7.33% permanent crops: 0.11% other: 92.56% (2001)
Irrigated land:	46,630 sq km (1998 est.)

Natural hazards:	permafrost over much of Siberia is a major impediment to development; volcanic activity in the Kuril Islands; volcanoes and earthquakes on the Kamchatka Peninsula; spring floods and summer/autumn forest fires throughout Siberia and parts of European Russia
Population:	143,420,309 (July 2005 est.)
Age structure:	0-14 years: 14.6% (male 10,704,617/ female 10,173,313) 15-64 years: 71.3% (male 49,429,716/ female 52,799,740) 65 years and over: 14.2% (male 6,405,027/female 13,907,896) (2005 est.)
Median age:	total: 38.15 years male: 34.99 years female: 41.03 years (2005 est.)
Population growth rate:	-0.37% (2005 est.)
Birth rate:	9.8 births/1,000 population (2005 est.)
Death rate:	14.52 deaths/1,000 population (2005 est.)
Net migration rate:	1.03 migrant(s)/1,000 population (2005 est.)
National holiday:	Russia Day, 12 June (1990)
Constitution:	adopted 12 December 1993
Legal system:	based on civil law system; judicial review of legislative acts